The **WISDOM** *of the* **ROOMS**

The WISDOM of the ROOMS

12 Months of Reflections for People in Recovery

Anonymous

Health Communications, Inc.
Deerfield Beach, Florida

www.hcibooks.com

**Library of Congress Cataloging-in-Publication Data
is available through the Library of Congress**

© 2019 Anonymous

ISBN-13: 978-07573-2160-3 (Paperback)
ISBN-10: 07573-2160-7 (Paperback)
ISBN-13: 978-07573-2163-4 (ePub)
ISBN-10: 07573-2163-1 (ePub)

Publisher: Health Communications, Inc.
       3201 S.W. 15th Street
       Deerfield Beach, FL 33442–8190

Cover design by Larissa Hise Henoch
Interior design and formatting by Lawna Patterson Oldfield

CONTENTS

INTRODUCTION

The rooms of recovery are filled with a wealth of collective spiritual and practical wisdom that is revealed in the hundreds of quotes and sayings heard daily in meetings around the world. Inspiring and insightful, these quotes help deepen the experience of recovery, enrich the spiritual journey, and provide a road map for living life one day at a time. The quotes in this volume have been collected from various Twelve Step meetings and programs and are a vital part of the spiritual tool kit each member of the fellowship carries.

The reflections in this volume are written in the familiar format of "What it was like, what happened, and what it's like now." Each daily reflection reveals the experience, strength, and hope members get from working the Twelve Steps and offers insight into what the program is, and how—by working it—the miracle of recovery and spiritual transformation takes place. Familiar topics such as sponsorship, commitments, going to meetings, and, of course, the challenges and gifts of working the Twelve Steps are all here. The quotes and meditations also reflect the experience of both newcomers and old-timers alike, and members will invariably find parts of their own journey within these pages.

As with all Twelve Step programs, and with all the sharing that takes place within the meetings, the reflections collected here are solely based on the experiences of individual members taking the Steps and working the program. These reflections are not intended to speak for the program itself but rather are presented as personal interpretations and offered in the spirit of giving back.

We hope you find the courage, strength, and direction you need, just when you need it, in *The Wisdom of the Rooms*. And if you do, then please pass on to others the encouragement and insights you find here. Remember, we don't do this alone.

JANUARY 1

"Humility is not thinking less about yourself, but rather thinking about yourself less."

I used to look down on people who were humble. They won't ever get anywhere, I used to think. It's a dog-eat-dog world, and if I wanted to succeed I had to be aggressive and take the things I wanted. When I combined alcohol with this attitude, my ego exploded, and my thirst for both success and drink was insatiable. Soon I was a pariah, shunned even by some of my closest friends.

In the program, while I was recovering from my disease, I heard a lot about humility. Rather than be open to the concept, my ego rebelled at the thought of it. I can still remember arguing about it with my sponsor. "If I'm humble, I'll be a nothing. People will take advantage of me, and I'll never get ahead," I whined. And that's when he defined it, according to the program. He told me, "Humility isn't thinking less about yourself, but rather it's thinking about yourself less." That was an aha moment for me.

The truth beneath this explanation has deepened for me over the years. What I have discovered is that I am much happier, have more freedom, and am more peaceful when I am thinking less about myself. In fact, the more focused on others I become, the more serenity I have. Today, whenever I find that I am anxious or upset, chances are I'm thinking too much about myself. The solution is simple: I seek humility by looking for ways to be of service. When I do, serenity returns to my life.

JANUARY 2

❧

"If I'm feeling hysterical, it must be historical."

B efore recovery, I often wondered why little things caused such big reactions in me. I was often filled with rage when somebody drove too slowly, or I hurt for days over someone's negative comments about me. Other things that didn't go my way often caused oversized reactions, leaving me confused and resentful. I suffered many painful emotional hangovers from these events, and this only fueled my drinking—which led to a different kind of hangover.

By doing my Step work, I began to untangle the strings of my emotional past. Through journaling and inventories, I learned to look beyond these events to the real causes of my feelings. What I uncovered were the old wounds and hurts from long ago, the historical causes and conditions of my hysterical reactions. Once I recognized that events were merely buttons triggering old feelings, my real emotional recovery began.

Today, I recognize uncomfortable feelings for what they are: guides into emotional areas that still need healing. I use questions to help me deal with these old wounds. "What is really behind this reaction?" "What can I do, right now, to soothe myself?" "Where is the path to recovery here?" These kinds of questions are the tools I use to help me heal, and so avoid the bigger-than-life reactions that used to make my life unmanageable. Today, I uncover, discover, and discard those old hurts.

JANUARY 3

*"Did God introduce me to the program, or
did the program introduce me to God?"*

I n the beginning of my sobriety, I spent a lot of time resenting that I had to go to all those meetings and do all that work. "Why do I have to go to ninety meetings in ninety days?" "Why do I have to write another inventory?" "Why do I have to make a Fourth Step list of resentments, and why, especially, do I have to look at my part?" "Why can't I just lead a normal life?" I cried. It took quite a while before the answer became clear.

What I finally realized was that all this work was part of the spiritual path I was on that led to a relationship with God, as I came to understand Him. All the work I had to go through was necessary because it enabled me to let go of my old self, and so become open to the healing and loving presence of a Higher Power. The freedom, the serenity, and the ability to live life on life's terms are the gifts of the indescribable miracle I found through recovery.

Today, whenever I find it inconvenient to keep going to meetings, or if I become resentful that I'm still an alcoholic, I ask myself, *If the program was the only way I would have found God, would I have chosen to be an alcoholic?* My answer is a resounding yes! Today, I'm one of those people who identify in meetings as a grateful alcoholic. It no longer matters whether God introduced me to the program or if the program introduced me to God. All that is important is that I found Him.

JANUARY 4

"If nothing changes, nothing changes."

In early recovery I heard someone say that, "If you get a horse thief sober, all you have is a sober horse thief." I learned that the Twelve Step program is a program of recovery because it is a program of change. Just getting sober isn't enough. I have known many people who came into the program and stopped drinking but either delayed or didn't work the Steps. They soon found that they still had all the old problems, feelings, and circumstances they had while drinking. Besides not drinking, not much else had changed.

"The same man will drink again." This was another saying I heard when I was new, and it reveals yet another danger of not working the Steps and of not changing. Driven and haunted by the pain of the old self, it is a short distance to the temporary relief and old solution of drinking. Once again, if nothing changes (besides not picking up a drink), nothing changes, and the same man *will* soon drink again.

"The only thing we have to change is everything." The miracle of the program comes as we work the Steps, abandon our old ideas, and discard our old self. The Big Book tells us that we become reborn as a result of working the Steps, and it is this new self that is capable of living a new life that is happy, joyous, and free. The good news is that this total change is much easier than it sounds, and it is a natural result of working the program. And ultimately, everything changes as *we* change.

JANUARY 5

"Let us love you until you learn to love yourself."

This is one of my favorite quotes, and it meant so much to me in early recovery. When I got to the program, the voices in my head were so filled with hatred and self-loathing that it was no wonder I was destroying my life. I remember sitting in meetings feeling down on myself, and then I'd hear this saying and a dim light of hope would shine in me and I'd think, *If these people are willing to love and accept me, then maybe I'm not the lost cause I think I am.*

I heard a speaker once talk about coming into the program with negative and destructive self-esteem. I could sure identify. He then said that after years of working the Steps, and after thousands of meetings, he'd been able to claw his way up to low self-esteem! We all laughed at this, but it taught me an important lesson: Developing healthy self-esteem is a process that takes a lot of work and time.

Thank God I don't have to do this work alone. People in the rooms are glad to help me and love me while I work, grow, and learn to love myself. It's not always easy, and I'm often my own worst critic, but by letting others in, listening to their perception of me, and by accepting their love, I've indeed learned to have love for myself. And what a precious miracle that is for me today.

JANUARY 6

"My mind is like a bad neighborhood—
I don't go in it alone."

O ne of the dangers of being alone for me is that I start thinking. Now, for a normal person, that may be okay, but for an alcoholic like me, that almost always means trouble. Colored by the disease of alcoholism, my mind seeks problems and reasons why nothing will work out. Even my so-called good ideas soon get me into trouble.

If I dwell in the bad neighborhood of my mind, I can also get depressed. I once heard that alcoholism wants me dead but will settle for drunk. If I get lost down its streets, soon I'm cut off from life and from the light of my Higher Power, and I start believing alcoholism's dark thoughts. Depressed and alone, my disease has seemingly won—*until I reach out.*

Today, I've learned to share my thoughts with others and to let them into my thought process. I'm no longer comfortable going into the neighborhood of my mind alone and find, over and over, that things always work out best when I have company. Today, when I'm feeling anxious or depressed, I ask myself if I'm in the dark neighborhood of my mind alone. And if so, I call you.

JANUARY 7

"If you stay in the middle of this program, it's hard to fall off the edge."

I don't know about you, but I see them. People who come to meetings late, sit near the door, smoke outside during the meeting, jet out the door right after the meeting. These people scare me because they seem to be half in the program and half out. One foot out the door, as they say. When I was brand-new to the program, I was like that, and it is a scary and dangerous place to be.

When people who have gone out come back in (those who make it back in, that is), I listen very carefully to the familiar story they share. It goes something like this: "I drifted away. First, I stopped calling my sponsor, then I stopped taking commitments, then I went to fewer and fewer meetings. Before I knew it, I had a cold beer or glass of wine in my hand." And their stories all descend to the same desperate place from there.

I was taught early on in my recovery that I needed to stay in the *middle* of the pack. The lion called alcoholism picks off the outside stragglers, but I'm safe if I stay in the middle. Today, I still arrive early to meetings and speak to newcomers. I sit at the very front of meetings, so I'm not distracted, and I take commitments, so I'm forced to show up even when I think I don't need to. Because of this I feel comfortable in my recovery, and I feel much safer than I would if I lived on the edge.

JANUARY 8

"If you still have some plans left, they suck, and you'll use them."

I hear some people share regularly at my Tuesday night meeting, and they always wish the newcomers one thing—desperation. At first this seemed harsh to me, but I realized that if I hadn't hit complete bottom, I, too, would have used the plans I had left. And when I think back to my old plans, none of them involved sobriety.

When I was new, my sponsor asked me what my back-pocket plans were, and I told him: "If this doesn't work for me in ninety days, I'm selling my house, cashing in my retirement savings, and moving to England. Once there, I'm going to buy, operate, and live above a pub." At the time, that was my best thinking, and I was dead serious. He looked at me, smiled, and just said, "Keep coming back." And I did.

Today, I'm thankful that was the only alternative plan I had left. I know it would probably have killed me, but I had reached such a bottom it didn't really matter anymore. If you're new, I hope you're out of any viable plans, desperate, and ready to give the program everything you've got. I guarantee you, it's the best plan you'll ever have.

JANUARY 9

"Listen for the similarities, not the differences."

Before my first-ever meeting of Alcoholics Anonymous, I was scared and didn't know what to expect. My friend made this suggestion to me, and it allowed me to pay closer attention; it also helped me to identify and see how I might fit in. I kept listening for the similarities during other meetings I attended, and each time I did I recognized pieces of myself, and I heard my story come out of the mouths of others. Soon I knew I belonged.

In addition to identifying with others in this way, I also saw the similarities in the different stages of recovery that people went through. Each time members shared their experience of using the Twelve Steps to meet life on life's terms, I saw how my own journey of recovery would soon mirror theirs, and this gave me the strength to begin dealing with some difficult situations in my own life. Seeing others recover through the program also filled me with the hope that I would recover also.

Like many of the lessons I've learned in the program, I now apply this one in all areas of my life. Listening for the similarities in other people's experience—at work, at home, and in relationships—has increased my empathy for others, as well as myself. Doing this has helped me feel not only a part of the program, but a part of life again as well. Today, I'm quick to see how my experience and life journey are similar to others, which helps keep me connected, humble, and happy.

JANUARY 10

"If you can't learn to laugh at yourself, we'll do it for you."

How serious everything seemed when I entered recovery. Overwhelmed by the problems I'd created—a home life that was in shambles, being unemployed and unemployable—I didn't find very many things amusing. But the people in the rooms sure did. I often sat in amazement as one after another would share horrible experiences of things they'd done, or that had happened to them, while the room roared with laughter! *What is wrong with these people?* I thought.

The way that people were able to laugh and make fun of themselves made me uncomfortable to say the least. Still filled with the secret shame of my own experiences and thoughts, I was much too self-conscious to share or reveal myself. I was sure that if you knew what I had done, then you'd banish me from the rooms, and I'd have nowhere to go. Once again, just like when I was out there drinking, I felt trapped and alone.

Thank God I jumped into the middle of this program and got active. As I worked through the Steps with my sponsor, and my life started to improve, I soon found myself identifying and laughing right along with everyone else. In fact, after a while I had enough distance and perspective on my life that I could even begin to see the humor in some of the humiliating situations my own warped way of thinking had gotten me into. I found I had developed compassion and empathy for myself, and this allowed me to laugh again—and what a gift that's been.

JANUARY 11

"People who try to figure it out,
go back out."

I like to think of myself as a pretty smart guy. When I was new to the program, I kept trying to figure out how the program worked and why my sponsor wanted me to do certain things. For example, when he told me to put the chairs away after a meeting or pick up cigarette butts, I was offended. I'd ask, "What's that got to do with me getting sober?" His response was, "Are you willing to do what we do around here to stay sober?" I was, and so I took his suggestions.

There are a lot of other pretty smart people who come into the program, and when given the same direction they balk and need to first figure out how it all works. They constantly ask questions, and when I give them the simple answers as to why it has worked for me and countless others, they just keep asking. Their resistance to follow direction, and unwillingness to do the work, hides an ego that hasn't surrendered yet. Unfortunately, this insistence on figuring it out often leads them to go back out.

Fortunately for me, I had hit a bottom that made me desperate and so allowed me to be completely willing and open to suggestions. I surrendered to the group of drunks (G.O.D.) because they could do something I couldn't—stay sober and improve their lives. As my sponsor once told me, "Your best thinking got you into the rooms, so stop trying to figure it out and just follow direction." I did, and my life got better. And thankfully, over twelve years later, I haven't found it necessary to go back out.

JANUARY 12

"Look for a way in, not for a way out."

When I was new to recovery, I constantly looked for a way out. I listened for the parts of others' stories that didn't match up with mine, and I knew they needed the program but I didn't. When my sponsor suggested I go to a meeting each day, I knew my schedule and other commitments would never allow me to do that. When I saw the word "God," I was finally convinced none of this was right for me.

The next time I saw my sponsor, I told him that the program worked for some people, but that it just wasn't going to work for me. He asked me how many days I had, and I replied, "Almost thirty." He then asked me how long it had been since I was able to stay sober for thirty days on my own, and I admitted I couldn't remember. He then suggested that something was working for me and said I might want to focus on looking for a way in, rather than a way out.

When I asked him how to do this, he suggested I might want to choose a home group and get a commitment there. He recommended I develop a regular meeting schedule and told me to share often so that people would get to know me. He told me I should go out for fellowship and that I should call other newcomers and ask them how they were doing. And it all worked! After many years in recovery, I'm so grateful my sponsor showed me a way in, so that I didn't have to find a way out.

JANUARY 13

"When I'm alone and by myself,
I'm outnumbered."

I remember the first time I heard about the committee. Someone shared that when she went to sleep, the committee in her head got together and started going over all the things that were wrong and why her life was never going to work out. They gathered evidence, put a solid case together, and then reached their decision. When she woke up in the morning, they handed her their verdict: guilty and sentenced to a miserable life!

I could certainly relate. I have my own committee of voices that constantly tell me things aren't going to work out, that my past mistakes are insurmountable, and that no matter how hard I try, I will never be happy. When I'm alone, the committee is especially active, and after a few days of listening to their decrees, I'm overwhelmed and defeated.

In recovery, I've learned that being alone and listening to my own thinking almost always leads to trouble. I was taught early on that my thinking is distorted by the disease of alcoholism. My best hope for right action and happiness is to run my thoughts by my sponsor and others in the program. Once I let others in, the committee disappears, and I am restored to sanity. Today, I recognize the danger of being alone and outnumbered.

JANUARY 14

"We're not bad people getting good;
we're sick people getting better."

I was attending a meeting the other night, and a newcomer raised his hand and asked what he could do to relieve the shame he felt. He shared that he hadn't been sober very long, and that the list of wreckage he had created was overwhelming. He was just becoming conscious of the damage he caused, and the feelings of remorse he felt were intense. He couldn't believe the things he had done, and his family wasn't letting him forget it either. "How could I have been so bad?" he asked.

And that is when a member shared this quote. This person reminded the newcomer, and everyone at the meeting, that alcoholism is a disease, not a moral failing. She said that when we are drinking and using, the things we do almost always lead to sorrow and remorse. And it is because we are sick, not because we are bad people. Once we treat the disease, the behavior almost always gets better, and so do we. The member ended by advising the newcomer not to focus on his old behavior, but rather to focus on the process of recovery.

This advice is right on, though it took me many years to see the wisdom in it. I was so used to identifying with my behavior that I rarely looked at the underlying motivation—a sickness called alcoholism. But once I committed to and focused on my recovery, I started to get better, my behavior changed, and my wreckage cleared up as well. I "grew a consciousness," so to speak, and these days I act differently. Today, I know that we're not bad people getting good. We're sick people getting better.

JANUARY 15

"Those who laugh—last."

I remember hearing the phrase "We are not a glum lot" when I was new in recovery. But I didn't believe it. I mean, here I was sentenced to attend meetings, prohibited from partying, and forced to develop a faith in God. Things looked pretty glum to me. If it wasn't for the laughter I heard in the rooms, I may not have stuck around.

At first, I couldn't understand what they found so funny. People would share embarrassing, demoralizing, and even tragic experiences, and the room would burst into laughter. Some of the things they shared I wouldn't even admit to myself. "I don't get it," I finally said to my sponsor. "Those who can laugh at themselves tend to last," he told me. It took a while, but I sure did find that to be true.

One of the most valuable lessons I've learned in recovery is not to take myself so seriously. Once I cleared away the wreckage of my past, I was free. Today, I allow myself to make mistakes, and if I step on someone's toes, I'm quick to make amends. Because of this, my life is lighter today, and I find it easy to laugh at myself. This not only makes the journey more enjoyable, but it's what's made it last so long, too.

JANURY 16

*"If you don't have hope, then
death is just a formality."*

Before recovery, my life was spiraling out of control, and each area just got worse and worse. I didn't have a job, and I didn't want one; I had no intimate relationships, and even my casual friends had stopped calling. Worse perhaps was that I had lost hope of my future ever getting better. In some of the darker hours, death didn't seem so bad. . . .

For a while, the only glimmer of hope I had came from the first few drinks I took. This instant euphoria didn't last, however, and soon I was once again mired in the pitiful and incomprehensible demoralization of my alcoholic bottom. Standing at a jumping-off place, I could either continue to spiral down, or I could reach out for help. It was only when I finally surrendered that some hope began to return.

I first saw this hope on the faces of people in meetings, and I heard it in their stories. One by one, I heard stories of fearful bottoms and of lives now reborn. It was exhilarating to witness the miracles taking place in their lives. Soon I believed there might be a miracle waiting for me, too. As I stuck around and worked the program, I found that I had begun to live again. Considering where I had come from, that was the miracle I had been waiting for.

JANUARY 17

"Putting down the drink was the easy part. Change is the hard part."

I used to say that stopping drinking was easy; I did it hundreds of times. After a particularly bad drunk, I would wake up with that sick hangover and with demoralizing memories of what I had done. Then and there I swore off alcohol. Sometimes I lasted a week or longer, but ultimately, I would end up with a drink in my hand. Stopping drinking was easy, staying stopped? Well . . .

When I got sober in the rooms, I told my sponsor that I already knew how to not drink, what I didn't know was how to live without always wanting to. He told me the key was changing who I was inside, so that the new man I became didn't want a drink any longer. *Why don't I just change my eye color*, I thought. *How in the world am I going to accomplish that?* He said we would do it one day at a time through working the Twelve Steps of recovery.

I must admit I felt skeptical, scared, resentful, and a thousand other emotions, but each day I took his suggestions and worked the Steps. I couldn't see the progress I was making sometimes, but slowly I did begin to change. I remember being at a restaurant watching other people enjoy cocktails, and I found that for the first time I didn't want one. The obsession to drink had been lifted! Now, that was a miracle. Many more followed, and over time many more things changed in me. Today, I am the new man my sponsor told me about, and I like who I've become.

JANUARY 18

"If you think you want a drink,
just roll the tape to the end."

Alcoholism is cunning, baffling, and powerful. It is the only disease that constantly tells me I don't have a disease. That's why sometimes, and without warning, I'll find myself nursing the idea that a drink might be a good idea—a nice cold beer at a barbeque, a glass of red wine at dinner, a colorful cocktail at a chic bar. If I just think about the drink, I could be thinking myself into big trouble. . . .

At the meetings I attend there are recovery slogans on the wall. "One day at a time," "Live and let live," and such. There is also a slogan that is hung upside down. It is "Think, Think, Think." When I asked my sponsor why it was upside down, he said it was to remind me that the problems of the alcoholic are centered in the mind. He said there would be times when I would have no mental defense against taking that first drink. He said that maintaining my spiritual condition, staying close to the program, and reaching out to others in the fellowship would be key in situations like this.

Other times, however, when I am able to think past the drink, I try to roll the tape to the consequences of where that first drink will lead me. Once I reach the inevitable end, I recoil as if from a hot flame. The illusion of fun and easy times is replaced by the hopelessness and incomprehensible demoralization I've experienced before, and that I know will come again from picking up that drink. Today, I try to think my way to the inevitable, miserable end and so save myself and others from the hurt and suffering that alcohol has always caused me.

JANUARY 19

"Stick with the winners."

In high school I was pretty much a loner until I discovered alcohol and drugs. The moment I did, I started ditching classes to get high with the stoners, and hanging out at night drinking and going to parties. I soon became the lower companion that parents told their kids to stay clear of. While other students were concerned about their GPAs and picking colleges, I was considered one of the losers who would be working a minimum-wage job after school—which is exactly what happened.

When I entered recovery and started going to meetings, I saw many different kinds of people in the rooms. There were the ones who participated by greeting or setting up the meetings, while there were those at the edge of the street smoking. There were those who sat near the front of the room and paid attention, and then there were those who sat in the back and talked or checked their phones. Some stayed and thanked the speaker, while others left early and were never seen at fellowship.

My sponsor taught me to "stick with the winners." He always sat me in the front row and told me to greet any newcomers after the meeting and ask them how they were doing. He taught me to take commitments that got me involved and encouraged me to interact with others. By doing these things, I was able to forge strong connections with other people who were committed to their recovery. As a result, I had a solid base of people and relationships to draw upon when things got tough, which they did. Today, I still continue to stick with the winners, and by doing so, I've become a winner myself.

JANUARY 20

"We either hang together, or we hang alone."

As my drinking got worse, I became more and more of a loner. After a close call of getting pulled over while I had been drinking (I somehow managed not to get arrested), I decided to stop going out to clubs. It was just easier to stay home and drink and listen to music. I also stopped receiving invitations to parties. At first, I didn't notice, then I didn't care. It had been a long time since I had been in a relationship, and since my family couldn't keep up with the way I liked to drink, I stopped hanging out with them, too. At the end, it was just me, my booze, and my resentments.

When my best friend finally took me to a meeting, I hated it. People seemed so fake and much too happy. *What was there to be happy about?* I thought. *You're at an Alcoholics Anonymous meeting!* And then some people came up to me and gave me their phone numbers and told me to call them. *That won't be happening*, I thought. Finally, after the meeting was over, my friend told me we were going out to "fellowship" at a restaurant. That was the last straw! I told him, "Some other time," and made my escape.

I stayed "out" another year, and when I finally crawled into the rooms, I was ready. Early on, I saw someone celebrate a six-year anniversary, and he said something I will never forget. He said, "Find someone you can tell the truth to; we don't do this alone." Thank God I took his advice. The moment I began to let the program in, the fellowship in, and a God of my own understanding into my life, I began to recover. By getting involved, I got out of me and got into "we."

JANUARY 21

"If at first you don't succeed, you're perfectly normal."

I used to be deathly afraid to try things because I didn't know how I would handle it if I failed. For years, I thought about getting a graduate degree, and I thought everything in my life would turn out well if I could just accomplish that. But during those same years I was afraid to start because I worried what would happen if I didn't get accepted to school, or couldn't afford it, or wasn't successful with it. For a long time, it was easier to live with the hope, the dream, and even the fear than it was to try.

I also knew I needed recovery, but what if it didn't work for me? For months I kept going in and out, staying sober for a couple of weeks and then drinking again. I felt like such a loser sometimes, but the message I always heard was, "Keep coming back." What I learned during this time was that even though I wasn't doing it perfectly, at least I was doing it. And once I stayed sober for good, I learned that this stage was just part of my journey and ultimately part of my success story.

The line in the Big Book that really helped me is, "It's progress not perfection." My sponsor told me the only thing we do perfectly in the program is not drink one day at a time. All else, he said, is part of our journey of recovery. As I put time together in the program, I found that I still made a lot of mistakes, but as long as I kept coming back and didn't drink, then I was already a success. I learned that it is perfectly normal not to succeed at first, and that the only thing that really counts is to keep showing up and keep trying.

JANUARY 22

"If everything else fails, try not drinking."

I tried countless things to make my life better before recovery. There was the gym phase. My buddy and I joined a gym and vowed to get healthy. I even started jogging. Then there was the healthy diet phase. I stopped eating junk food and instead drank protein shakes with raw eggs. Then there was the meditation phase. I started attending ashrams and bought some tapes on meditation. I even got a special meditation timer. Nothing worked, though. After each phase, my drinking and my life got worse.

Next I turned my attention to controlling and enjoying my drinking. My brother told me his brilliant idea of drinking a glass of water between drinks. I tried it. I peed a lot. Then I tried drinking only premium tequilas. I even bought a book on how to cook with tequila. Drinking and cooking with tequila got me pretty drunk. Finally I tried the Dr. Bob beer experiment. Surely beer was safe. Off to Costco I went to buy cases of beers from around the world. I drank a lot of beer, and peed even more, and stayed drunk. My life didn't improve.

When I entered recovery, you made a novel suggestion: Don't drink! Wow, that was new. *Surely, that couldn't be the total problem,* I thought. Turns out, it was. After many inventories, I finally made the connection that I have the disease of alcoholism, and when I drink, bad things happen. Further, I discovered that if I am trying to control my drinking, I'm not enjoying it. Today, my solution is simple because everything else has failed. Now I just don't drink, and my life gets better.

JANUARY 23

"The First Step is the only Step a person can work perfectly."

I have been a perfectionist most of my life. When I'd start something, I would do it slowly, carefully. If it started going wrong, or not to my perfectionist standards, I'd quit. Because of this, I just thought I was a quitter, a failure. When I look back on my life before recovery, I see a string of projects, goals, and opportunities started, but rarely finished. Driven by an obsessive need to be perfect, I had a low opinion of my accomplishments and entered recovery with low expectations for success there as well.

When I read through the Twelve Steps for the first time, my perfectionism kicked in. Reading Steps Two and Three, I already felt defeated because I had very mixed feelings about God. Reading Step Nine made me want to give up, as there was no way I could make complete amends without declaring bankruptcy and going to prison. I was ready to go back out until my sponsor reassured me that nobody works the program perfectly. He said the only thing we do perfectly is stay sober one day at a time. I told him that was something I could try to do.

Over the years, I've come to see how important following Step One is. While I may not do the rest of the Steps perfectly, as long as I'm sober, I have a chance to do them better tomorrow. Giving up the obsessive need to work my program perfectly has allowed me to persevere and do it to the best of my ability. And doing so allows me to continue growing in sobriety. My recovery continues to be a work in progress, and it starts by being perfect where I can—with Step One.

JANUARY 24

"Live life today as though you knew you were dying."

W e've all heard sayings like this before, and for many years my reaction was, "Yeah, but it's not my last day and the rent is due at the end of the month, and my relationship isn't getting better, and blah, blah, blah." As the many worries of the future consumed me, the precious days and years passed by without me, and now, at thirteen years of sobriety, I wonder where the time went.

I remember when I got thirty days, an old-timer with twenty-four years shook my hand and congratulated me. I said, "Gee, I wish *I* had twenty-four years," and I'll never forget what he said. "I'll trade you my twenty-four years, right now, for your thirty days." It took me many years to see the wisdom in this: it's about the journey, not the destination.

These days, I'm very aware of the gift of another day alive and sober. I've seen a lot of people go out or even die, and today I live from a place of supreme gratitude. Life is precious, beautiful, and filled with opportunities to help people and make a real difference. I appreciate my life today, and I'm grateful that I'm present enough to enjoy it. Today, I live life as though I were dying, and I'm fully alive because of it.

JANUARY 25

*"We must learn from the mistakes of others
because we won't live long enough
to make them all ourselves."*

I used to be very judgmental. I especially liked pointing out other people's mistakes and making fun of how stupid they could be. When I made a mistake, I was quick to blame circumstances or others, and rarely did I take responsibility or admit that perhaps I was to blame. After years of avoiding or evading the consequences of my mistakes, they finally caught up with me and I had to surrender.

When I entered recovery, I was still in denial about my behavior, and each time I heard someone share I would think, *I wasn't that bad*, and, *They sure need to be here.* My sponsor reminded me to listen for the similarities, not the differences, and soon I began to identify not with their actions but with their feelings. Once I identified with their feelings, I learned the powerful word "yet." I hadn't made those mistakes yet, but if I had continued drinking and using, I probably would have.

Over the years, I've learned to listen to and benefit from other people's experience. Now when I hear of the mistakes others have made, I'm quick to see how I've done something similar, or how I could have easily made the same mistake given similar circumstances. Today, I'm grateful for the mistakes I've made and for what they have taught me, and I'm even more grateful for the mistakes of others. You see, I understand that we must learn from the mistakes of others because we won't live long enough to make them all ourselves.

JANUARY 26

*"Find someone you can tell the truth to;
we don't do this alone."*

Over the twelve months when my life crashed around me, I shut myself off more and more from the people I cared about. On those rare occasions when people who knew me asked how I was, I lied and told them I was fine. The truth was that I was isolated, desperate, and utterly without hope. I knew the end was near, and I didn't care; in fact, when it came I was actually relieved.

When I entered the program, my life became the antithesis of what it had been before. Rather than isolating, I went to meetings. Instead of eating alone, I went out with groups of people afterward. And instead of lying about things being fine, I learned to speak my truth and tell people what was really going on with me.

Today, I know that the only way I can stay comfortable in my own skin is by letting other people into my life and sharing with them what I'm going through. Alone, my head will still lie to me, but when I reach out to others and tell them honestly what I'm thinking, feeling, or doing, that's when the miracle of recovery takes place. Today, I know about the importance of finding someone you can tell the truth to, because we can't, and don't, do this alone.

JANUARY 27

"If you are sober today,
you are tied for first place."

When I was new to the program, I used to compare the amount of sober time I had against others. When I had 60 days, I felt less than those who got chips for 120 days. When I got 120 days, I envied those who made it to a year. When I finally got a whole year of sobriety, I watched the next person on the stage take a cake for three years, and I felt like a newcomer again.

When I confided these feelings to my sponsor, he told me I was comparing my insides with someone else's outsides again. He told me this was a twenty-four-hour-a-day program, and that if I was sober today, I had just as much time as anyone else. Besides, he said, it's the quality of your sobriety, not the quantity of days. As I started watching people with several years drink again, I felt the gravity of his words.

Today, I have what some consider to be long-term sobriety. Some newcomers talk to me as if I have it all figured out, and they tell me they wish they had the recovery to stay sober like I do. I quickly tell them that if they have today, they have exactly the same sobriety I do. I remind them, and myself, that I am just as close to a drink as they are, and that my daily solution is the same as theirs. For those who are still comparing, I tell them if you are sober today, you are tied for first place.

JANUARY 28

"When all else fails . . .
the directions are in the Big Book."

One of the first things my sponsor suggested I do was read the first 164 pages of the Big Book. The entire program of recovery was in these pages, he told me. After I did, we started working the Twelve Steps, and we followed the directions as laid out in this basic text of A.A. By adhering to the Steps as explained in the Big Book, and by relying on the suggestions, directions, and experience I found there, my life greatly improved.

After years of recovery, and after working the Steps again with another sponsor, I felt like I was launched into the world with the foundation I needed. I continued going to meetings (and still do), but I wasn't as focused on my Step work as I had been. Slowly, some of my old ideas crept back in, and in some situations, I unknowingly began handling things in ways that were based on ego rather than on spiritual principles. And each time I did, my life grew a little more unmanageable.

Thank God I still have a sponsor, people in the fellowship, the Big Book, and meetings. What I constantly find is that when things aren't working out the way *I* think they should, all I have to do is return to the first 164 pages of the Big Book to find the solution. And as soon as I become willing to follow its direction, the situation, and my life, improve once again. Sometimes I still try to do things my way, but when that fails, I know where to find the directions.

JANUARY 29

"I can't handle it, God;
You take over."

Before I had a program, a fellowship around me, and a Higher Power, I was in charge of my life. I made all decisions based on self and ego, constantly planning, scheming, and manipulating people and things to get what I wanted. When I added alcohol, my wants became demands, and soon the situations I created spun out of control. When I finally hit bottom, I surrendered and began to learn a better way.

Step One of the program laid the foundation for recovery by helping me admit to my innermost self that I am an alcoholic. Once I accepted this fundamental truth about myself, I clearly saw the consequences of it—that my life had become unmanageable. After taking Step One, I became open to the real solution for my disease and my life: a belief in and surrender to a God of my own understanding. Once I turned my will and my life over to Him, I began to recover.

Throughout my sobriety, my life has continued to improve in direct proportion to how much of it I am willing to turn over. In each area, the more I harbor and hold on to old ideas, just to that extent does my life remain unchanged. Even when things seem to be going well, I can limit the goodness available to me if I insist on coming from ego or self. The sure sign of this is unmanageability, either in my own life or those near to me. The solution is as it has always been: to let go and let God. The gift is, I'm much quicker to let God take over these days.

JANUARY 30

"Welcome to A.A., the place where
you grow up in public."

After a few months in the program, I began hearing people share that their emotional development stopped at the age they started drinking. They said they felt as if they had the coping skills, and the emotional responses to situations and people, that they had when they were teenagers—or younger. I was seventeen when I started drinking, and I, too, felt baffled by how to deal with people, places, and things. Many of my reactions were that of a selfish and self-centered teenager.

Later, I heard people say they also felt as if they had missed that day at school when they handed out the instruction manual to life. I really related to that. The good news, my sponsor assured me, was that the Twelve Steps would provide the best instruction ever, and I only had to be rigorously honest and willing throughout the process. As I uncovered, discovered, and discarded my old self, and built a relationship with my Higher Power, I began to grow up. But it wasn't always pretty.

I made a lot of mistakes as I evolved and changed over the years. It was often embarrassing, and sometimes even a little humiliating, to admit my mistakes and some of my ongoing selfish thoughts and behaviors during meetings with other people. But the acceptance I found, along with the the identification and support I received, made it safe to discover myself and grow into the man I am today. And the laughter! When I learned to laugh at myself, I learned to forgive myself. And that's what made growing up in public possible, and even enjoyable at times.

JANUARY 31

*"If you are bored in the program,
then you're boring."*

I remember when I entered the program; I thought my life was over. No more parties, nightclubs, or wild, fun times. And worse, I was condemned to meetings where there were cliques of people who knew each other; I felt like I was back in high school. Sure, some people reached out to me, but I mostly wanted to isolate and keep to my secrets. And that's when I told my sponsor how boring the program was.

I'll never forget how patiently he listened to me. Once I was done, or had started repeating myself for the third time, he asked me some questions. "Are you asking to join people after the meetings for coffee or a meal?" No. "Are you offering to help set up or clean up after?" No. "Are you going to any of the picnics, roundups, dances, and parties that are offered?" No. "Then no wonder you're bored. You're boring!"

My sponsor explained that alcoholism is a disease that wants to keep us isolated so that it can kill us. He told me that people in the program insist on having fun, and as a group we're not a glum lot. Just look at the laughter and friendships you see. But you have to take contrary action and join in if you want to be a part of it. And deep down, I did. So I did get active. And what I found to be true in the program is also true in life: You get out of it what you put in to it. Today, I'm too active to be bored, and because of that, I get to live a life that is happy, joyous, and free.

FEBRUARY 1

"You have to feel to heal."

I learned to hide from my feelings at a young age. Raised in an abusive, alcoholic home, I checked out early in front of the TV set. In my teenage years, I discovered alcohol and used that to keep uncomfortable feelings away. Over the years, I used other things—relationships, food, shopping, and so on—to avoid feeling. Unable to escape them, and without the tools to deal with them, my feelings became overwhelming and threatened to engulf and destroy me.

When I entered recovery and stopped drinking, my feelings descended on me, and I sometimes thought I was losing my mind. I can still hear my sponsor tell me, "Feelings aren't facts—they are just feelings." While that may have been true, it was also true that my feelings were still there, and they were really uncomfortable. The solution to dealing with them, I learned, was to ask my Higher Power to help me sit with my feelings, and to listen to what they were trying to tell me. It wasn't easy at first.

Through inventory, though, and sharing with others, and listening to my Higher Power, I have learned to respect rather than run from my feelings. Today, my feelings are like little guides that lead me into the depths of who I really am, and I am no longer afraid to go there because I know that at my core I am a child of God. Today, I know that the key to healing in a profound and sacred way is to honor my feelings and truly hear what they are trying to teach me.

FEBRUARY 2

"There are two sure ways to get out of fear:
Either make a decision or take action."

I don't know about you, but before recovery it was easy for me to be paralyzed by fear. Fear of the past, the future, an event, or a situation. Often, I would find myself numb, indecisive, and unable to do anything except obsess over the numerous negative outcomes I feared were awaiting me. Fear dominated my life, and I didn't know how to escape its dark prison. But that changed when I began to recover.

One of the first things I began building when I started working the Twelve Steps was a spiritual tool kit. The tools in this kit helped me to begin living life on life's terms and taught me how to handle situations that used to baffle me. And two of the most important tools taught me how to deal with my fears.

The first tool I use to get out of fear is to make a decision. Since most of my fear is in my head and gains power by my obsessive thinking, I find that simply making a firm decision often disconnects the two and so frees me from fear's grip. Decisions usually point to the second tool of action. Once I put this tool to work, it immediately dissolves the fear and puts me into a solution. As with all my tools, these are simple and effective but not always easy to practice. But like all spiritual tools in my tool kit, they work when I work them.

FEBRUARY 3

"I'll never be happy as long as I keep comparing my insides with someone else's outsides."

I t is very easy for me to feel less than. I'm constantly comparing myself to other people and asking why I don't have a better car, a bigger house, or more money. I'm convinced that most people are happier than I am, know something I don't, or are having a better life. While I've always felt something was wrong with me, it wasn't until I entered recovery that I found out what it was.

I remember having this discussion with my sponsor who told me that alcoholism is a disease of perception. He said there are three beliefs most alcoholics have that will forever prevent them from being happy. First, he said that we believe that what we don't have is almost certainly better than what we do have. Second, no matter how much we have of something, we're sure that having more of it would be better. The third belief is that when we finally get what we want, then we'll be happy.

Now, I don't know how he read my mind, but that sure described me! When I asked him what I was supposed to do next, he told me that God could and would restore me to sanity if I was willing to work Step Two. I was. It's taken some time, but today I have an attitude of gratitude, I'm comfortable in my own skin, and I have a peace and serenity that no car or amount of money could ever give me. And best of all, I'm truly happy because I no longer feel the need to compare my insides with someone else's outsides.

FEBRUARY 4

"When I get the flu, I forget I was ever healthy."

I've heard that the "ism" in alcoholism can stand for many things, but my favorite is *incredibly short memory*. In sobriety, this presents a double problem. First, having a disease that is constantly telling me I don't have it is hard enough, but because of its incredibly short memory, I also forget how bad things were. The trouble, the demoralization, and the hopelessness are all quickly forgotten when my memories are painted with the brush of alcoholism.

Second, my incredibly short memory also quickly forgets the good times I've had in sobriety, the possibilities, and the hope I felt even a few hours ago. An event like getting a cold or waking up in a bad mood—or other minor things—can trigger my alcoholism, and the vibrant color of my life quickly drains, leaving me in a black and barren place. With no hope for the future, and no memory of the painful past, alcoholism has me right where it wants me.

This is why I continue going to meetings. In meetings, I get the constant outside reminder of what it was like, what happened, and what it's like now. I get to hear the various parts of my story come out of the mouths of others, and suddenly my memory returns—it was bad, and I belong here. I am also reminded of the hope and possibilities I have as I see and participate in the miracles happening to others. And that's when the miracle of recovery happens for me, too.

FEBRUARY 5

"You're not who you think you are."

I was in a meeting the other day when a woman shared that early in recovery she told her sponsor she was going to commit suicide. "If you did that you wouldn't be committing suicide, you'd be committing homicide," her sponsor said. "What do you mean?" the woman asked. "You have no idea who you are yet, so you'd be killing someone else. That's why it would be homicide." Boy, did I relate.

I remember early in recovery struggling to discover my real self as well. At first, I identified with my past actions, and the self-loathing and shame I felt convinced me I was a bad person. As I worked through that and began feeling better about myself, my ego was unleashed, and I suddenly thought I was better than everyone else. My new mantras became, "Don't you know who I am?" and "Where's mine?"

It took me a long time to realize I wasn't as good or as bad as I thought I was. With over a decade in recovery now, and with a multitude of personality shifts, I've come to realize that identifying with who I think I am is a waste of time. I now know that at my core I am simply a channel of God, and the more I focus on being of service the more I come to know my real self and true purpose. I am not who I think I am today—good or bad. Instead, I am just a child of God.

FEBRUARY 6

*"A God small enough for me to understand wouldn't
be large enough for me to trust."*

What a stumbling block the "God" thing was for me in the beginning of my recovery. Having a religious upbringing, I was afraid of God and after a while rejected the whole idea outright. I mean, how could there be a God if children got cancer and wars in His name still ravaged the world? And now I was told that my very life and recovery were dependent on my ability to forge a relationship with God? What was I going to do?

The key for me was reframing the "God concept" as simply a Power greater than myself. This put the mystery back in it for me, and suddenly I didn't have to understand how God worked, and I didn't have to explain anything either. My proof of God was now clear enough. God could do something that I alone couldn't do, and that was relieve me of the desire to drink and use.

Today, my concept and understanding of God doesn't get clearer, it gets more expansive. I've become more accepting of God's will, and time and time again, I find that things often work out for the best—despite what I initially thought. I've stopped trying to explain who or what God is and know that the infinite reality of the divine will always be beyond my finite understanding. Today, I am able to live in faith.

FEBRUARY 7

*"I have to change what I want,
to get what I want."*

When I was new in the program, my sponsor suggested that I make a list of all the things I wanted and hoped I'd get from being sober. That was easy because there were a lot of things I wanted. I went ahead and made my list, and things that would feed my pride, or give me property and prestige, were at the top. I then attempted to share it with him, but he said, "Just put it somewhere safe, and we'll look at it after we work the Steps."

As I worked my way through the program, my outside world started to improve. After a while, I began accumulating some of the things on my list, certain that I would begin feeling better. But a curious thing happened; they didn't fix me. In fact, the more I got what I wanted, the more I realized that I didn't really want those things anymore. What I found is that I had changed.

My sponsor told me that because the program worked from the inside out, to get what I wanted, I had to change *what* I wanted to match the new me I was becoming. When we pulled out my old list and we went over it together, I understood what he meant. Happiness, serenity, friends, and security don't come from having certain things. They come from acting in alignment with the true self I discovered as a result of the Twelve Steps.

41

FEBRUARY 8

*"The good part of recovery is that you
get your feelings back; the bad part is that
you get your feelings back."*

A h, the paradox of recovery—one of many. When I was out there, I had an easy way of dealing with my feelings: I'd numb them with alcohol. Unable to feel or even acknowledge my feelings, I drifted through the complexities of relationships and situations, neither growing nor evolving. In fact, I've heard it said that we come into the program emotionally frozen at the age we started drinking and using.

So here I was, a thirty-seven-year-old man with the emotional maturity of a seventeen-year-old. And here came a bewildering onslaught of *feelings*. Shame, hurt, fear, rage, regret, resentments—the range, depth, and color of my feelings were overwhelming. At first, I didn't think I would survive, but I followed my sponsor's direction and kept coming to meetings, and I stayed sober.

Over time, I learned that my feelings were not going to kill me. I learned that, although sometimes painful and unwanted, all my feelings were valid, and each had something valuable to teach me. Through working the Steps, I developed tools to process my emotions and soon learned to give them the space and respect they deserved. Today, my feelings are teachers, and all teachers are welcome.

FEBRUARY 9

*"Trying to understand God just
makes His job harder."*

I can't tell you how much time I've spent trying to figure out who or what God is. I've spent years trying to understand the God I was raised with, and even more years trying to define God from a philosophical perspective. Then I spent some years denying the whole idea of God by becoming an agnostic, and even a part-time atheist. It seemed the more I tried to understand God, the further away from Him I got.

Even in early recovery, I tried to figure God out, this time through the open assignment of defining a God of my own understanding. You can imagine how that went. I thought about, analyzed, and tried once again to understand who or what God was. After a while I grew just as despondent and felt just as far away as before. And that's when I finally surrendered.

Once I gave up trying to understand God and instead looked at the evidence of God's presence in my life, I began to develop a knowing that went beyond understanding. Suddenly, I just knew that a force was working miracles in my life, that it was always available to me, and that it would never let me down. This knowing is what I now call faith, and now I understand why trying to figure God out just makes His job harder.

FEBRUARY 10

*"Recovery is the only place where you can walk into
a room full of strangers and reminisce."*

When I began going to meetings, I remember how uncomfortable it was being around so many people I didn't know.
As soon as they found out I was new to the program, many of them
came up to me and gave me their phone numbers, asked me how I
was doing, and wanted to know all kinds of things that I didn't want
to tell them. It was all overwhelming.

As I sat and listened to people share, I was pretty sure I didn't
belong because I hadn't done half the stuff I was hearing. That's when
my sponsor told me I hadn't done them *yet*. He asked me if I identified with the other half, and I admitted I did. He suggested I should
look for the ways I was the same rather than the ways I was different.

It's amazing how that little piece of advice has changed my life.
Now, no matter what part of the world I am in, I can always find a
part of myself in the strangers I meet in the rooms of recovery. Even if
I don't know you personally, I know I can identify with many of your
experiences and with the way you feel and think. This is what allows
strangers like us to start reminiscing the first time we ever meet.

FEBRUARY 11

"The bottom started falling out faster than I could lower my standards."

The last few years of my drinking were sure ugly. It had stopped working long before I got sober, but I had failed to realize it. Instead, I debased myself more and more as I obsessively pursued my disease. All those things I said I would never do passed by quickly, just like the floors of a tall building do to a man who has just jumped off. Hurtling toward real oblivion, I had lost all self-respect, and I was about to lose my life.

As I sat in meetings during early recovery, I used to hear people talk about hanging out with their "lower companions." This brought to mind all the "nowhere" people I had taken to hanging around with, too, and I was disgusted that I had stooped so low. I'll never forget the shock I felt when my sponsor pointed out that I had been their lower companion as well. That put me in my place.

When I look back on my past, a wave of deep gratitude washes over me. I don't know why I get to be one of the lucky ones, but I do. As I look at my life today, I smile because most people think I'm a pretty okay kind of guy. I'm a contributing member of society with real friends, a solid career, and a great marriage. And today, not only do I have standards again, but they keep getting higher. How's that for a true gift of recovery?

FEBRUARY 12

*"Recovery isn't for people who need it;
it's for people who want it."*

After I was sober awhile, I started thinking about all the people I knew who could really benefit from—and, in fact, really needed—the recovery I had found in the program. I began thinking of some of my family members, my drinking buddies, and especially the newcomers who kept relapsing. "They really need this program," I'd say to my sponsor. "Why can't they get it?"

And that's when he told me that this program isn't for people who need it; it's for people who want it. He said that if everyone who needed the program attended meetings, we'd have to rent out stadiums, not just rooms and dining halls. He told me that only the desperate can become willing enough to do what we do to get what we have. And that's when I thought about my own journey.

For years I needed recovery, but I still had better ideas. It wasn't until I had hit my bottom, and was willing to abandon myself to this program, that I began to recover. I now understand when someone says to a newcomer, "I wish you desperation," because it is only by bottoming out that one can go from needing this to wanting it. Today, I realize that everyone is on their own journey, and that although many may need recovery, until they want it, they won't be able to get it.

FEBRUARY 13

*"Be as enthusiastic about your recovery as
you were about your addiction."*

When my sponsor asked me if I was willing to go to any lengths to get sobriety, I balked. I had been going to meetings for almost sixty days, and I had an idea what he meant. He was suggesting that I go to "ninety in ninety" meetings, get a home group, take commitments, write inventories, be willing to go on Twelve Step calls when it wasn't convenient, and so on. Sounded like a lot of work to me. I wasn't sure I could make that much of an open-ended commitment.

As I continued to resist the idea of going all in, he asked me about my drinking and drug use. He asked if I had been willing to do whatever—whenever it was necessary—to party, drink, and score drugs. "Oh, yeah!" came my enthusiastic reply. I then recounted many instances when I drove miles and miles, at all hours of the day or night, to get loaded. It didn't matter if it was raining or hot, if I had to ride a bicycle, take a bus, or walk. I was totally committed to my addiction. After we finished talking, I got what he was driving at.

Once I dived into my recovery with the same level of commitment I devoted to drinking and using, things quickly turned around for me. I did get that home group and commitments, and very soon I learned to look forward to them. I made many fearless and thorough inventories, and I owned up to my side of the street. I soon experienced the freedom and hope that came from doing that. By becoming as enthusiastic about my recovery as I had been about my addiction, I became enthusiastic about my life again. And today, I still am.

FEBRUARY 14

❧

"Feelings are not facts."

E arly sobriety was extremely uncomfortable. A universe of feelings greeted me each morning when I woke up, and I would lay in bed and obsess over each one. My emotional life became unmanageable very quickly. Frozen with fear before my day had even begun, I called my sponsor, and he urged me to let my feelings go. He tried to convince me that feelings were not facts, they were just feelings. I still wasn't buying it and insisted that it was a fact that I was having the feelings, and that made them real enough to me. I paid a heavy price for my stubbornness as my feelings would hit me like a freight train and drag me down their tracks.

After I got a little recovery, I learned to put some space between having a feeling and impulsively acting on it. I began to realize that my feelings only became facts if I acted on them. For example, if I felt like drinking, that was just a feeling. But if I acted on it—by taking a drink—then that feeling became a fact in my life. What I eventually learned is that I could sit through and survive my feelings. Like clouds in the sky, they would always move on if I could just wait them out.

Today, I'm not immune to having a full range of feelings. Especially when life gets busy and stressful, lots of uncomfortable feelings still come up. But now with some recovery and lots of experience, when I see the freight train of feelings approaching, I simply step aside. Today, I sit and watch as the train passes, and I can almost feel the wind from it as it whizzes by. Today, I know my feelings really aren't facts, and if I pause long enough, they will always pass by.

FEBRUARY 15

"You are exactly where God wants you to be."

When I was new to the program, I used to complain to my sponsor about where I was in my life. I told him I couldn't believe I was in my late thirties and my life was such a mess. I was unemployed, and more importantly, I was unemployable. I had no savings and was borrowing money to pay my expenses. I had never been married and hadn't had a serious relationship in years. My family didn't want to have anything to do with me, and I had few friends left. I was at the bottom of my life.

And that's when he looked at me and said, "You are exactly where God wants you to be." *How can that possibly be?* I thought. *What kind of a deranged God would want me to be so miserable, so desperate?* My sponsor told me that I had finally reached a place where I had fully surrendered, and it was only here that God could reach me and begin the miracle that would transform my life.

While I understood what my sponsor meant, my ego continued to struggle against where I was and where I thought I should be. As I slowly pieced my life back together, I still resented that I had to take an entry-level job, or wait a year before getting into a relationship, or sweep floors after meetings. But after a while, the wisdom of these baby steps revealed themselves. By starting over, and doing things the right way—selflessly, fully present, and grateful for the opportunities—I began to appreciate and cherish the new life I had a second chance at building. Even today, when I get anxious or impatient, I remember that I am exactly where God wants me to be.

49

FEBRUARY 16

"God never gives me more than I can handle—
I just wish He didn't trust me so much!"

Early in sobriety, I was told I'd have to learn to live life on life's terms without drinking. *How was that going to happen?* I wondered. I was convinced I could never stay sober through life's tougher times. What would happen if my child died? Or if I was diagnosed with cancer? Or if my house burned down? There was no way I could stay sober through any of that.

As the months and then years went by, I began experiencing life without drinking. First, I lost my career. Then my dad had a major stroke and was confined to a nursing home. Then my first significant relationship in sobriety broke up. By not drinking through these things, I learned how to turn to and trust in my Higher Power, and I learned I could make it through without picking up a drink.

Today, I know how to handle life on life's terms. While I may not always like what life has in store for me or others, I know that God will always give me the strength, the wisdom, or the acceptance to get through it. Today, I've come to rely on God to help me make it through life, and I know that He relies on me to make it through sober. While I know God never gives me more than I can handle, sometimes I just wish He didn't trust me so much!

FEBRUARY 17

*"Just because you're having a bad day doesn't
mean you're having a bad life."*

I t's amazing the way my mind used to work. When things were good, it told me they wouldn't last. When things were bad, it told me they were going to get worse. When I was having a bad day, it told me every other day was going to be just as bad, and that no matter how hard I tried, my life would end in failure.

When I entered recovery, the first thing I learned was that alcoholism was a disease of perception. I was told that what was happening in my head didn't always reflect what was happening in my life, and I was given tools to help me tell the difference. Gratitude lists helped me see the good instead of the imagined bad; running my thinking by others helped me see past my insanity, and working with others always helped me feel better no matter what was going on.

It took a long time to develop a new perspective with my thinking, but by being willing to change, and by working hard at it, I now know that much of what my mind tells me is a lie. To counter this today, when I wake up I turn my thoughts over to my Higher Power, and I let Him direct my thinking. If I'm having a bad day, I know I can start it over at any time, and I do that by saying to myself, "Thy will, not mine, be done." This always works. Today, I know that if I'm having a bad day, it doesn't mean I'm having a bad life. It just means it's time to turn it over.

FEBRUARY 18

❧

"God, grant me the serenity to accept my own rate of recovery."

When I got into the program in my late thirties, I looked around at all the twenty-year-olds, and younger, and got depressed. I felt like such a loser to have wasted so much time. It didn't help that I was also unemployed, had no direction, and essentially didn't even know who I was. Years of drinking had robbed me of the growth and progress I saw others making. When I started counting days of sobriety, I felt like I was in kindergarten again.

None of this was good for my fragile ego. It didn't take long for the resentment and anger I felt to be turned inward, and soon the person I hated most was me. I constantly judged how I felt and how much progress I was making, and whether someone with the same amount of time was doing better. Unable to accept my own rate of recovery, my sponsor reminded me that I was exactly where I should be. This was hard to accept, especially when I didn't like where I was most of the time.

As the years have passed and I have stayed sober, I realize how much I learned through my journey in recovery. I've learned to accept that I got sober when it was right for me, and that the bottom I hit was necessary for me to do the work ahead. As I look back on things, I'm glad I didn't get that job or that girl I thought I needed. Instead, my recovery took the route it needed to for me to become who I am today. Even now, when I get anxious or impatient, I remember that I'm still exactly where I should be. And when I accept that, I am granted serenity.

FEBRUARY 19

"You can't save your face and your ass at the same time."

After a meeting the other day, a newcomer with seventy-one days asked me to sign his court card. "How's it going?" I asked him. He told me it was tough: his wife and kids and job were demanding, and all his friends were still drinking and using. He said he was just trying to hang on. I asked him how sobriety was going, and he said he felt awkward in meetings—he didn't really know what to share and was afraid of looking uncool or stupid, so he just didn't say much. That's when I told him that he couldn't save his face and his ass at the same time.

When he asked me what that meant exactly, I told him my experience when I was new. When I got to the rooms I was quietly dying inside, but I was desperate for people to like me. I wanted to fit in, to say the right things, and to be a part of the group. I was sure that if I told you how I really felt—scared, ashamed, angry—you wouldn't want me there. So instead I smiled and just said I was fine. I was saving my face, but my ass was on fire and falling off.

When my sponsor directed me to start being honest, to share what was really going on, things immediately changed. First, others didn't reject me; instead they opened up to me and let me know that they felt the same way, too. After being honest, I also felt great relief and my days started going better. Most of all, though, I learned that it was okay to have feelings and that my feelings weren't going to kill me, and they weren't going to drive people away either. Suddenly I saw the wisdom in saving my ass first. By doing that, I was able to discover my real face and found that it would be accepted for who I truly was.

FEBRUARY 20

"You can't fix your thinking with your thinking."

When I was new to recovery, I began to make plans for my life again. Now that I wasn't drunk all the time, I suddenly thought of all the money I could make and how happy I would be in that new home I would someday buy on the beach. I began thinking about finding and marrying "her," and thought that within a year I would have that perfect relationship. I was also convinced that I would have a bestseller published and would probably even be flying around the world as a circuit speaker in the program.

As I began sharing these thoughts with my sponsor, he suggested I concentrate on turning my will and my life over to God instead. When I tried arguing with him about how my vision for the future was probably better, he reminded me that my own best thinking got me to a seat in the program. When I pointed out that I was sober now and that my thinking was clearer, he asked me what Step I was on. "Two," I replied. "You might want to wait until you work all the Steps before you think about becoming a circuit speaker," was his suggestion.

He also suggested that I not make any major changes in the first year, and I am so glad I took that advice. The more time in recovery I have, the more I don't want what I thought I did. I now know that money, property, and prestige will never fill the hole I feel, and the answer I'm looking for won't come from my own thinking. Today, I know that my really good ideas are rarely that, and that my best thinking is almost always centered on me. I know that only God can fix my thinking and my life, and today, I let Him.

FEBRUARY 21

"Try not to place conditions on your sobriety."

The first time in the program, I had a lot of conditions on whether I was going to stay sober or not. First of all, if I wasn't noticeably better within ninety days, I was going to quit. Next, if I wasn't happy in six months, I was going to move to England and buy that pub and live above it. Last, if I made it to one whole year and wasn't a hugely successful Hollywood producer, I was going back to drinking forever. Needless to say, I was drunk after ninety-one days.

When I finally got sober again and committed myself to working the Steps, I had a new set of conditions. To start with, if I were suddenly diagnosed with terminal cancer, I was going to get loaded. If my family were to die tragically, I was also going to drink and denounce God. And if things got so bad that I ended up in prison or on the streets, I was probably going to drink as well. My sponsor listened with amusement as I recounted my conditions. He had heard this all before. And that's when he told me to try not to place conditions on my sobriety.

What I learned in the program is that my sobriety must come first, no matter what. All the scenarios I painted are part of life, and could indeed happen, but none of them would be made better if I took a drink. As I worked through the Steps and moved closer to my Higher Power, I discovered a peace and a strength I had never known. What I found is that my new spiritual condition is without a doubt the most valuable thing I possess, and as long as I hold on to that, I can get through anything with grace and even serenity. Today, sobriety is the only condition of my life, and so long as I have that, I have everything.

FEBRUARY 22

"Around A.A. or in A.A.?"

When I slinked into A.A., I arrived just as meetings were starting, and I sat in the back of the room, near the door. When they ended, I made my escape before the final prayers and was driving out of the parking lot as the first smokers arrived at the edge of the sidewalks. I didn't call any of the phone numbers people had managed to pass to me during my brief attendance, and I was horrified at the thought of fellowship. After a few weeks of being *around* A.A. in this way, I found myself drunk on my couch on a Monday afternoon.

When I sneaked back in after a particularly demoralizing couple of weeks, someone cornered me as I was once again making my escape and declared himself my sponsor. He offered to drive back to my house to help me "clean up" the place, meaning to pour all my liquor out and flush my drugs down the toilet. I declined. He got a promise from me to call him the next morning, and to meet him at a meeting that night, and to not drink or use in between. I thought he was pretty demanding, but I didn't have any better ideas, so I agreed.

Over the next several months, my sponsor taught me how to be *in* A.A. He suggested we meet an hour before meetings to read the Big Book together. He then suggested I get three to four commitments at various meetings I attended during the week. Once we got to a meeting, he taught me to sit in the front row with him so that we wouldn't be distracted. Afterward, we either thanked the speaker or reached out our hands to a newcomer. Today, I know there is a big difference between being *around* A.A. and *in* A.A.

FEBRUARY 23

"It is what it is, but it will become what you make it."

Before recovery, I mistook my reality of how things were for how they were always going to be. When I found myself in a dead-end job, I felt as if I had missed my chance all those years ago at getting a college degree and bettering my life. I could envision years of waking up and dreading my terrible job. When a relationship ended, I was alone and could project myself years into the future as a sad, old bachelor. Toward the end of my drinking, all I could see of my future was a lonely drunk who would die a miserable death. And if I hadn't gotten sober, much of that might have come true.

It was rough when I started working the Steps. Many uncomfortable feelings came up, and I confused how bad I felt with what recovery was like. I remember telling my sponsor that if this was what being sober was like, I'd prefer to just keep drinking. He told me this wasn't what being sober was like, and that if it was, many other people might choose to keep drinking as well. Instead, he said this was what *getting* sober was like. He said if I was willing to keep working the Steps then I would soon experience the joys of recovery.

And that was my experience. One of the enduring gifts I've been given is the knowledge that this, too, shall pass. No matter how bad things seem, or how I'm feeling, it will pass. The freedom I've received is the choice to make things better. By working through the program, turning things over and taking the next right actions, my life has consistently gotten better. I now know that it may be what it is, but it will become what I have the courage to make it.

FEBRUARY 24

"Directions to recovery:
Just go straight to hell and make a U-turn."

When I was new to the program, I heard a word I didn't know the definition of. The word was "perdition." As the fog began to clear, my sponsor recommended I look it up. When I read its meaning, I knew it accurately described my state of being: Perdition means complete spiritual bankruptcy.

During the final, dark months and days of my drinking, one by one I abandoned my self-respect, my self-care, and ultimately the light of my spirit. I was on the way to a private hell where hope—and life itself—would soon disappear forever. In a desperate moment, a part of me reached out for help, and I made the U-turn that led me to recovery.

The miracle that I found in recovery is the miracle that awaits us all, no matter how far down we have fallen, no matter the state of despair or the depths of the abyss into which we have descended. Our collective experience is we will recover if we are willing to work the Twelve Steps. When we do, we find that the very experience that nearly took our lives enables us, over time, to help and save another. This is the enduring miracle that is available to all who keep coming back. No matter what, don't leave before the miracle happens for you, too.

FEBRUARY 25

*"When I wake up in the morning, 80 percent of the
things in my head are none of my business."*

I don't know about you, but some mornings when I wake up, I'm
so overwhelmed with what I'm thinking that I can barely get out
of bed. "What if I don't make enough money this week?" "What's
going to happen if the economy tanks again and in six months I have
to sell my home?" "What if my sore throat turns out to be cancer?"
On and on I go until I'm frozen with fear and defeated before I even
begin the day.

When I heard today's quote, it was explained to me that what's
going to happen a week or even two days from now is none of my
business. My job is to suit up and show up today, do the very best
I can, and then turn the results over to God. I learned that I have
absolutely no control over the future, but I do have control over the
actions I take today, and this is where my energy and focus need to be.

While I sometimes find this hard to practice, I always find that
when I do, my day and my life go much better. First of all, action is the
answer to all my fears. Just doing something—anything—instantly
makes me feel better. Second, God does exist; He's working in my life,
and He's never let me down. Just spending five minutes in the morning in meditation remembering this changes my entire day. And once
I clear out 80 percent of the thoughts that are none of my business,
it's easier to focus on and expand the 20 percent that make up my life
on any given day.

FEBRUARY 26

"Before you do something stupid,
wait 24 hours. . . ."

Restraint of pen and tongue was a foreign concept to me before I entered the program. Instead, I was impetuous and acted on feelings of jealousy, fear, anger, or hurt pride. Fueled by resentment, it was easy for me to justify my actions and ignore the repercussions and reactions of others. When I got into the rooms, I was at odds with most people and alienated even from myself. My life had become unmanageable.

When I began working the Steps, I learned to take the focus off what other people were doing and saying and look at my own behavior instead. It was hard at first not reacting to the many perceived wrongs I felt people were doing to me, but when I finally learned to put a space between what I felt and how I reacted, my life began to dramatically improve.

Today, I've come to rely on the wisdom and the miracles that can happen in between my thoughts and my actions. Time after time, situations will automatically clear themselves up if I only wait, pray on them, and turn them over. I am much less likely to become excited or agitated, and I'm much less likely to make things worse if I can just pause before I react. Today, I've learned that before I do something stupid, I should wait at least twenty-four hours.

FEBRUARY 27

*"It is easier to resist the bait than
to struggle on the hook."*

I can't tell you the number of times I swore I wasn't going to drink. Then I'd begin reasoning that just one drink wouldn't be so bad. In a matter of minutes, I'd rationalize that two drinks—okay, maybe three max—for an evening or party should be perfectly controllable. But once that first drink went down my throat, the phenomenon of craving took over, and then the allergy of the body left me utterly defenseless as to how much I would end up drinking. One drink, and I was hooked.

I didn't know anything about alcoholism when I entered the rooms. I had no idea about the allergy or about the craving. And I especially couldn't understand it when I heard people say, "It's the first drink that gets you drunk." *But it's the sixth or seventh drink that gets you drunk*, I'd think. And that was when my sponsor had me do an inventory on my drinking career. Turns out, they were right.

I now know that, as an alcoholic, I cannot take that first drink. Even with years of recovery, I know that I am still defenseless against the disease, and that one drink would once again kick-start the allergy and the craving. My only hope is to resist the bait. I shiver to think what it would be like to be hooked on the disease again. It's truly frightening. Today, I'm grateful that my spiritual condition gives me the strength to resist picking up that drink. It truly is easier to resist the bait than to struggle with active alcoholism.

FEBRUARY 28

*"It will take me at least as long to get out
of this mess as it did to get into it."*

I drank like an alcoholic from the first time I took a drink. I didn't drink socially or for the taste; instead, I drank to get wasted. And I did this for nineteen years. During that time, everything in my life suffered. My career went nowhere; my relationships deteriorated; my health declined. By the time I was finally at my bottom, my life was in shambles, and my choice was to either keep drinking and die or get sober.

After about four months in the program, I began to get restless. As I surveyed the state of my life, I was frustrated it was still a mess. I began to feel entitled for it to be better already. I mean, I was sober for four months already! As I saw other people in the program improve their lives, I developed a serious case of, "Where's mine?" When I brought this up to my sponsor, he asked me how my Step Two inventory was going.

The lesson I had to learn was that my life would—and did—improve, but it wasn't going to happen overnight. I was reminded that it took nineteen years to get to my bottom, and that it would take some time to dig myself out. Thankfully, the program gave me the tools to stay present, to work on what was in front of me, and to have faith in the process. These tools not only worked then, but they remain the way I deal with a goal or challenge today. These days, I give myself at least as long for something to improve as it took to get messed up.

FEBRUARY 29

"G.O.D.: Good Orderly Direction."

Like many newcomers, I had a lot of conflicted feelings and ideas about the God concept in early recovery. I didn't trust the God I had grown up with so I had a hard time turning my will and life over to Him. My other concepts of spirituality were vague and not very useful to me. I was growing pretty discouraged when, once again, my sponsor came to my aid.

He told me to first stop trying to figure out who or what God was. "Your job is simply to come to believe that there *is* a Power greater than you out there somewhere. Who or what that Power is isn't important. What is important is that it's not you." That put me in my place. "How do I do *that*?" I asked.

The answer, he told me, was to take Good Orderly Direction. He suggested that I start by attending regular meetings, and that I refrain from drinking in between those meetings. Next, he said I should begin reading the literature and start working the Twelve Steps. He encouraged me to begin sharing my feelings honestly with him and with others in recovery. "If you continue to go in a Good Orderly Direction, you'll come to know God," he said. It took me years, but my sponsor was right: G.O.D. has led me to God.

MARCH 1

"A.A. spoils your drinking."

When I was drinking, I didn't know anything about Alcoholics Anonymous. I had vaguely heard of it, but my image was of old men in trench coats smoking cigarettes and drinking lots of coffee. I had never heard of the Twelve Steps, and when I saw car stickers with the triangle in the circle, I had no idea that it referenced the A.A. program. I didn't even know my best friend had gotten sober until I needed help. Thank God he and the A.A. program were there for me.

When I left the life of drinking, I entered a whole new world. There were meeting rooms, slogans on the walls, Twelve Steps and Twelve Traditions, and lots of happy, sober people who had a solution. I began learning a new way of life, but at ninety days I wasn't ready for it. I went back out and drank. But the A.A. program had already begun to work because suddenly my drinking wasn't the same.

I experienced what I'd heard in meetings: A head full of A.A. and a belly full of alcohol don't mix. I had become aware of the disease—the physical allergy of the body coupled with the obsession of the mind. I had also become aware of the solution—the loving help of a Higher Power and the freedom from bondage the Twelve Steps offered. I kept going to meetings, and finally my sobriety took hold and I stopped drinking for good. Today, I'm glad that the A.A. message spoiled my drinking, because if it hadn't, I might not be here.

MARCH 2

*"The difference between my will and God's will
is that my will starts out easy and gets hard, while
God's will starts out hard and gets easy."*

A perfect example of this quote is the program itself. When I was new, my will often told me that it would be much easier to just keep drinking and doing what I had been doing than to work the program and take all those Steps. Of course, my will had always seemed easier, but when I bottomed out I saw how hard that path had really been. By staying sober, I found that God's will for me was to recover, and though early recovery was hard at first, my life got infinitely better and became more fulfilling.

What I learned in recovery is that the main problem with my will is that it is driven by my incessant wants and needs. It tricks me into thinking that I deserve to satisfy myself first, and only then can I be available to help another. As I pursue my will and trample over others to get what I want, I find that my will is insatiable, and I quickly become lost in its demands.

God's will, on the other hand, is about focusing on and helping others first. When I pray for the knowledge of God's will and the power to carry that out, I become interested in what's right for all concerned, the whole picture of which I am just a part. I find that as I become truly focused on helping others get what they want and need, my wants lessen, and soon I realize that I have much more than I need. Because helping others brings such peace and serenity into my life, I know this has been God's will for me all along.

MARCH 3

*"When fear knocks on the door, and
faith answers, no one is home."*

When I was new in the program, I was afraid most of the time—afraid I wouldn't stay sober, afraid I wouldn't get a job, afraid "she" would leave me, and so on. It was a revelation to me when my sponsor told me that I couldn't be in fear and faith at the same time. He taught me that, in recovery, I had the choice to either dwell in my fear or to nourish and live in faith. I didn't know how to do that, but he showed me that the way to faith and freedom was through the Twelve Steps.

In the Big Book, there is a simple yet powerful line: "God is everything, or He is nothing." When I read that sentence, I realized I had one of the most important decisions in my life to make. I could either decide to keep living and practicing my self-will, and so continue cultivating fear, or I could turn my will and my life over to the care of God. The choice I make leads to a path of either fear or faith.

By working the first three Steps on the unmanageability of my thoughts and life today—"I can't, He can, let Him"—I make a conscious decision to choose faith. Then, when life turns challenging and fear once again comes knocking, as it always does, my faith answers the door and fear is not invited in. Living in faith gives me the freedom and courage to live life on life's terms. And as a result, I'm much more comfortable in my own skin today.

MARCH 4

"I learn to stop trying hard, and learn to try different."

We alcoholics are a stubborn lot. When I entered the program, I was a big ball of self-will run riot, and there was only one way to do something—my way. And if that didn't work, I would just try harder: I would manipulate, lie, convince, or cajole until I got what I wanted. My ego convinced me I could get anything I demanded, and even though it was exhausting for me and many others, much of the time I succeeded.

Unfortunately, the things my self-will got me didn't make me happy. In fact, they generally made me miserable and got me into trouble. And that's when my sponsor said that instead of trying hard to get what I wanted, I might want to try different. He suggested that I pray for the knowledge of God's will and the power to carry that out. While I was unconvinced this would make me happy, I was beaten down just enough to be willing to try.

Recovery, like life, is a process. Sometimes it's one step forward and two steps back. But I've found that as I kept praying and taking right actions, my life did get better. I also found that the new things God gave me made me happier and more fulfilled than the other things I thought I wanted. As I worked the Steps and got a few years of recovery, I realized that the easier and softer way was to try different. And because of this, I now know what the "road to happy destiny" means.

MARCH 5

"H.A.L.T.:
Hungry, angry, lonely, tired."

One of the things we get in recovery is a spiritual tool kit that contains new ways of thinking about and dealing with life. Before recovery, so many situations and people used to baffle me, and I was ill-prepared to deal with them and the emotions they brought up in me. My lack of coping skills was fully revealed once I put down my old solution of using alcohol to mask my feelings.

Thankfully, the Twelve Steps provide me with all the tools I need to deal with life on life's terms. One of my favorites is "H.A.L.T." I was taught early on that if I was feeling anxious, worried, angry, or out of sorts in any way, then there was a good chance I hadn't taken care of myself. I was to "H.A.L.T." and ask myself, "Am I hungry, angry, lonely, or tired?" If so, then it was my job to stop and attend to these first.

What a wonderful tool this has been for me. I have learned that it is my job (and within my power) to take care of myself, and I have learned how to self-soothe. Once I am feeling centered, the outside stuff is much easier to sort through and deal with. It's amazing how often I rely on my spiritual tool kit, and how it has become second nature to H.A.L.T. when something is bothering me. Today, my solutions start on the inside and work their way out.

MARCH 6

"The Power behind me is bigger than the problem in front of me."

I n the past, I faced life alone. It was up to me to manage everything I had, to arrange things to get what I wanted, and to solve the problems I encountered. This was an exhausting task, and at times the mere thought of my current problems, or problems unforeseen, would overwhelm me, leaving me depressed and listless. *How can I keep getting up in the morning feeling this way?* was a thought I often had.

In the rooms of recovery, the first great relief I had came from the energy of the collective spirit I felt from all the people who had already recovered. Suddenly, I was no longer alone, and now I, too, had access to solutions and a new way of living and dealing with life. Most important of all, I discovered a Power greater than myself, and I grew to trust and rely on this Power that I now call God.

Today, after years of trying and relying on this Power, I have the confidence that comes from faith, because I know that by relying on God's solutions to my life and problems, I am always taken care of. Whenever I remember to include or turn to God for life's answers, I am amazed and delighted by how problems melt, situations change, and my life flows like the river of peace I believe God is. Today, I have faith that the Power behind me is bigger than the problem in front of me.

MARCH 7

"When I entered recovery, I was dropped
into the landscape of Grace."

M y life used to be a living hell. Driven by an obsessive mind and a disease that wanted me dead (and settled for drunk), I was controlled by a hundred forms of self-centered fear and I felt alone and defenseless. I had no tools for living, no hope for the future, and darkness filled my thoughts and painted my days. Finally, I hit bottom.

When I entered the rooms of recovery, I felt as if I had been lifted out of a sinking life raft and dropped into a great big, safe ship. Meetings gave me (and still give me) support, comfort, hope, and help. The program provided me with the owner's manual to the life I had always wanted, and the greatest gift of all was a relationship with a loving and nurturing Higher Power.

Today, I begin my days by turning my will and my life over to my Higher Power. By surrendering my will, asking for His guidance, and then seeking to do His work, I experience a freedom, a sense of purpose, and a state of serenity that is beautiful. It is Grace. Today, I get to choose to live in this landscape of Grace, and for me that is the miracle of recovery.

MARCH 8

"If you don't go within, you go without."

L egend has it that the deepest wisdom was once freely available to man, but he ignored it. The Gods, growing tired of this, decided to hide this wisdom so that only those determined to use it would search for it and find it. They considered hiding it on the tallest mountain, then underneath the deepest sea, and even burying it in the earth, but they decided that man would eventually stumble upon it. Finally, they decided on the perfect place, inside man himself, a place he would never think to look.

This certainly describes me before recovery. I was constantly searching outside myself for the answers to my life. I was convinced the right job, the right relationship, or more money would fill the hole I had inside me. Eventually I turned to drugs and alcohol, thinking the temporary relief would work, but it never did. In the end, I didn't know where to look anymore, and once alcohol stopped working, I entered recovery.

I remember the first time I heard this quote: "If you don't go within, you go without." My sponsor explained that it meant not only were all the answers inside me, but that if I didn't go inside for them, then I would keep searching outside myself and would continue to go without the solutions. It has taken years for me to consistently search within—the Gods did find the perfect hiding place! Each time I go within, however, the wisdom is there waiting for me. Now I know what they mean in the program when they say, "It's an inside job."

MARCH 9

❧

"Everyone has a Higher Power,
and it's not me."

What a relief it was when I heard this quote for the first time. I've spent a lot of time thinking about what's best for you, a lot of energy trying to arrange things for you, and a lot of time worrying about what's going to happen to you. In other words, I was pretty sure that I knew what was best for everyone else, and I felt like it was my job to bring that about.

When I heard this quote, it restored me to my proper role in your (and everyone else's) life. It relieved me of a lot of responsibility. It reminded me that you have your own path and that my role is to support and love you, not direct and control you. And it relieved me of responsibility by reminding me that you have a force in your life far greater in power and wisdom than me, and that is your Higher Power.

Once I stopped playing God, I stopped trying to direct life and instead learned to let go and let God. Today, when I worry about the challenges those I love and care about are going through, I recognize that I can be of the most service simply by being there for them, by helping them, and by loving them. But their ultimate solace, strength, and hope will always come from their own Higher Power. Today, I let go and let God work in my life and in the lives of others.

MARCH 10

"Go to ninety meetings in ninety days.
If you're not satisfied, we'll gladly
refund your misery."

I'll never forget how crazy I was when I was new! My poor sponsor had to listen to my endless rants, my objections to his suggestions, and all my "better ideas." Worst of all, he put up with my constant doubts about whether the program would work for me. That's when he told me to give it ninety days, and if I didn't feel better he would gladly refund my misery.

I thought he was just being a smart aleck when he said that, and I became determined to prove him wrong. So, I did what he told me to do—I got a home group, took commitments, worked the first Three Steps, and I went to a meeting every day for ninety days. At the end of all that, I was amazed that not only did I feel better, but my life was improving as well.

When I next asked him how long I'd have to keep coming to meetings before I could drink again, he smiled and said, "Why don't you try the program for twelve months, and if you don't like it, we'll gladly refund your misery." While I balked at the thought of staying sober for a whole year, I secretly imagined toasting my anniversary with a glass of champagne. Nine months later when I took my one-year cake, I looked at my sponsor and told him I didn't want my misery back. And that's when he told me I never had to go back to that way of life again, as long as I kept working my program, one day at a time.

MARCH 11

"If God is your copilot, change seats."

Before the program, I wouldn't even let God on the plane. I was the pilot and copilot of my life, fueled by self-will and self-seeking. I took off and flew through the lives of others like a tornado. My thoughts were focused on what I could get or take, or how I could control you to get what I wanted. At the time, it seemed strange to me that the harder I tried to manipulate everything, the less I got what I needed or wanted.

When I started working my program, the idea of putting God in charge of my life seemed downright irresponsible. Fueled by a hundred forms of self-centered fear, I couldn't fathom giving up control of my life. I was still under the delusion that I controlled not only my thoughts and actions but the results as well. For me, faith was slow in coming. The key was willingness, and the more I turned things over, the better my life got.

Today, one of the greatest gifts I've been given is a life of true freedom as the result of turning my will and life over to the care of my Higher Power. When God is the pilot, experience has proven, time and time again, that life flows more smoothly for me as well as for those around me. Plus, it's easier being the copilot. My job now is just to suit up and show up and let God take care of the rest. And He always does. These days, when my life is getting a little turbulent, I look to see if God is my copilot, and if He is, I quickly change seats.

MARCH 12

❧

"Things aren't necessarily going wrong just because they're not going my way."

This is *still* hard for me to accept. My ego tells me that my plans and ideas about how things should go, and how you should act, are 99 percent right. And if everybody would just fall in line, then everything would be great, and I'd be happy. But how many times has my self-will twisted or bullied things into place and got me what I thought I wanted, only to discover it wasn't what I wanted? The short answer is, "Most of the time."

There is an old gypsy curse that goes, "May you get everything you think you want." Once again, my ego hears that and says, "That doesn't sound like a curse!" But my experience understands the wisdom in it. One of the gifts I've received in recovery is the willingness to pray for the knowledge of God's will—not mine—and the power to carry that out.

And that's when the miracle truly happens for me and countless others. It becomes apparent that the wants and needs of my ego are limited and shortsighted, but God's will is vast and includes infinite possibilities for happiness and fulfillment. By developing the faith to truly seek God's will, I have been able to let go of controlling others, to show up and look for ways to be of service, and to let go of expectations. Doing this has enabled me to see that things aren't necessarily going wrong just because they are not going my way.

MARCH 13

"If you are feeling far away from God,
you are the one who moved."

I remember sitting in meeting after meeting hearing people describe their concept of God. The one that resonated with me the most wasn't a God who caused or allowed good or bad things to happen, or who punished or rewarded behavior, but rather the concept of a peaceful river. One woman spoke of her God whose love and peace flowed like a river, and the river was always there. It was always available to her as a constant source of serenity, understanding, and forgiveness.

She shared that whenever she was feeling scared, agitated, or discontented, it was a sure sign that she had wandered away from the river of God. The further she strayed and got caught up in chasing people, property, or prestige, the worse she felt. Sometimes she traveled for days and would find herself lost, seemingly alone, and quite afraid.

During those times, she needed only to stop and listen for the distant sound of the river. Immediately she would make her way back, and as she drew closer, the familiar feelings of peace and comfort would return. Once she was back at the river's edge, serenity returned, and she was filled with gratitude knowing that God's grace and love were always available to her. For me, the presence of God is like this river. And I know that if I'm feeling far away from God, then I'm the one who has moved.

MARCH 14

*"Is this going to help me stay sober,
or help me get drunk?"*

When I was a newcomer I asked my sponsor if I could still hang out with my drinking buddies. He suggested that might not be a good idea in the beginning of my sobriety, and that instead I should go to as many meetings as I could and establish a foundation in recovery. I'm glad I took his direction. It was very difficult staying sober at first, and the experience, strength, and guidance I found in the fellowship were crucial to me.

By attending family barbeques and get-togethers, I discovered a whole new threat to my sanity and sobriety: long-standing relationships with family members. Unable to deal with the onslaught of old patterns, new resentments, and unhealthy boundaries, I withdrew from those situations. Someone suggested I might find some solutions by attending Al-Anon. I took direction and learned invaluable ways of honoring myself and my process, and by detaching with love, I learned to set appropriate and healthy boundaries.

After many years in the program, I still run into situations that challenge my sanity and sobriety: intimate relationships, work-related events, exciting vacations, sitting in traffic, and so on. Whenever I am unsure of how to behave or what to do, I check in with other sober people and with my sponsor. I often find their suggestions come down to a very simple question: Is this going to help me stay sober or help me get drunk? Once I answer that question, the choice is clear.

MARCH 15

"When you are in fear you should remember to T.R.U.S.T.:
Try Really Using Step Three."

When I first heard this quote, a great release and calm came over me. I was at a meeting, anxious and afraid, and all at once I let go of the fear, dread, and self-pity I had been carrying. In an instant, I shifted from my will to God's will, and the peace and comfort I felt reminded me, yet again, that it works when I become willing (or desperate enough) to work it.

There is so much power and wisdom in Step Three. It first reminds me that the peace and serenity I get from turning my will and life over to God are just a decision away. I always have the choice of either staying in fear or surrendering my will to the care of my Higher Power. And although I'm often reluctant to let go of control, when I remember I am turning my will and life over to the "care" of God, the decision becomes easier.

After years of working this Step, I have come to trust that God's will for me is always better than anything I can think of for myself. It's hard to remember this sometimes, as I still get wrapped up in self-centered fear and try to control life to suit myself. But I do have a way out; my experience is that, when I use the Third Step, relief and release always come. Today, my way out of fear is to T.R.U.S.T.

MARCH 16

"Expectations are premeditated resentments."

Even after all my time in recovery, I often find that I still try to control people, places, and things. Even though the First Step teaches me about my powerlessness and the Third Step gives me direction for dealing with life, I still find myself resentful when things don't go my way. And I can usually trace my resentments back to my expectations.

When I can get calm and take a sober look at a situation, I realize that my expectations are indications that I haven't fully turned my will and life over to God. It means that I have tried to control everything again, and that I have forgotten my true role in life: to suit up and show up, do the best I can, and leave the results up to God. Since expectations are just results in disguise, it's no wonder they so easily lead to resentments.

Today, I recognize expectations for what they are: reminders to refocus my energy and thoughts on the actions I am about to take rather than trying to direct and control the results. It helps to work the First, Second, and Third Steps, as doing so allows me to remain open to God's lessons and gifts that show up in the results. They are always there if I am open to them, and appreciating and learning from them keeps me safe from unnecessary resentments.

MARCH 17

❧

"Relationship:
Real Exciting Love Affair Turns Insanely Obsessive;
Now Sobriety Hangs in Peril."

Someone once said that getting into a relationship in early recovery is like throwing Miracle-Gro on your character defects. The danger comes from not having developed a proper relationship and reliance on a Higher Power; what happens is that the other person quickly becomes your Higher Power. Because people aren't perfect, this total reliance on someone almost always ends in frustration and hurt feelings.

The other problem comes from our self-obsessive natures. Self-centered in the extreme and new to recovery, we obsessively use the other person to fill the tremendous void we still feel. We soon find, however, that our self-seeking continues to get us nowhere, and before long we stand at the precipice with our nascent sobriety in danger.

Over time, we come to understand the importance of developing and relying on a relationship with God. We learn to turn our character defects over to Him and to give of ourselves unselfishly, knowing that our true purpose is to be of service to others. Once we are on this right footing, all our relationships flow smoothly, and we finally experience the peace and serenity we always sought. Now, we can bring this sense of peace to a relationship rather than relying on the relationship to give it to us.

MARCH 18

"God will never give you more than you can handle—but life will."

Before recovery, life was pretty overwhelming. It seemed that no sooner had I put out one fire that two more started. Without a Higher Power in my life, it was up to me alone to handle everything, and before long I became resentful at how unfair life was. This caused me to drink even more, and after a while my life was completely unmanageable. Desperate and out of options, I surrendered.

When I got sober and started working the program, my life became *more* unmanageable at first. Still without a Higher Power, I tried to solve all the old problems of my life, as well as some unforeseen challenges, while handling all the new emotions I felt. Doing this quickly brought me to another level of surrender. This was when my sponsor taught me about the importance of working Steps One, Two, and Three.

He told me to get up each morning and say, "I can't, God can, let Him." By doing this each day, I was taking the First Three Steps, and that's when I began turning my will and my life over to a Higher Power. The miracle of this was that even though life continued to overwhelm me, with God in my life, I could find ways to deal with it with courage and grace. Today, I know that life will still give me more than I can handle alone, but with God, I can handle it all.

MARCH 19

❧

"I'd rather go through life sober believing
I'm an alcoholic than go through life
drunk trying to prove I'm not."

I love it when newcomers share at meetings that they don't think they are alcoholics. Sure, they like to party, they admit, and perhaps they had a DUI or two, or lost a job, or made a bad scene, but they can control their drinking when they have to. Eventually someone points out that people who don't have a drinking problem are rarely at meetings trying to defend or explain their drinking!

For a long time, I also resisted the idea that I might be an alcoholic. The longer I stayed sober and learned about the disease, and the more I compared my behavior with the alcoholics around me, the more I had to admit that I probably was one, too. Rather than become a sentence, though, this turned out to be the key that set me free. I truly had found the easier, softer way.

Today, I've stopped debating whether I'm an alcoholic or not, and I choose to live a sober life. It's kind of like that saying about whether to believe in God or not: "I'd rather live my life believing that there is a God and find out in the end there isn't, than live my life believing there isn't a God and end up finding out there is." In the end, it's about living a fulfilling and meaningful life, and that's what sobriety allows me to do.

MARCH 20

❦

"Meeting makers make it."

When I was ninety days sober, I saw a guy take a seven-year anniversary cake. He talked about how grateful he was, about his sponsor and sponsees, and how he still went to at least five meetings every week. I was appalled! Seven years sober and he still went to that many meetings?! In fact, still went to meetings at all? If he could go seven years without a drink, wasn't he better by now?

After the meeting, I asked my sponsor how long I would have to go to meetings. He said I'd have to keep going until I *wanted* to go to meetings. This made no sense to me at the time because going to meetings didn't seem to be an option, but rather an obligation. I knew that if I didn't go, then I'd soon be drinking and using again. I also harbored the idea that one day I would graduate. I'd learn how to control the urge to drink and would be normal again. I soon learned differently.

The longer I went to meetings, the more I discovered that those people celebrating anniversaries for longer-term sobriety were the same ones who consistently went to meetings. The other people whom I saw occasionally, and then stopped seeing, eventually went out. And that's when I made the connection: Meeting makers make it. I realized that to retain the sense of ease and comfort I'd found, I needed to keep receiving the message of experience, strength, and hope I heard in meetings. Today, gratefully, I want to keep attending meetings, and now as an "old-timer," I realize that by consistently making meetings, I've been able to keep making it.

MARCH 21

❧

"Keep it green so that you don't forget where you came from."

I used to have an amazing ability to recover from a night's—or a weekend's—worth of debauchery. While there were days when I would swear off that kind of behavior and make promises to never drink that much again, inevitably I forgot the pain and demoralization and did it all over. Having the physical ability to bounce back was good, but not being able to remember the ugly consequences of my drinking caused my life to become unmanageable. Finally, I looked for a better way.

After thirty days, I felt great physically and began to forget about my inability to control my drinking. Soon I was thinking that while there had been some bad incidents lately, these were isolated, and surely now that I had some time and knew more about alcoholism I would be more careful and could probably control and enjoy my drinking again. My sponsor suggested I work my First Step more thoroughly by writing an exhaustive inventory. Most of all, he recommended I didn't drink, one day at a time.

I'm glad I didn't. What I found is that the more sobriety I got, the more I realized how bad things really were for me. I also learned that alcoholism is the only disease that tells me that I don't have it, and it's waiting for me to let my guard down. It chills me still when I hear of people going back out after long-term sobriety. To avoid that terrible fate, I've been taught to keep doing the things that got my life good rather than the things that got good. Regularly doing so allows me to keep it green, because I don't ever want to forget where I came from.

MARCH 22

"I can't, God can, let Him."

I remember how unmanageable my life used to be. The more uncontrollable it became, the more I tried to control it. This only made it worse. I felt like that Dutch kid who sticks his finger in the dike to plug up the hole, but when he does, two more sprout up. As I tried to control the ongoing deluge, I finally became overwhelmed and gave up. Peering up from a very deep bottom, I could barely make out a pinprick of light—and that light was recovery.

When I entered the program, I thought that—besides not drinking —I would be taught how to manage and control my life better. Instead, I was told the craziest thing: to "let go and let God." That sounded way too esoteric to work in my case. I mean, God wasn't going to fix my career, pay my rent, and repair all the damage I had caused. "That's right," my sponsor said. "Your job will be to take the action. The results, however, you will leave up to God." That seemed even crazier, but I was willing to learn to try.

I only let go a little bit at first. But each time I did, things got better. And what was truly miraculous was that when I completely trusted God and let go of the results, things turned out better than I could have imagined. My sponsor taught me that by doing this I was working the first Three Steps, and he recommended I try it not only on my problems but in my life as well. He said the shortcut to remembering Steps One through Three was to simply say, "I can't, God can, let Him." And I've found that it works when I'm willing to work it.

MARCH 23

"The biggest thing I have to do today is not take a drink."

When I was new to recovery, I felt overwhelmed by all the things I felt I needed to do. First there was staying sober and finding a sponsor and trying to figure out the Steps and all that entailed. Then there was the immediate wreckage of my life and the worries I had about my finances, my relationships, and even my health. Next, I would lie in bed at night worrying about the long-term consequences of my years of drinking, and I would replay the regrets and resentments I had. I was an emotional wreck.

As I started opening up to my sponsor about all this, he listened patiently and then gently nudged me back to the present. He always began with the same question: "Are you sober today?" I answered that I was, and then tried to add, "But . . ." He quickly interrupted me and told me that being sober was the most important thing I could do, and once I made sobriety my priority, everything else would, over time, work out. Secretly I didn't believe him, but I was out of options.

What I came to understand was that all the things I worried about, and all the problems I had, were mostly the result of my alcoholism. I caused most of the pain and suffering in my life by being selfish and self-centered, and by my grandiose thinking. The solution, I found, started when I quit drinking and started working the Steps. Day by day, my life did improve, and I finally understood what people meant when they said that if I put my head down on my pillow at night and was sober, then regardless of whatever else was happening, I was a winner. Today, I know that the biggest thing I have to do is not take a drink.

MARCH 24

"Once you change the way you look at things,
the things you look at change."

I've always heard that alcoholism is a disease of perception. For example, when I first got sober I kept hearing that it was a disease, but I never really saw it that way. Once I started to work my program and learned more about it, I began to look at it differently, and sure enough it changed! Now I see alcoholism as the disease it truly is.

As I continued to work the Steps and recovery, I began changing the way I looked at a lot of things, and they also began to change. For example, my past used to be a source of shame and remorse. But when I looked at it as a source of experience, strength, and hope that I could use to help another, my feelings about it changed as well. Through this new perspective, I gained a new appreciation for it, and my very past seemed to change along with it.

Today, I know that every situation in life is open to interpretation, depending on how I choose to look at it. To help me gain perspective, I sometimes pretend I'm part of a debating club and have been assigned the task of building a case for the opposite point of view. Forcing myself to look at something differently changes my opinion and, seemingly, the thing itself. It always comes back to how I look at things. Once I change that, everything else changes as well.

MARCH 25

"I have not found a God I understand;
I have found one who understands me."

I had a love/hate relationship with God before recovery. My image of God was as an old, wise man with a white beard sitting on a throne judging and keeping score of all my thoughts and activities. I was constantly trying to keep track of whether I was heading toward heaven or hell. In college I denounced the concept of religion and of God and briefly became an atheist, but then moderated to an agnostic. All the while I felt guilt and resentment at a God I didn't understand and who I was sure didn't understand or like me.

When I read the Twelve Steps on the walls of my first meetings and saw "God" in them, I almost left. And then when people said the Lord's Prayer at the end of meetings, I felt lost and discouraged. I was sure the road I had been on led straight to hell, and the idea of getting sober only to be condemned by my old God didn't appeal to me. When I turned to my sponsor, he stressed that we all had the freedom to discover a God "as we understood Him."

While this offered a glimmer of hope, I found it exceptionally difficult to do. With an open mind, however, I turned my will and my life over to the program of A.A. first, and then to a Higher Power. Oddly, as my faith grew and as I came to believe in a Power greater than myself, I still couldn't clearly tell you what He or It was. I just know that my life worked better when I had faith. In the end, I still may not understand God, but I know He understands and cares about me.

MARCH 26

❧

"Easy does it."

I heard a lot of recovery slogans when I got sober. "One day at a time" and "Think, think, think" were a couple of them. But the one that caught my eye, and that I had the most trouble with, was "Easy does it." This was the exact opposite way I lived my life. Instead, because of my need to control everything, I tried hard every second of the day. I was busy thinking, planning, scheming, reacting, and trying to control and direct outcomes. I thought it was all up to me, and as such I drove myself, and everyone else, crazy.

In recovery, I thought it was all up to me again. I was the one who needed to stay sober, work the Steps, fix all my relationships, figure everything out, and so forth. I was exhausted halfway through my first meeting. That's when I saw this slogan: "Easy does it." When I finally accepted that I couldn't control people, places, and things, I became willing to turn my life over to a Higher Power. And that's when I began to make real progress.

One of the most precious gifts I've been given in recovery is my relationship with God. Having this relationship restores me to my proper place in this world—to be a channel of His love and grace. My job isn't to control and manipulate life to suit myself; rather, it is to suit up and show up. It's to seek to be of service. And when I do this, not only am I always taken care of, but I'm fulfilled in wondrous ways. Knowing my proper place in life allows me to relax, enjoy, and finally take it easy.

MARCH 27

"If you don't change, your sobriety date will."

When I was new, it was suggested that I begin making some changes. First, it was recommended that I go to ninety meetings in ninety days. Next, it was suggested I get a sponsor, read the first 164 pages of the Big Book, and start working the Steps. My sponsor also suggested I stop hanging around my drinking buddies—and not start dating for at least a year. A lot of my life was changing except the most important part: me.

For the first several months, I felt like I was auditing the program more than I felt like I was totally committed. The old me couldn't wrap my head around the concept of never drinking again. When you told me I needed to be willing to go to any lengths to get what you had, I wasn't sure what it was that you *did* have and wasn't sure I wanted it. It's no wonder that at ninety days, facing the Fourth Step, I chose to drink again.

Luckily I took your suggestion and kept coming back to meetings. I didn't do it perfectly—I drank between meetings sometimes—but I did keep trying. Finally, someone I respected confronted me after my regular Saturday night meeting. I had raised my hand as a newcomer yet again, and afterward he got in my face. While everyone else had been understanding and encouraging, he had had enough. "Quit f@#king around!" he snapped at me. "This isn't a game. You need to stay sober and work the program." Well, that was the wake-up call I needed. I committed to the program and all the changes that were asked of me. And I haven't had to change my sobriety date since.

MARCH 28

"The 'why' questions keep us in the problem."

In recovery, I have learned that the "why" questions always keep me in the problem—questions like, "Why did that have to happen?" or "Why didn't/couldn't she do this?" or "Why does it always have to turn out that way?" or "Why can't I catch a break just once?" "Why" questions not only keep me focused on the problem, they almost always turn me into a victim as well.

As I worked the Steps of the program, many wonderful things began happening in my life, beginning with an awareness of my thinking and self-talk. My sponsor taught me about the "why" questions and encouraged me to look for solutions using who, what, how, and where questions instead. It was hard at first to break my old habits of thinking, but I got better as I learned to ask better questions.

Today when I have a problem or situation I don't like, I ask questions like, "What are three things I can do right now to remedy this?" or "Who might have experience with this that I can call for help?" or "What lessons are here for me to learn and grow from?" or "Where can I get a solution for this?" These questions help me get out of the problem and into the solution. Today, I know how to ask better questions.

MARCH 29

"The minute I take control, that's
when I lose control."

I used to try all the time to control my drinking and using. I'd give myself a limit as to how many drinks I would have; I'd practice drinking a glass of water between cocktails; I would use only on the weekend (that didn't work because soon Friday and then Thursday became part of the weekend), and on and on. What I found was that as soon as I tried to control it, I lost control.

When I entered recovery, I learned about the concept of powerlessness. Even though I had countless examples of how I was powerless over drugs and alcohol, I secretly hoped that one day I would be able to control and enjoy them. After countless inventories and Step work, I learned that I lost that dubious luxury long ago. Whenever I tried to control my drinking, I didn't enjoy it, and when I enjoyed it, I couldn't control it.

Just as I was coming to accept my powerlessness over alcohol, I faced an even more daunting idea—that I was powerless over just about everything else in my life as well. The way I've come to accept this is to take responsibility for the things I can control (my thoughts and my actions) and to leave the results up to God. This always works, when I remember to work it. And the minute I don't, the minute I try to take control of the outcome, that's the minute I lose control once again.

MARCH 30

❦

"Wisdom is knowledge you learn after you know it all."

You couldn't tell me anything before I entered recovery because I knew it all. I had all the answers for my life; I also had all the answers for your life, and I was quick to tell you about it. One of my favorite sayings back then was, "Those who think they know it all are really annoying to those of us who do!"

When I came into the program, I brought all my opinions into the rooms with me. At first I tried to do things my way and thought I had better answers than you. I mean, "Turn it over"? "Let go and let God"? That may work for you, but I was sure I knew better. Soon afterward, though, I was drunk.

When I finally admitted that I didn't know how to stay sober, I became willing to admit that perhaps I didn't know everything after all. That was the moment I became teachable, and it was the moment I began to recover. The longer I'm in the program, the more I realize that many times what I think I know just isn't so. Today, I'm quick to admit that I don't have all the answers, and when I do that I become open to the wisdom that lies beyond.

MARCH 31

"God is the answer, so now,
what is the question?"

When I was a newcomer, I had a hard time with the God part of the program. "Higher Power" made it a little easier, but I still had trouble turning my drinking—and so the only way I knew how to live—over to something I didn't quite believe in yet. My sponsor suggested I make the group of drunks (G.O.D.) in the meetings my Higher Power because they could do something I couldn't: stop drinking. With that I was able to make a start.

While I began to see that the G.O.D. concept was working and that there might be something else helping to keep me sober, there was no way I was going to turn other areas of my life over. "God isn't going to give me money to pay my bills today, is He?" "It's up to *me* to make everything better in my life," was part of my early attitude. Only slowly did this change as I found that the more I did turn over, the better my life got.

Today, I understand the full meaning of the Third Step and prefer to turn as much of my will and life over to God as I can. Without exception, any answer or direction I receive from prayer or meditation with God turns out to be the best for me and all involved. Now, whenever I'm anxious or uncertain about something, I'm grateful to turn to God. And when I dwell with Him long enough, I usually forget what I was worried about to begin with. God truly is my answer today.

APRIL 1

"Fake it 'til you make it."

If life is a self-fulfilling prophesy, then I used to believe my life was destined for failure. I always thought I had been dealt a bad hand: broken family; alcoholic, abusive father; poor education; menial jobs, and so on. And once I discovered alcohol, my downward spiral accelerated. I believed and acted as if my end would come quickly, and that it would be worse than I could imagine.

Thankfully, when I hit bottom, I stopped digging. I entered the program, and with the help of my sponsor and the Twelve Steps, I began uncovering, discovering, and discarding my old ideas. In limbo between who I had been and who I was yet to become, my sponsor suggested I "fake it until you make it." When I didn't believe the program would work for me, he suggested I act as if I did and to keep coming back. When I didn't think I'd get a better job, he suggested I act as if I did and to suit up and show up and go on interviews. By taking a lot of contrary action, my life improved.

When it came to the God concept, I didn't know if I could turn in the Academy Award–winning performance it would take to fake faith. But then my sponsor told me something I remember to this day. He said that he would rather live believing there was a God and then die to discover there wasn't, than to live as if there wasn't a God and die to find out there was. When I heard this, I made a decision to believe, and when my faith wavered, I faked it until I made it. It worked, and today I believe in God and that my life is destined for good. And if I ever doubt it, I just fake it until I make it.

APRIL 2

"When I did my Fourth Step, it felt as if my life was being turned upside down—but it was really being turned right side up."

I first heard this saying right when I needed it most—when I was in the middle of my Fourth Step and I thought I was losing my mind. I remember sitting in my Wednesday night meeting after just having written some inventory, and I literally thought my life was coming apart. That's when someone shared this, and at once I was filled with hope and thought maybe, just maybe, I will survive this.

The "fearless and thorough moral inventory" of the Fourth Step not only rocks our very foundation, it shakes loose the shame and the secrets that make up our fragile and distorted sense of self. This sober examination of our core defects of character causes us an overwhelming amount of pain, and once we begin looking at and seeing how these defects drove us, it's no wonder we feel our very lives are being turned upside down, because they are.

The good news, however, is that a thorough Fourth Step is the very thing needed to turn our lives right side up. Before this process, it was all your fault, and because I couldn't control you, I was always the victim. But by seeing and taking responsibility for my role, which I do have control over, I can now make changes, thereby giving me control and hope over my future. The Fourth Sep indeed made me crazy at first, but then it turned my life around and set me free.

APRIL 3

"What other people think of me is none of my business."

How much of my time and energy have I spent worrying about what other people think of me? "Too much," is the short answer. Before recovery, I had few boundaries and little sense of self. How I felt about myself and my life was largely determined by whether other people approved of me or not. With no internal awareness, other people's likes and dislikes, moods and opinions were the compass I used to evaluate and direct my emotional life. This exhausted me and contributed to the bottom that drove me into the program.

Thank God for recovery through the Twelve Steps. In particular, while writing my Fourth Step inventory, the "my part" fourth column, I found the freedom and encouragement to discover and validate my own feelings. This process continued as my sponsor helped me take the focus off others and taught me to look within for my own truth. At first this was an unfamiliar and uncomfortable process, but it was the only path to the security, confidence, and peace I had always craved.

Today, I've come to honor and welcome my feelings, and I now trust and rely on them as the ultimate validation for my sense of self. I recognize that other people have their own thoughts and opinions, and they are valid for them. But today, there is a boundary between the two, and my opinion and acceptance of myself are no longer linked to other people's approval. Today, I enjoy the freedom and empowerment that come from respecting, and even loving, myself.

APRIL 4

"My recovery changed when I forever gave up the hope of having a different past."

I have spent a lot of time thinking about my past—alternately feeling sorry for myself or being outraged by the wrongs—real or imagined—that were done to me. A constant theme in my thinking is how much different, better, and happier I would be if only I hadn't had these parents, or these stepparents, or these siblings, and so on. My angst over my past fed resentments that fueled my alcoholism, and that nearly ruined my future.

But it will never *be* different. My past will always be my past, and, good or bad, it is uniquely mine. When I got to the program I was taught that in recovery we stop fighting everybody and everything; in other words, we surrender. At first I saw surrender as a sign of weakness, but soon I found it to be the path to freedom. By releasing myself from the pain of my past, I could see it in a new light, and the miracle of my recovery had begun.

By working the program, I am able to make peace with my past, to look at my part, and see the lessons and gifts it has to offer. And what I find is that no matter how painful or unjust my past was, with time I have seen how valuable my experiences are, and how I can use them to help another. A therapist once told me, "Our deepest wounds, integrated, become our greatest power." Once I have healed my past, I begin to see how it can help heal someone else's.

APRIL 5

"R&R stands for rest and relaxation, not rehearse and rehash!"

If only my mind would leave me alone, I often think. I have what I call a *digging mind*. Like a dog at the beach, it digs and digs and digs in a problem, a worry, or in some other imagined potential problem area or scenario, often without my approval or even awareness. It loves to uncover negative thoughts, feelings, and fears, and then rehearse ugly scenarios or rehash old problems. In the past, the only way of quieting my mind was to drink.

My digging mind is not only relentless, it is consistently negative as well. When I got sober, I rarely found it digging in a positive or hopeful place. During early recovery, it wasn't dwelling on how great my life would turn out, or how all the damage I had done would get straightened out. Instead, I learned that I was driven by a hundred forms of self-centered fear, and I watched as it searched and dug away at the beaches of disappointment, past regrets, and failure.

Thank God I was given tools to rein in my mind and things to do that kept me focused on the positive aspects of recovery. I learned to take my mind off myself by helping others. I started dealing with my resentments of the past by doing inventories and looking at my part. And I found relief by clearing away the wreckage of my past and making amends. Today, I know how to give myself a break, and when my mind starts digging I direct it to uncover God's will for me. Today, I've learned how to truly rest and relax.

APRIL 6

***"There are no victims, only volunteers.
You always have a choice."***

This was a tough lesson to learn. When I was new to the program, I felt like a victim in many situations and relationships. When I started complaining about my job or what my family was making me do, I expected to get some sympathy and understanding. I was shocked to be told that I was a willing volunteer in much of the drama and even the pain in my life. That was a hard pill to swallow.

And it didn't go down easily. I had to do many fourth columns of the Fourth Step—my part—before I clearly understood that I had a choice, and so a role, in the uncomfortable situations in my life. As I began making different choices by not engaging in old family dynamics, or by making better decisions elsewhere, other people got pretty upset. They were used to me playing a certain role and so grew angry and resentful as I began to stick up for myself.

The breakthrough came as I continued to honor myself and make healthy choices. The miracle was that as I changed and recovered, the dynamics of my relationships changed. Soon, as I took more responsibility for myself, other people took responsibility for their actions as well. Together, we became less codependent, and through my recovery others experienced recovery also. And it all started when I accepted my role as a volunteer and began making different choices.

APRIL 7

"Put the magnifying glass down and pick up the mirror."

Oh, how I love focusing on you. If you would only stop doing this or that, or if you'd start doing this or that, then finally, maybe, I'd be happy. Relieved of the responsibility of self, it was so easy to be critical, resentful, and dependent on you. "If you only knew what you were doing to me. If you loved me, you wouldn't act this way. Don't you care about me?" These were my constant thoughts.

When I first entered the program, my sponsor told me something shocking—he told me that my happiness and well-being were *my* responsibility. He told me it was and always will be up to me to make my life enjoyable and safe. "But what happens when they do this, or they do that?" I protested. "Put down the magnifying glass and pick up the mirror," he told me.

It took me a while to see the profound wisdom of this new way of thinking. Once I put the focus on me, I regained the power to influence and direct my life and happiness. If I spend my time focusing on trying to control others, then I will forever be a victim. But when I place the power and responsibility where I do have some control—over my own life—that's when I begin to recover and regain hope. It's about the mirror, not the magnifying glass, today.

APRIL 8

"FEAR: False Evidence Appearing Real,
and more . . ."

There are a lot of great acronyms in the program, and three of them describe the progress I've made with respect to fear. The first is: *"F@#k Everything And Run."* This is how I dealt with fear before recovery, and as a result, many unresolved issues became big problems. These problems begat more problems until they piled up on themselves and overwhelmed me, making my life completely unmanageable.

When I entered the program, I was taught that most of my fears were nothing more than *"False Evidence Appearing Real."* Through working the Steps, I found that many of my fears were just that: stories my head made up and elaborated on based on situations and evidence that didn't even exist. Through my recovery I learned to look at the facts and stay in the moment, which helped me see fear as it mostly is: *False Evidence Appearing Real.*

As I made progress through the Twelve Steps, I learned that fear could also stand for *"Face Everything And Recover."* By following the basic tenets of this program—trust God, clean house, and be of service—I have discovered that I can face and get through anything life throws at me. And this is especially true when it comes to fear. My approach today is to look for the solution that is contained in the Steps. And when I do, I find a way to grow through fear rather than run away from it.

APRIL 9

*"When one door closes, another opens,
but it's hell in the hallways."*

I have never been comfortable with change. Before recovery, I had few tools or healthy ways of dealing with it. For example, if something ended in my life, it often felt like the end *of* my life. Once I entered the hallway, it was scary indeed. As I flailed around those dark hallways, I reached out to the only thing that brought me relief: alcohol. But soon, even that flickering light went out.

When I entered recovery and began working the Steps, I learned many valuable life lessons. The first was, "One day at a time." Even though life was still scary, I learned that I could get through anything just for today, and if I kept my focus on what I was doing in the moment, I could handle my anxiety. The hallway doesn't look so long or so dark when I do this.

Perhaps the biggest thing I learned is that "this, too, shall pass." No matter how bad things seem, or what is happening, it, too, will pass, and things will change. And with change comes new openings, new opportunities, and new beginnings. Today, when one door closes, I have tools to deal with the hallways while I wait and watch for the new doors to open. And in my experience, they always do.

APRIL 10

"If I'm not the problem, then
there is no solution."

When I came into the program, I had a lot of problems, and most of them were your fault. My girlfriend didn't understand me, my boss didn't appreciate me, the police didn't like it when I drove after just a few drinks (I was fine!), and on and on. *If everyone would just get off my back, then I'd be fine*, I thought. After a while, I felt like the whole world was against me.

As I began working the program, I was introduced to the Fourth Step and was instructed to make a searching and fearless moral inventory. My sponsor showed me how to make a list of all the persons and institutions I resented. Finally, I could document how I had been wronged. *Perfect!* I thought. But then he slipped in a fourth column called "my part" and told me to include my role in all my resentments and interactions. *Now, that was unfair*, I thought.

With his help, however, and my willingness to be fearless and thorough, I was able to see that I did have a part in them all. And what a gift that turned out to be. I discovered that if it was all your fault—and I certainly couldn't control or change you—then I would forever be a victim, and nothing would change. But if I took responsibility for my part, which was something I could control and change, then I was released from the bondage of resentment and was finally free to live a new and better life. Today, I understand the wisdom in this quote and choose to keep my side of the street clean.

APRIL 11

"Honesty without compassion is hostility."

Before recovery, I had a lot of resentments I was unaware of, and the burden of these buried feelings was heavy. They were often expressed in a passive-aggressive way when I gave my opinion or offered unasked-for advice. I thought I was just being honest, but I've come to see I was often lashing out and being mean. Unaware of the impact of my "honesty," I unintentionally hurt a lot of people.

When I started working the program, I discovered a tool for uncovering, discovering, and eventually discarding these resentments. It's called a fearless and thorough Fourth Step. When I started writing my inventory, I imagined I had one or two resentments at most, but soon found that I had hundreds. I almost needed a whole notebook just for my family! No wonder I was so spiteful.

By working the rest of the Twelve Steps, I've been able to let go of these resentments, and something miraculous has happened: I've developed compassion for others and for myself. Freed from petty resentments and imagined wrongs, I now identify with the struggles we all share as we make our way through life. I'm not better or worse than anyone else. Newfound compassion now allows me to be open with and thus deeply connected to others. Today, my honesty is based on true compassion.

APRIL 12

"The people who are the angriest are the people who are the most afraid."

I t took me a long time to make the connection between my anger and my fear. For years, I drowned my fear in alcohol and lived quite detached from my feelings. Any extended periods of abstinence usually left me feeling agitated, edgy, longing for, and needing a drink. I craved the instant calm and temporary sense of ease that my addiction provided me.

When I entered the program, I was unprepared for the shock of emotions that grabbed me and tried to pull me apart. Chief among these were my feelings of dread and fear, which manifested initially as anger, and then as rage. After I completed my Fourth Step fear inventory, I began to understand that the reason I was so angry was because I was full of a lifetime of unacknowledged fear.

One of the gifts of my recovery is that now I am quick to trace any discomfort, agitation, or anger back to a specific fear. If I am complaining about a line being too long or someone driving too slowly, or if I'm angry at my boss or spouse, I stop and ask myself what is making me afraid. When the answer comes, as it always does, I use the tools I have developed in the program to deal with it. Today, I have empathy for people who are angry because I know they are just people who are in fear of something.

APRIL 13

"Without tolerance for another, it's hard to have empathy for myself."

"Tolerant" was one of the last words you would have used to describe me before I entered the program. Instead, I was quick to find fault with what you said, or how you dressed, or what you did. My opinion of myself was so low that I constantly had to rip you down to build myself up. Living this way made me bitter, isolated, and resentful.

As I listed my resentments in the Fourth Step, I began to see how much fear and low self-esteem drove my decisions and actions, hurting both myself and others. As I worked with my sponsor, I developed an awareness and acceptance for myself. And as I listened to others sharing honestly and openly about similar struggles and fears, I began to feel a connection with them. For the first time, I experienced true empathy for others.

I once read a description of empathy as being an emotional echo that is sent out to the center of another person and returns with pieces of yourself. When I began finding pieces of myself in other people's stories, I began to find the shared humanity in our experiences. And that is when I developed real tolerance and compassion for others, as well as for myself. Today, I understand that without tolerance for another, it's hard to have empathy for myself.

APRIL 14

*"Resentment: Taking poison and
hoping the other person dies."*

This was sure a shocker the first time I heard it. I was new in recovery and I had so many resentments that I didn't even know about them all yet. What I also didn't realize was that the people, places, and things I resented didn't know or care about how I felt. The only person suffering from my resentments was me. And after years of drinking over them, they finally brought me to my knees.

In the program, I learned a whole new way of living. When I started working the Fourth Step—making a searching and fearless moral inventory—I began to see all the resentments I had secretly been harboring. At first there were some I vowed I'd never let go of, but as I uncovered, discovered, and began discarding them, I felt a new freedom and a sense of peace and happiness flow into my life.

In my recovery today, I have a new understanding of the danger and futility of holding onto resentments. I much prefer to remain comfortable in my own skin, so that whenever I'm upset or feeling slighted, I look for my part and clean my side of the street. If I'm still feeling resentful, I pray for the other person for two weeks; this always works if I'm willing to work it. Today, I no longer let resentments poison me, because today I choose to live happy, joyous, and free.

APRIL 15

"I may not be much,
but I'm all I think about."

If I add up all the time I spend thinking about myself, at least 70 percent of the time I'm thinking (usually worrying) about my future, 20 percent of the time I'm thinking about my past (usually wishing I had made different choices), and about 10 percent of the time thinking about what I should do next. It's easy to see why I don't have time for others. I'm busy! And oddly, the more I think about myself, the more miserable I become.

The paradox is that all this self-centeredness isn't driven by a big ego or high sense of self, although they are certainly contributing factors. Rather, it's the low self-esteem of alcoholism that fuels my thoughts. This is why most of my thinking is negative and self-defeating. Self-loathing is a core characteristic of this disease, and when combined with self-obsession, it becomes a depressing and deadly combination.

Thank God the program offers me a way out. I was taught early on that self-centeredness is the root of my trouble, and that true recovery comes from thinking about and being of service to others. I've found that when I'm focused on others, I'm not thinking about me, and that's always when I begin feeling better about myself and life in general. And when I feel better about myself, it's easier to think more about helping and working with others.

APRIL 16

"You can't experience victory if you refuse to surrender."

The concept of surrender was—and sometimes still is—a hard thing for me to accept. I mean, how could I possibly win or succeed at something if I'm told to give up and surrender? I've always been taught that the things worth having were the things worth fighting for, yet the program told me to surrender. What was up with that?

I remember trying to figure this out when, during a meeting, I heard someone define "surrender" this way: "Surrender means laying down your arms and joining the winning side." Suddenly it made sense. I looked around at all the winners who had surrendered and overcome their addiction, and I realized that if I stopped fighting, stopped resisting, and surrendered, too, then I could recover as well.

Today, I have come to see the wisdom in the saying "We ceased fighting anything or anyone." I now understand that the majority of my pain and discomfort comes from fighting and resisting things as they are, and that immediate peace and serenity are mine the moment I surrender. Once surrendered, I can pray for the right thought or action, and the solution always comes if I remain open to it. Today, I'm on the winning side, and I have the tools to stay there.

APRIL 17

"My brain is like a photographer's dark room;
the only thing it develops is negative."

Toward the end of my drinking, I was as much addicted to negative thinking as I was to drugs and alcohol. Alcoholism robbed me of hope and took away possibilities of happiness, and the only snapshots of the future I could see were dark and blurry. As I descended further into the abyss, I was convinced that things weren't ever going to get better, and somewhere deep inside I had given up. When I finally got some help, my sponsor told me I had reached my bottom.

As I began to recover by working the Steps, I learned that alcoholism is a disease. At first I didn't believe that; instead I thought I was just weak-willed. But after listening to hundreds of other alcoholics share my same dark fears and feelings, I realized the common characteristics of alcoholism: self-loathing, negative thinking, and utter defeat. To recover from this seemingly hopeless state of mind, my sponsor told me I needed to work the program and experience the spiritual transformation that God makes possible.

While I didn't believe that would happen for me, I am grateful to report that it did. Today, I have a different, more positive voice inside that comes from my true self, the child of God who I truly am. Recovery has returned the hope and happiness I believe God wants for me, and now I experience those feelings by doing what God wants me to do: help other alcoholics recover and discover His light. Today, in the darkroom of my mind, I develop some beautiful images and pictures of a life that is happy, joyous, and free.

APRIL 18

"Keep the broom on your side of the street."

It is so easy for me to point my finger and judge. "He's not open-minded enough," "She should stop telling people what to do," "He's driving like a jerk," "She's not raising her kids right," and so on. By constantly criticizing and condemning others, it's also easy to avoid looking at my own behavior. It's easy for me to become self-righteous, and from that high perch I ultimately find myself disliked and alone. When my big ego isn't getting the attention it thinks it deserves, it's easy to get on my pity pot and think *Poor me, poor me, heck, I should pour myself a drink!*

When I entered the program, I was still pointing fingers: "I drank because she didn't understand me." "I used because my boss was unreasonable and demanding." "I'm an alcoholic because my dad was one." My sponsor showed me that when I was pointing my finger at others, three fingers were pointing back at me. He encouraged me to work my Fourth Step to see what my part might be in my resentment and judgments, and that's when my recovery began.

By turning my magic magnifying mind away from others and onto myself, I began to see that I wasn't as perfect as I thought I was. I soon found that I wasn't so open-minded either. I loved telling people what to do, and I was often the one behind you honking my horn. My sponsor taught me that by working hard to eliminate my own character defects, I would be able to free myself and others from unkind and unnecessary judgment. By doing so, I finally learned the wisdom and benefit of keeping the broom on my side of the street.

APRIL 19

❧

"Pain transformed by the Twelve Steps is no longer pain transmitted."

When I came into the program I carried a lot of pain with me. There was the pain from living daily in an abusive alcoholic household, and then years of self-inflicted drug and alcohol abuse. The pain I had was palpable, and every relationship I had felt the impact of my pain. I was passive-aggressive at work, jealous and tyrannical in relationships, and toward myself I was self-destructive and self-loathing.

When I was introduced to the Twelve Steps, the Step I feared the most was Step Four. To me, doing a Fourth Step was like climbing down a ladder into myself, into the pit of pain, shame, and fear that I was sure was going to swallow me up. I couldn't imagine that there was another side to that darkness, and it took months for me to complete that fearless and thorough inventory. Once through Step Five, however, I began to see a new light in my life, and I began to sense the freedom I had heard others talk about in the program.

Through working the rest of the Twelve Steps, I was able to shine the light of a healing and loving Higher Power on the pain and secrets that fueled my character defects. As I made amends, my connection to others, to God, and to myself was restored. As the promises came true for me, I realized that the Steps had transformed not only my pain but my whole life. For the first time ever, I was able to live comfortably in my own skin, and today what I have to transmit is experience, strength, and hope.

APRIL 20

"All unhappiness is the result of comparison."

I used to constantly compare myself to others. As I drove along Pacific Coast Highway, I'd look at all the homes on Malibu Beach and envy and resent the people who had such wonderful lives. At restaurants, I'd see couples enjoying a romantic dinner, and I'd feel sorry for myself alone at the bar. I was constantly comparing myself to what I didn't have, and as I did, what little happiness I did have slipped through my hands like sand in a sieve.

My best friend made a recommendation to me when I got sober. He told me to look for the similarities and not the differences. He knew how critical and judgmental I was and knew that if I focused my magnifying mind on the differences, then I wouldn't stay. This was sage advice. As I listened for the similarities, I stopped comparing and began identifying. Once I learned that most of us felt less than and that comparing ourselves to other people, places, and things was just another way that alcoholism fed our discontent, I found a solution.

The gratitude list is a tool in my spiritual tool kit that gets used often. Whenever I'm feeling less than, or when I begin comparing myself to others, I stop and make a written or mental list of twenty-five things for which I'm grateful. These include my health, my sobriety, my awareness of and relationship to my Higher Power, my beautiful marriage, and all the other things I have, including my ability to dream and have goals again. When I'm done counting my blessings, I'm also done comparing and my happiness returns.

APRIL 21

"No one owes you anything."

I can remember sitting at bars stirring my drink while I stirred my resentments. I resented my boss who promoted someone else over me when I deserved it more. *After how hard I worked, he owed it to me*, I thought. As I kept drinking, I looked at all the couples in the restaurant and thought about how lonely I was. Surely I deserved to be in a relationship, too. As I ordered another drink, I started counting the resentments I had over past affairs that never worked out. The more I drank, the more the world owed me, and soon I was consumed with self-pity.

When I got sober, I simmered and seethed with these resentments. As I worked the Steps with my sponsor, I began to share my belief with him that the world owed me a lot and that one of the reasons I drank so much was because I had so little. He quickly told me that the reason I drank so much was because I was an alcoholic, and the reason I had so little was because I rarely worked hard enough or long enough for it. He told me no one owed me anything.

This was hard to hear at first. But after working Steps Four and Five, I discovered that my part was the most important part in the equation of what I had and didn't have in my life. I found that others who had the things I thought I deserved did indeed do the things I didn't: They worked and sacrificed for them. When I finally accepted that I was responsible for my life, I gave up the fantasy that the world owed me anything. And once I did that, I was free to begin working for and achieving the things that were truly meaningful to me.

The WISDOM of the ROOMS

APRIL 22

"Nothing is so bad that a drink won't make it worse."

In my limited tool chest of coping skills before recovery, drinking was the number-one solution to my problems. When I lost a job or relationship, straight to the bar I would go. My problems melted away as the warm glow of alcohol went down my throat. After a few more rounds, I entered that "king of the world" state where nothing would ever go wrong again. So secure in that delusion was I that I continued to drink to oblivion. After years of carrying on this way, my original problems soon paled in comparison to the damage my alcoholism caused me.

As I got a little time in the program, I quickly forgot the negative consequences of my drinking. When I was at a restaurant, for example, I saw people laughing and enjoying their drinks. At parties, I saw how alcohol was indeed a social lubricant, and I began to miss the easy times I sometimes enjoyed. And when I had to deal with my problems in sobriety, I was tempted to think a drink would make them easier to address.

That is when my sponsor had me pull out my Step One inventory. In it, I recounted the real consequences of my disease. After sober examination, I realized that at no time did drinking help me; in fact, over and over again, it just made my problems worse. This sobering reminder drove me back to the real solution I found in the Twelve Steps. Today, I know, without a second thought, that regardless of the problems I'm facing, a drink won't help. It will only make things worse.

APRIL 23

*"There are people in jail who
have done less than I."*

I remember being in a meeting when the speaker shared that prisons are mostly filled with unrecovered alcoholics. These alcoholics, he said, were the same as you and me—only they either got caught or their alcoholism had driven them a little further than ours had. Also, he said that if we found ourselves saying, "I have never done the things some of them have," we should always add a "yet" to it. He ended by saying that prisons are just one of the places alcoholics who don't get sober wind up.

As I thought more about this, I wrote an inventory of all the close calls I had. I remember when I was seventeen, I had been drinking and driving after work and just missed hitting a woman pushing a baby in a stroller in a crosswalk. I hadn't noticed that others had stopped in the lane next to me, and I barely missed her as I sped through. Over the next twenty years of my drinking, there were multiple times when my disease could easily have landed me in jail—or worse.

When I think about how fortunate I am to have escaped the desperate consequences of my alcoholism, I am indeed filled with a deep sense of gratitude. As I sit in meetings, I know we have all survived a similar, darker fate, and the idea of sharing the bond of shipwreck survivors that I read in the Big Book resonates with me. Whenever I find myself on my pity pot for not yet getting the things I think I deserve, I remember the things I didn't get that I actually did deserve. It makes me think of another saying: "There but for the grace of God, go I."

APRIL 24

❧

"If the grass is greener on the other side, it's because they are putting fertilizer on it!"

I've spent a lot of my life envying what other people had, resenting that I didn't have it, too, and feeling I deserved it. I've always felt smarter, more talented, better looking, and more suited for the success I've seen others enjoying. I never understood why others seemed to have all the breaks until I entered recovery, and then I got a harsh lesson. . . .

As I started sharing my feelings of entitlement with my sponsor, he asked me some difficult (for me!) questions. "Why didn't you stay in college?" he asked. "Money is in sales, not college," I answered. "If you think you'd be such a great actor, why haven't you taken acting classes?" "Ah, it's not what you know, it's who you know," I scoffed. After a while, he pointed out that I had all the answers except the one that mattered.

It took me a long time before I could admit that perhaps the reason I wasn't successful was that I wasn't doing the things that successful people do. As childish as it may sound, I learned that the world wasn't waiting to give me things just because of who I thought I was. It took a while, but now I get it: If the grass is greener on the other side, it's because they are putting fertilizer on it!

APRIL 25

"The longer I'm sober, the drunker I was."

Denial is an amazing thing. When I first entered the program, I had no intention of staying sober longer than a few months. I just needed to pull things together a little, get myself under control again. I wasn't like the real alcoholics I heard share in meetings, and I was sure I could control my drinking again once I cooled it a bit. *After all, it hadn't been that bad*, I told myself.

As the fog cleared, though, and I began journaling and working the Steps, more began to be revealed to me. I especially remember sitting in meetings listening to people share about being arrested for drunk driving and thinking *That never happened to me.* I was sober over a year before I remembered that when I was seventeen I crashed my car into two parked cars and was arrested for reckless drunk driving. That was a humbling memory.

As I peel back the layers of my past and uncover the truth about my drinking and using history, I'm amazed at how lucky I've been. I know that hospitals, institutions, and prisons are packed with alcoholics and addicts who never found sobriety, and I now know I could easily have been one of them. Today, my denial is gone, and the longer I stay sober, the drunker I realize I was.

APRIL 26

❧

"When you own your part,
you own your power."

When I was new to the program, I dreaded doing my Fourth Step inventory. *What possible good could it do me to list all my resentments?* I wondered. When my sponsor told me there was an invisible category called "my part," I was sure this was going to be a useless exercise. I mean, I didn't have a part in choosing my parents or my siblings, or in what happened to me at school, and on and on. Just thinking about it made me resentful!

After months of painful and exhaustive writing, I finally finished the first draft of my inventory. I remember reading it to my sponsor during the Fifth Step and becoming more and more irritated each time he asked me about my part. "But I'm talking about what he, she, or it did to me," I complained. "Yes, but yours is the only part you can change," he said. And that's when I began to understand.

I had spent a lifetime blaming other people, places, and things for the misery in my life, and all that did was make me a perpetual victim. Once I learned to focus on my part, however, I began to see the role my own behavior played in the destructive patterns in my life. And that's when I discovered I had the power to change them. And this is what finally set me free. You see, I learned that when you own your part, you own your power.

APRIL 27

"It's okay to look back.
Just don't stare."

A few weeks ago, my brother published a memoir about the early years of our family's life in this country; we emigrated from England in the late 1950s. It tells the story of the rapid and painful breakup of our family due to my father's alcoholism, and there are some harrowing scenes that were painful for me to read. When I finished the book, I was pretty shaken up, but after a few days I felt myself again. I was grateful for this and remembered that it wasn't always this way.

Before recovery I was lost in the resentment, fear, and misunderstanding of my upbringing. I spent many years secretly wishing it had been different, and many more hating what had happened and what had been done to me. When I looked back on it, I would dwell on the wrongs that had been done, and the loathing I had for "them" soon turned into the self-loathing of my own alcoholism. Without recovery, it surely would have destroyed me as it had my family.

Through recovery, I have learned to sift through my past to find the lessons and even the gifts it has to offer. I know now that my upbringing and my experiences allow me to help others in a way that no one else can. This is one of the miracles of recovery. Today, I don't have to relive my past, but I don't have to shut the door on it either. Today, I know that it's okay, and even valuable, to look back—as long as I don't stare.

APRIL 28

"People have the right not to recover."

The first time I heard this saying, I thought it was cruel and insensitive. I had been in another program about six months and was still convinced that I not only could help other people in my life recover but that it was, in fact, my job to do so. Learning to detach with love was still foreign to me, and the idea of allowing people to destroy their own lives was unthinkable. When I asked my sponsor what to do, he told me to look at my own experience.

As a double winner (in both programs), I knew firsthand how ineffective others had been in trying to get me to see the dangers of my drinking and using. The more they tried to warn me or control my behavior, the more I resented and avoided them. In fact, their attempts had the opposite effect: They drove me to isolate and drink even more. In the end, what I learned to be true is what I've since heard in meetings a thousand times: Until we admit to our innermost selves that we're alcoholics, we won't do the things we need to do to get and stay sober.

Over the years, one of the things that continues to baffle me is why some people recover and others—who so obviously need it and would benefit from it—don't. I've had to accept my powerlessness over others, but it's still hard to see those I care about ruin their lives. My sponsor once told me that I needed to respect someone's decision to drink themselves to death. That still sounds harsh, but there's a strange, sad truth to it. It's a reminder that people have the right to not recover.

APRIL 29

"If you stay on the train long enough, the scenery will change."

Whenever I talk to a newcomer, I remember the insanity of my early recovery. I used to talk in endless circles about my problems and about the people, places, and things responsible for them. I went on and on about how I could never stop drinking, and I was convinced the program wouldn't work for me. I didn't believe it when people told me, "This too shall pass," but I was out of options so I kept showing up, hoping the people were right.

It took many months of staying sober and working the program, but things did begin to change. I began feeling better physically, my head cleared, and I became open to a new way of living. As I took different actions, I got different results, and after a while my life improved. More importantly, I developed the perspective of recovery, and I learned firsthand that things do change as long as I'm willing to change first.

Today, I know that I can only keep changing and keep growing if I stay on the train of recovery. No matter what the scenery looks like today (and sometimes it's not so pretty), as long as I continue to grow along spiritual lines, I know that it will change, and things will get better. This has been my consistent and enduring experience, and I now live by and trust in the knowledge that if you stay on the train long enough, the scenery will definitely change.

APRIL 30

"You know you'll be back, so why don't you just stay?"

When I had a few months of sobriety, I went out. I copped a resentment at my home group meeting because they ran out of the anniversary chip I was due, so I stormed out, went home, and drank. I still remember the feelings of relief I had as I drank that big glass of port wine: I was off the program and no longer had to descend into the pit of shame the Steps were leading me into. Even so, I also knew there was no other way to recover and that I would be back.

After several months of drinking and yet still going to meetings, I finally quit for good. Once again, I started working the program, all the while dreading the Fourth Step. When I got to it and started making a list of resentments and my part in them, I truly felt I had descended into hell. I was sure that once my sins and secrets were revealed, I would be shunned, abandoned, or even arrested.

What I found instead was amazing. Where I thought I would be alone, I found that people trudged the road with me, helped me, and even understood what I had been through. Where I thought I would find the darkest parts of myself, I found my connection to my Higher Power. When I thought I'd be abandoned, I found a great fellowship and now know that I don't ever have to be alone again. Today, I encourage others who want to go out to stay—you know you'll be back anyway.

MAY 1

"Don't take a drink and go to meetings."

When I was new, I was still in a fog. Most of my life was just as it had been: I still had a ton of problems, there was wreckage everywhere I turned, and the impending doom I felt only grew and grew. I needed solutions, and I needed them fast. I began attending meetings daily, and at the end I'd always be given the same message: Don't take a drink and keep going to meetings. *That's fine*, I'd think, *but where are the solutions I so desperately need?*

As I got thirty days sober, and then sixty, and even ninety days, the fog began to clear, but my life didn't get much better. In fact, as I approached my Fourth Step inventory, I thought I would get lost in the wreckage and never survive. When I pleaded with my sponsor for help, he told me the same old thing: Don't take a drink and keep going to meetings. He assured me that if I kept doing that and kept working the Steps, I would be okay.

Fast-forward a few years, and even though I highly doubted it, his advice worked. What had seemed like too simple of a solution for my complex life and problems turned out to be the exact solution I needed. All the problems I had were resolved, and all the promises came true for me. While my life isn't perfect today—no one's is—and while problems and challenges still come up, what hasn't changed is the solution: Don't take a drink and go to meetings.

MAY 2

❧

"Let it begin with me."

At my morning meditation meeting, a newcomer has a commitment to clean the room before the meeting starts. That's great. The problem is that the bleach solution he is using is strong and toxic. I approached an elder of the meeting to complain and was surprised when he intimated that it wasn't all about me. He suggested I speak to the newcomer and work it out. I didn't, and instead I sat and quietly fumed over the whole situation.

Before recovery I used to feel this kind of frustration a lot. The problems in my life were always someone else's fault, and for much of the time I played the victim and swallowed resentments. Over time, these resentments and perceived wrongs, combined with my drinking, almost killed me. Thank God for the fourth column of the Fourth Step. It was there that I learned to identify my part—and my responsibility. Turns out, if I take care of my side of the street, things tend to work out.

By the end of the meeting, I had chosen how to handle the situation. Unfortunately, the newcomer left early, but I have decided to speak with him next week. First, I'm going to acknowledge his service and see how his sobriety is going. Then I'm going to bring him a less toxic cleaning solution so that he and I and the rest of the group aren't breathing in harmful chemicals. I remember the lessons of my Fourth Step and know that if something is to be changed, then let it begin with me to help make it that way.

MAY 3

"God can't give you anything new until you let go of the old."

O h, how I love to hang on to what I think I know. I came into the program filled with opinions, ideas, resentments, attitudes, beliefs, and more. Many of them were literally killing me, yet I fiercely defended them and resisted letting them go. When other people tried to reason with me, I was obstinate and defensive. Luckily, I was also desperate and had hit a bottom, and because of this, I was willing to try something new.

That willingness was the crack in my personality through which God's energy and grace entered. I learned that with willingness comes the ability to surrender. And so, one by one, I began peeling back the layers of the onion that were my old ideas. As I uncovered, discovered, and discarded them, God gave me new ways of looking at, thinking about, and acting in my life. Slowly, a new man was being born.

What I have found over the years is that letting go is a constant, ongoing process. Each new relationship, job, situation, or season brings me face-to-face with some old ideas or opinions that I've not yet examined. When I become stuck or unhappy these days, I now know to pray for the willingness to be open, so that God can give me something new. Today, I'm not as resistant to letting go because I know that God always has something better for me.

MAY 4

"Overheard at a meeting: 'How are you?'
'Probably a lot better than I think.'"

This quote resonated deeply with me when I first heard it. What an accurate and appropriate way to answer a question I get asked so many times a day. And isn't it true? Most of the time I walk around with a completely different picture of how I'm doing and what's going on in my life. For years my disease distorted the thoughts I had about my life versus the reality of it. It's no wonder I drank so much.

When I got sober, my thinking wasn't completely restored to sanity. In fact, this quote reminds me that my thoughts are still driven by the disease of alcoholism. Even today, my head rarely tells me the truth; instead, it's busy painting dark scenarios and building cases for why and how things won't work out. It's always planning a way and a reason for me to drink.

And that is why, even after many years in recovery, I still go to meetings and work the Steps. I've been told that while I'm sleeping, alcoholism is doing push-ups beside my bed. It keeps me discontented and craving a drink, and the road to ruin is still my distorted thinking. Today, I use the tools I have to stay spiritually fit. Today, I focus clearly on how good my life really is, and when asked how I'm doing, I realize that things are a lot better than I think.

MAY 5

"Many of us get to heaven by backing away from hell."

At a meeting the other day, someone was going on and on about how he hated being an alcoholic. "What a curse," he kept saying. "Why couldn't I be like normal people?" Someone else then shared the extreme gratitude she felt for being an alcoholic, and she said that if having alcoholism was the only way of finding and establishing a relationship with God, then she would have gladly chosen to be an alcoholic.

This made me think about my own journey and attitude about my disease. In the beginning, I, too, was resentful that I had to work a Twelve Step program and attend meetings and get commitments. I was uncomfortable doing inventories and constantly looking at my side of the street. I could never understand when someone identified themselves as a grateful alcoholic. *Grateful for what?* I'd wonder.

Now that I've been sober awhile, I have come to understand and appreciate what the Big Book means when it says that our past becomes our greatest treasure. This has many implications, of course, but one is that if I hadn't been dying, and if alcoholism hadn't driven me to a bottom, I may never have reached out for life, for the program, and for God. It is indeed true that many of us get to heaven by backing away from hell. Today, I know what it means to be a grateful alcoholic.

MAY 6

"Keep coming back and don't drink."

I had a lot of problems in my life before I got sober. I had job problems (what I was doing wasn't exactly legal), I had relationship problems (with everyone from my neighbors to my family to my friends), and I had tons of other stuff I was juggling that caused me constant stress. Oh, and then there was the continuous drinking, the blacking out, and all the mess that went with that. To say the least, my life was complicated.

When I entered the rooms, I couldn't wait to tell people how much was going on in my life. I told my sponsor, my best friend, and any other poor soul who asked that dangerous question of newcomers, "How are you doing?" What I wanted so desperately was solutions. I needed answers and advice, and frankly an offer of a good job would have been helpful as well. All I got, though, was, "Keep coming back and don't drink." What? Aren't you listening? That wasn't going to solve my problems. I need some real help!

What I learned, however, was that it took many years for my life to go so wrong, and that it was going to take some time to fix it as well. The most important thing I needed to do was stay sober so that it *could* get better. What I've also learned over the years is that as long as I keep showing up and going to meetings, I will hear the solutions I need and often just when I need them. In fact, I've found that the more I change, the more the solutions I need change, too. My life has gotten a lot better, but it wouldn't have been possible if I hadn't followed the advice I got early on: "Keep coming back and don't drink—one day at a time."

MAY 7

"We found we couldn't help ourselves, but we could help each other."

Before sobriety I did everything I could think of to get better on my own. I tried not drinking during the week, and then only four days a week. I joined a gym, exercised, and even started eating better. I went into therapy and worked on myself, and I started journaling to get to my real feelings. At the end of all of this, though, I stopped going to the gym and gave up therapy as both began to interfere with my drinking.

When I entered the program, I thought I might finally learn how to help myself. Instead, I was given directions that made no sense. "Wash the coffee cups after the meeting," I was told. "Get a commitment to arrive at the meeting early to set the chairs up." "Become a greeter and ask other people how they are doing." *What about me?* I thought. *How am I going to get better if I'm focused on helping others rather than myself?* Even though I didn't understand it, I was desperate so I followed directions.

And that's when the miracle took place. Over time I came to see that alone I couldn't make my life better, but together we could recover. I learned that the solution began when I got out of myself and helped you. I discovered that when two alcoholics got together, that is when the power of God flowed and healed us both. Ultimately, I learned that when I was helping you, you were helping me, and that was the solution I could never find by myself. Today, I know that while I can't help myself, I can always help you—and together, we can help each other.

MAY 8

*"There are only two times when you
should go to a meeting: when you feel like going,
and when you don't feel like going."*

I t is hard living with a disease that tells me I don't have it. When I'm in between meetings and life is busy, it's easy for me to think of going to a meeting as an imposition. *I'm fine. I don't want to drink, haven't in years, and I'm too busy for a meeting!* That kind of thinking can get me into big trouble, and if I listen to it, I can grow irritable, restless, and discontented. And that can put me in real danger.

One of the most valuable lessons I've learned in the program is to take contrary action to what my head is telling me. In fact, I've learned that when my head is telling me I don't need a meeting, it actually means that I *really* need one. Thankfully, I learned in early recovery to take that contrary action, and when I follow it and go to a meeting, without exception, I always feel better.

I've heard that the only thing an alcoholic does in moderation is work the Steps. Because this disease is cunning, baffling, and powerful, and constantly tells me not to do something that will make me feel better, I have to remain vigilant and ready. This is why I just take the right actions regardless of what my head is saying. So, for me, there are two times when I should go to a meeting: when I feel like it and when I don't.

MAY 9

"No God, no peace.
Know God, know peace."

Lately, I've been having a rough time with my business. So many companies have tightened their budgets because of the economy, and that means my sales (and income) are way down as a result. This has led to many restless nights, getting up and worrying at 4 AM, and having a knot in my stomach most of the day.

As I went to bed last Sunday night, I could feel the familiar dread descending. As the knot began tightening, I suddenly remembered to reach out to God. Why had I been trying to go it alone? I immediately asked God to be with me right then and told Him I didn't want to wake up again alone. I asked Him to be with me in the morning, to comfort me and to allow me to know His peace.

As soon as I said that prayer, I felt my body relax and the knot dissolve. I felt a calm and a peace I hadn't known for many nights. While I still woke up early, the difference was that I wasn't worried as on previous mornings; rather, I knew that the presence of God was with me. As I lay there I just kept thinking, *Remember, it works if you work it.* I also remembered, *No God, no peace. Know God, know peace.*

MAY 10

"Anger and resentment are masks for fear."

When I came into the program, I was pretty angry. With the alcohol gone, I very quickly got in touch with my feelings, and for me that meant my anger quickly turned into rage. Oh, and resentments—I had a lot of those as well. Without having developed the spiritual tools to deal with my feelings yet, I soon became defiant. You could say I wasn't very fun to be around.

As I began working my way through the program, I learned in the *Twelve Steps and Twelve Traditions* book that we are driven by a hundred forms of self-centered fear. After doing a thorough Fourth Step that included a fear inventory, I found I was driven by way more than just a hundred! It took years, though, for me to realize the connection between my fears and the anger and resentment I felt.

Today, I not only see the connection, but I feel it all the time. In fact, today I know that whenever I'm feeling uncomfortable, impatient, quick to snap at people, or just generally irritable, I'm usually in fear of something. The good news is that now I have a solution. Today, when I'm feeling angry or resentful, I stop and ask myself what I'm afraid of. Doing this allows me to take the mask off my fears and allows my Higher Power to present a solution.

MAY 11

❧

"In recovery there are no losers,
just slow winners."

I remember being in early recovery and feeling bad because I felt it wasn't working. I'd tell my sponsor about it, and I can still hear him saying, "You're exactly where you should be, and that's exactly what you *should* be feeling right now." At first, I thought he was just handing me a line, but after a while I believed him and learned to trust in the slow progress I was making in recovery.

Years later, I'd hear other newcomers complain about how bad they felt and about how terrible a day they were having. I can still hear the old-timers ask them if they had a drink that day. "No," they would respond. "Then no matter how bad you think you're doing, when you lay your head on your pillow tonight, you're a winner." It was comforting to hear that back then, and it still is today.

Now that I've been sober a while, I understand the wisdom in today's quote. It doesn't matter what you're going through in recovery or how you feel. The fact that you *are* in recovery, that you have a program, and that you are developing or improving your conscious contact with a Power greater than yourself means that you're a winner. You may feel like a loser sometimes, but more often, and in the long run, you'll live a life filled with the joys and miracles of recovery.

MAY 12

❧

"The less full of ourselves we are, the more room there is for others."

During my first year of recovery, I worked as a municipal bond broker. I hated every minute of it and barely made enough money to survive. As I drove to a meeting one night, I was obsessed over a sale I had just talked someone into, and I was worried sick that the prospect might cancel the order. As I drove along, consumed with self-centered fear, I had a moment of clarity.

From out of nowhere my thinking shifted to today's quote—I had heard it a few weeks before—and I suddenly now knew exactly what it meant. I realized that if I arrived at the meeting obsessed with this sale, then I wouldn't be present for the people at the meeting who needed my time and attention. In that instant, I had my first God shot, and I've remembered that lesson to this day.

Today, I realize that thinking less about myself not only helps me to feel better, but it does something even more important: It allows me to be present for others. And being there for others allows the miracle of God and the program to work through me. I also know that my only hope for long-term recovery and happiness depends on my continued ability to be of service to others. That's why today I try to make more room for others by being less full of myself.

MAY 13

*"Those who piss us off the most are
our greatest teachers."*

In my pre-recovery days, a lot of people, places, and things really pissed me off. To start with, I resented my family for always trying to tell me what to do (thinly veiled as, "We're just trying to help you"). Schools, jobs, or any other institution that tried to dictate my behavior also pissed me off. I guess you could say I was kind of angry before I got sober.

When I entered the rooms, there was a whole new set of rules to follow (thinly veiled as suggestions), and I transferred my rebellion and resentment to them. Several months into sobriety, while I was still pretty angry, my sponsor told me something I didn't get at first, but which is a principle I now live by. He told me that whenever someone or something made me upset, it was always because there was something spiritually unbalanced in me.

What I've come to understand today is that whenever I get pissed off, resentful, or upset in any way, I can almost always trace it back to self-centered fear. I'm either afraid I'm going to lose something I have or not get something I think I deserve. When I'm spiritually centered, however, and close to my Higher Power, I realize I already have everything I need, and that this essential completeness can never be taken away. Today, when someone pisses me off, I realize that person is just a teacher, and I begin looking within for what I am afraid of.

MAY 14

"Take my advice. I'm not using it."

Before I had a program, I thought I knew everything. I knew the right way you should be living your life, the right diet to eat, the right way to vote, and so forth. And because I knew everything, I was quick to tell you about it. Problem was, I rarely practiced what I preached because I thought I had a better way, an easier, softer way of getting what I wanted. Turns out I was wrong.

When I started working the Twelve Steps, the biggest obstacle I faced was letting go of my old "good" ideas. My sponsor always used to ask me what my back-pocket plans were, and I'd tell him my best advice for living. "And how's that working for you?" he'd ask me. Not too well was my inevitable reply. It took many more bottoms for me to finally release my know-it-all attitude and listen to others' solutions for living.

Nowadays, I keep my advice to myself and let my life and my actions speak for themselves. If I have a good idea, I discuss it with others before I try it out. If it works for me, I let it be another living example of what works *for me*. When asked for my advice, I now offer my experience, strength, and hope instead. If it helps you, great; if not, that's fine, too. Today, I'm quicker to take advice than to hand it out, and I've found it works out a lot better this way for everyone.

MAY 15

"Just another Bozo on the bus."

All my life I've been taught to do whatever I could to be the best. In school my parents drove me to work harder than everyone else so that I could get As and stand out. When I began working professionally, it was very clear that average performance would get you fired, and that if you wanted to excel and move up, you had to work harder and be better than everyone around you. Even when I partied, I prided myself on being able to out-drink and out-use others as well.

When I entered the program, my ego was accustomed to comparing and to finding ways of proving I was better than you. When I heard some people's stories, I immediately felt better than them because I had never done *that*. And when it was suggested that I clean the coffee mugs after a meeting, I thought that was beneath me: *I mean, don't you know who I am?* My feelings of entitlement nearly sabotaged my recovery, but luckily I heard today's quote and was able to humble myself long enough to truly understand it.

My sponsor explained to me that if I wanted to get and stay sober, then I had to deflate my ego and learn to become "right-sized." He told me that I wasn't any worse or any better than anybody else; I was simply a child of God. He suggested that I would get along with people better and live more comfortably in my own skin if I could strive to become "average." It took a lot of years for me to see the wisdom in this kind of thinking and living, but now I'm truly happier being just another Bozo on the bus.

MAY 16

"'No' is a complete sentence."

Having been raised in an alcoholic home, I didn't learn much about boundaries. My mother, an untreated Al-Anon, scurried about the house trying to make everything okay. I learned that the best way to avoid trouble and get my limited needs met was by stuffing my feelings, letting everyone else have their way, and never saying no.

As I grew older, these very adaptive living and defense strategies became character defects that caused me to be insincere in relationships, continually unhappy, and ultimately unable to form meaningful bonds with other people. Without healthy boundaries, I couldn't stand up for myself and make my true needs known. Instead of looking at my role in this, I just blamed other people and formed a lot of resentments.

When I entered the program, boundaries, self-care, and responsibility for my own happiness were new ideas to me. One of the most helpful concepts was learning that my needs and well-being were not only my responsibility and right, but that I didn't have to justify or defend them to anybody. I learned that if something wasn't right for me, I could simply say no; I didn't need to argue, convince, or explain why. More importantly, I didn't need to feel guilty for stating my truth. Today, "No" is a complete sentence.

MAY 17

*"When I am in my head, I am with the
last person I got drunk with."*

When I hear this quote, I remember that my best thinking can't get me sober—that by myself, my solutions to my problems are still self-serving and often driven by fear. Before recovery, this inner voice drove me, and just as long as I followed its advice, for that long I was going to remain selfish, alone, and drunk. It wasn't until I surrendered my thinking and let someone else inside that I began to recover.

When I was new to sobriety, I was desperately afraid of telling people what was really going on in my head. If others knew what craziness brewed in there—what resentment, hatred, and despair went through my mind—I was sure they would ban me from the rooms. But they didn't. When I finally began to reveal myself, something miraculous happened. I was accepted, along with all my crazy thoughts and faults, and I was shown the way to freedom from bondage of self. That path, I learned, was to let others in.

I was taught right from the beginning that this is a "we" program, and for me to recover I needed to find someone to whom I could tell the truth. By letting others know what was really going on inside my head and by surrendering my thoughts and actions to God, I began to change. By growing in this way, I began feeling a part of the fellowship and a part of life. Today, I try to stay out of my head, because when I'm alone with myself, I know that I'm with the last person I got drunk with—and I know where that can lead.

MAY 18

❦

"When I'm filled up with me, there is no room for God."

This quote reminds me of the story of a novice who once met with a Zen master for tea. As the novice went on and on about everything he thought he knew about the practice and meaning of Zen, the master just kept pouring tea into his cup until it overflowed onto the tray. The master then just kept pouring. Shocked, the novice stopped talking and asked the master why he continued pouring when the cup was obviously full. The master replied, "You are like the cup. Your mind is so full of ideas and preconceptions that I cannot pour anything new into it." The master then stood up and left.

When I got into recovery, I was also a novice. I was so full of my own selfish ideas, I couldn't take in much recovery. The best I could do was to stay sober one day at a time. Thankfully, this was enough for me to realize that I didn't have all the answers, and by continuing to come to meetings, I became humble enough to listen and learn a new way of life. By working the Steps, I was slowly able to empty myself of me, which created room for God to come into my life.

Today, it's still easy for me to get wrapped up in my own life, my old ideas, and silly demands. What saves me—what always works to get me outside myself—is to work with others. As soon as I get together with someone, I am emptied of ego, and God rushes into that void. Suddenly I become calm, useful, and genuinely concerned with helping somebody else. It is in this state that the miracle of recovery takes place. They say A.A. is simply one drunk talking to another, and that is the simple truth and power of the program.

MAY 19

"If you keep it in, you'll go out."

T oward the end of my drinking, I had a lot of secrets. As my alcoholism progressed, I did more and more things I swore I would never do. Soon shame, remorse, and resentment became my companions, and after a while I stopped confiding in others. *Besides,* I thought, *who would want to be friends with someone as terrible as me?* Even I couldn't stand myself at the end. As my world grew smaller and smaller, I finally hit the bottom.

When I snuck into the rooms the first thing I noticed was how alive everyone seemed. Happy even. As the speakers shared their stories, illuminating the demoralizing and shameful things they had done, the audience roared with laughter. *Are these people nuts?* I wondered. Months later when I shared these thoughts with my sponsor, he told me that we were only as sick as our secrets. He told me that by letting the shame out, it loses its power over us. And that's when we begin to recover.

Letting another person in by revealing myself and the things I had done was incredibly hard. The Fourth and Fifth Steps took everything out of me, and it was only later that I understood the importance of these Steps. I learned that the more I could empty myself, the more I could let the light and love of God back in. I also learned that the things I still kept in—the character defects I wanted or thought I still needed—kept me sick, stuck, and uncomfortable. And for a sober alcoholic, that is a dangerous place to be. After years of sobriety, I know that if you keep it in, you'll go out.

MAY 20

"Another big *lie:*
I can do this on my own."

When I entered recovery, it was very hard for me to ask for help. I had been taught not to trust others, so when someone suggested I get a sponsor, I didn't think I'd need his help. The Steps, after all, were clearly laid out. Surely I could follow such easy instructions. For the first few months, I tried to go it alone, not calling any of the phone numbers people gave me, checking in with my "temporary" sponsor only when I saw him at meetings, and so on. Before long, I was isolated and desperate, and I went back out.

When I got sober again, I took the suggestion to get connected and started telling others what I was experiencing. At first I felt like I was bothering people when I called them. But very quickly something else happened: I felt better. I also started relying on my sponsor's guidance more, and together we began working the Twelve Steps. Slowly my defenses came down, and gradually I became more open to asking for help.

Even after many years in the program, my first instinct is still to go it alone and figure things out for myself. But I also have a tried-and-true tool as well, which is to ask for help when I need it. What I have found especially helpful is to share a problem I am having in a meeting. When I do, other people share similar situations and what they did to deal with them. This has helped me immeasurably and given me solutions I never would have come up with on my own. Today, I try to avoid the *big* lie and reach out to others instead.

MAY 21

"I can prove the world is a miserable place."

A s I approached my bottom, I perfected the art of negative think-ing. Fueled by the disease of alcoholism, my mind searched for and found the reason my life sucked, and then proved to me that it was never going to get better. It then went on to confirm why the whole world was such a miserable place, what with the wars, the suffering children, the crooked politicians, special-interest groups, and more. At the end of my drinking, it didn't matter if I lived or escaped the whole mess.

I didn't have much hope that sobriety would change my life for the better. I thought that even if I did manage to stay sober, I would still have all my problems, the world would still be a mess, and I still had more proof of the negative than the positive. I acquired some invaluable tools, though, as I began working the Steps. I learned to focus on just today, just this moment, and to stay out of the future. I learned to be a positive influence in the lives of others by helping them and giving of myself. And most of all, I learned how to develop a relationship with a Higher Power.

Fast-forward now to many years of recovery. The world is still a mess, I still have problems in my life, but something has changed—and the change is within me. Today, my internal landscape is based on the spiritual ideals of the Twelve Steps, and today, I seek to be a channel of God's grace. Today, I look for the good in people, places, and things, and because of that, I have a choice of what kind of proof I gather—and I know that there is plenty of good in the world as long as I'm willing to recognize it.

MAY 22

"A snail can climb Mount Fuji."

I used to get so overwhelmed by my life. I wanted to make so many changes, but where to begin? I didn't want to be in sales any longer, and instead I always wanted to get a graduate degree so that I had more options. But the thought of even applying for college, getting the financial aid, and then spending years in school was overwhelming. Even getting healthy seemed out of reach. I'd have to join a gym—and then even go regularly!—and probably have to greatly reduce my drinking. Impossible. Every change seemed monumental, so I just stayed drunk.

"One day at a time," "First things first"—these were new concepts to me, and they saved my life. That's because I applied them to the most important change of all—getting sober. While the thought of remaining sober for a whole month, and then a whole year, was unthinkable at first, I could manage the thought of staying sober that day. And, one day at a time, as I put first things first, like praying in the morning to God to keep me sober, I began accumulating first weeks, and then months of continuous sobriety.

I've been able to apply these lessons to other changes in my life. I did go back to college and earned my graduate degree. I did it one day at a time, starting by first downloading the college admission forms. I've also learned to "take the next indicated action" when I become overwhelmed or afraid. It always keeps me moving in the right direction. Today, no goal or life change seems impossible as long as I remember how even a snail can climb Mount Fuji—one step at a time.

MAY 23

*"Things might not get better for me, but
I can get better despite things."*

When I was a newcomer, I was convinced that because I was now sober, things in my life would get better. I was sure my career would finally get on track, my relationships would improve, and so on. And I thought that as those things came together, I would finally be happy. In fact, I secretly felt like I deserved for things to improve now that I was being "good." In the beginning, though, it didn't turn out that way…

What happened was that my life started to spiral out of control. It was as if things had a natural momentum to them, and even though I wasn't acting the same way, the wreckage of my past was beginning to catch up with me. As I grew more and more miserable, my sponsor taught me something that set me free.

I remember he sat me down and asked me if I could make it through the day without a drink or a drug. I told him I could, and that's when he taught me that while I may not be able to control all the things in my life, I could control the most important thing of all—my sobriety and my recovery. He told me that if I took care of that, then all the other "things" would work out. While at first I didn't believe him, it turns out he was right. Today, I know that while things may not always get better for me, I can get better if I focus on the one thing that matters: my sobriety.

MAY 24

"For every nut in the program,
there is a bolt."

When I first entered the rooms of recovery, I was a little taken aback by some of the strange characters whom I heard share. Some had been to prison, some had lived on the streets, some had been prostitutes, some were ex-gangsters, and some were still pretty crazy. "These people have nothing in common with me," I told my sponsor. "How are *they* going to help me get sober?"

"Some of these people may not be able to help you directly," he said. "But the fact that they can get this thing and stay sober shows that you can, too." I saw his point. "Besides that," he continued, "even if they don't have the exact experience you've had, there will be someone else who will. No matter what's going on with you, there will always be somebody who has the experience, strength, and hope you will need."

Over the years, I've found this to be so true. One of the things I've learned to count on is that there is always someone who can help me regardless of what I've been or am going through. This has taught me the value of everyone in the program, not just those whom I can identify with. Now I know that there is a bolt for every nut in the program—even me!

MAY 25

"Sit down, shut up, and listen."

When I was brand-new to the program, I had a lot to share. I liked going to participation meetings because I thought you needed to hear what I thought I knew about drinking, and even about regaining control. I didn't buy that alcoholism was a disease, and I harbored the belief that as soon as I got things settled down, I could probably resume drinking more moderately. Finally, my sponsor pulled me aside and gave me a suggestion.

He told me, as nicely as he could, that for the time being I might want to listen more rather than share. He suggested that the people in the rooms could do something I never could—stay sober and happy for many years. He told me that if I wanted what they had, then perhaps I should listen to their experience and take the actions they took. He encouraged me to share my thoughts and feelings with him, one on one, but at meetings he essentially suggested I sit down, shut up, and listen.

Once I became willing to take things in, I started making better progress in my recovery. As I began working the Steps, I found I really needed the experience, strength, and hope I heard from others in meetings. After a while, I began sharing again, but I was taught to only share my experience on a topic, not my opinion. By following the early direction I was given, I have been granted the gift of recovery. And it all started by sitting down, shutting up, and listening.

MAY 26

"Don't compare—identify."

Comparing my insides—how I feel about myself and my life—with someone else's outsides—what I think they have and the kinds of lives I imagine they are living—has always kept me feeling less than. As I struggled in my career or relationships, I'd see others wearing nice suits, driving nice cars, or enjoying romantic dinners in restaurants. Not only did I not have those outside things, but inside I was miserable, so I kept drinking.

The night I attended my first meeting, my friend advised me to look for the similarities rather than the differences. This was good advice, and when I listened to the speaker's story, I identified with many of his thoughts, feelings, and actions. Deep down, I thought we had much in common. As I began working the Steps, I began comparing what I had in early sobriety to what I saw others had attained because they had more time sober. Soon I was feeling less than, again.

My sponsor came to my aid. He suggested I stop comparing and that I start identifying with others instead. He told me to listen to people sharing and to identify with their hopes, dreams, struggles, and fears. Once I did, I discovered that despite how different our outsides may be, inside we're all the same. Today, whenever I'm feeling less than—or more than—I stop and try to identify. When I do, I feel equal to, and that helps me feel a whole lot better about myself.

MAY 27

"Formula for failure:
Try to please everyone."

I used to drive myself crazy trying to please everyone. In my insane alcoholic home, I learned that if I didn't make waves, and just agreed with everyone, then maybe for a little while there would be some peace. But it didn't last long. Soon I would have to change, adapt, and give in again to placate the prevailing mood or attitudes of others. It was exhausting, and in the middle of it all, I lost my sense of self.

In working the Twelve Steps, I discovered something else: I had a lot of resentments. I used to consider myself an easygoing guy, but what I learned by doing a Fourth Step inventory was that by acquiescing to others by trying to please them, I was untrue not only to myself but to others as well. By looking at my part in the fourth column, I realized that if I was to be happy and free, it was up to me to change.

Changing the way I interacted with others, especially with my family, was very uncomfortable for a long time. Suddenly, I was no longer the pushover, and when I disagreed or refused to go along with their ideas, I suffered their wrath. But at least I didn't hate myself or hold the familiar resentments anymore. After years of being true to myself, I've healed my relationship with myself and with others. Today, I have successful relationships because I am no longer trying to please everyone.

MAY 28

"Sometimes you don't make progress; you just hold on."

Early in sobriety, there were many days when I felt I just wasn't going to make it. I would see others take chips and cakes on their anniversaries, and I was pretty sure I'd be drunk tomorrow. When I met with my sponsor, he told me that even if I couldn't see the progress I was making, others could. When he saw my look of disbelief, he asked if I was sober that day. I told him I was, and he told me the program was working for me even if it didn't feel like it.

As I made my way through the Steps, it continued to be a roller-coaster ride. Sometimes the pink cloud returned, and I was filled with hope and gratitude. But other times I descended into the pit of despair and felt like I was going backward. During these dark times, my sponsor told me to just hold on. "Don't drink today, and I guarantee it will pass," he said. And it always did.

After many years of sobriety, there are still times in life when I don't feel as though I'm making the progress I would like. What I've learned is that it is okay to just hold on during these times. I have found that the solution is for me to stay sober, turn things over to God, be grateful for what I do have, and be open for what His will holds next for me. Each time I do this, I find that holding on is part of the process that leads to the progress I was hoping for.

MAY 29

"All that pain has value."

When I came into the rooms, I was buried in shame. Without alcohol to escape into, I was overwhelmed with remorse over many of my actions. As I moved toward working the Fourth Step, I was desperately afraid of what I would find in the abyss of self. I was sure that once I uncovered how bad I really was, no one—including myself—would accept me. I was definitely at a jumping-off place.

As I began putting my inventories together, I discovered something else, though. Yes, I had acted poorly and had made many selfish decisions, but I learned that much of my behavior had been driven by the disease of alcoholism. What I found was that my actions weren't necessarily who I was; they were just my actions. And if I was willing to own those actions, make amends, and stay sober, then I could recover through working the Twelve Steps.

As I continued to uncover, discover, and discard my character defects, I found something even more important. I learned that all my experiences, especially the "bad" ones I felt shame over, would turn out to be the most useful in reaching out to and helping others. I learned that my pain was often the key that allowed others to come to terms with and overcome their own pain. All the experiences I had tried to run from had value, and in God's hands they uniquely qualified me to be of service to His other children. Today, I no longer wish to shut the door on my past or on my pain.

MAY 30

"Alcoholism is an equal opportunity destroyer."

I never thought of myself as an alcoholic. My idea of an alcoholic was a bum living in the gutter downtown, or someone wearing a dirty raincoat drinking from a paper bag. I owned a home, had a retirement account, and dined at fancy restaurants. I just drank too much sometimes—it could happen to anyone. After years of what I've now discovered to be the slow progression of the disease of alcoholism, my life hit a bottom, and I started attending A.A. meetings.

When I got to the rooms, the people I met didn't fit the profile of what I thought of as alcoholics. There were no dirty trench coats, and the guys who had five-day-old beards wore them carefully cut and shaped. I met people in all lines of work: attorneys, dentists, actors, housewives, and more. They were full of life—laughing, sharing, and giving freely of themselves. As I listened to their experiences and feelings, I identified with them, and I felt like I belonged.

I remember being in a meeting and hearing a newcomer share that he didn't think he was an alcoholic. Someone else shared that nonalcoholics rarely found themselves in an A.A. meeting on a Saturday night denying they were alcoholics. The suggestion was to keep coming back. As I kept coming to meetings and working the Steps, I discovered that I, too, had the disease. I found that it is an equal opportunity destroyer, and that no one was immune. I also found that we all have a common solution that works every time we work it. I thank God daily I was willing to try it.

MAY 31

*"The worst bottom can become
the greatest beginning."*

A woman once shared in a meeting that she used to keep a breathalyzer in her house to help her control her drinking. One day she started drinking too early, lost track of time, and her husband caught her using it. She was upset the dogs hadn't given her a warning that he was coming. The husband, naturally, was aghast, and it seemed like the end of her marriage and family. Instead, it led to her recovery.

I've heard people describe all kinds of bottoms. Some have shared that they came out of a blackout in jail, scared and confused, and not knowing if they had killed anyone while driving drunk. I've known others who lost their businesses, their families, and even their freedom. Bottoms come with demoralization, shame, embarrassment, and bewilderment. All these situations seem like the end of the world, and they are.

But the world that ends is a dark one, one that was ultimately unsustainable and led to ruin. The new world that recovery brings is one where hope, love, and faith are restored. Through the Twelve Step program, a God of our own understanding performs the miracle of transformation in our lives. He turns what seems to have been the worst day into the greatest, and so begins our new life. No matter how dark your life seems right now, take our advice: "Don't leave before the miracle."

JUNE 1

"But by the grace of God, there go I."

In early sobriety I sometimes had trouble identifying with other people's alcoholism, and often wondered whether I belonged. After all, I had never been to prison for manslaughter while driving drunk. I never robbed a liquor store in a blackout or woke up in a different state—or country—not knowing how I got there. There were countless other things that had never happened to me either. As I discussed this with my sponsor, he said I hadn't experienced these things—yet.

As I started working the Steps and writing inventories, I began to see what he meant. First of all, I remembered I crashed a car while drunk, and I had been arrested for it when I was a minor. Thankfully, I hit an unoccupied parked car, and no one in my vehicle was injured. Other inventories revealed plenty of times I blacked out and came to in strange circumstances. As I looked deeper, I identified more with the stories I heard, and I felt the gravity of the word "yet."

Today, I know my stories could have ended very differently if I had continued drinking, and any of the outcomes I heard others share could easily have been my fate as well. Moreover, I also know that any of these terrifying endings could be in my future also—they are only one drink away. Today, when I see or hear these stories, I say a quiet prayer of gratitude, for I know that "but by the grace of God, there go I."

JUNE 2

"What's the most loving thing I can do for myself today?"

My drinking career was filled with a series of self-destructive situations, actions, and events. When I was drinking, I didn't like myself very much, and I didn't care what happened or how much trouble I got into. Part of me even felt like I deserved bad things. Because I didn't care about myself, I also didn't care much what happened to others either. As my life caved in on itself, and my demoralization was complete, I hit my final bottom.

In the sober light of day, I began my Step work and explored my drinking years through the use of inventories. I uncovered some dark resentments, discovered the character defects that I used to deal with them, and eventually found a way to discard the old self that had been driven by the disease of alcoholism. The most painful part of that whole process was how much self-hatred I had. Ultimately, what I learned is that the core characteristic of this disease is unrelenting self-loathing, and an unbelievable obsession for self-destruction.

The power of the Twelve Steps is that they have released me from this prison of hatred. By working through the layers of the disease— the shame, the complete incomprehensibility of my feelings and actions—I finally arrived at the truth of who I really am: a child of a loving God. In my core, I am not the dark illusion of the disease. I am, instead, a shining beacon of God's light. Today I ask, *what is the most loving thing I can do for myself?* Just the fact that I can ask that question evidences the profound change the program has made in my life.

JUNE 3

"Instead of telling God how big your fears are, start telling your fears how big your God is."

I never knew how much fear ruled my life before I entered recovery. After writing many inventories while working the Steps, my sponsor had me write a fear inventory. I found that I was afraid of not only other people but places and things as well. As these fears boiled up inside me—fear of disease, of the IRS, of the police, of my boss, and so on—I began to understand part of the reason I drank so much. But now that I was sober, what was I to do with all these fears?

As I worked my way through Steps Six and Seven, my sponsor helped me see that fear was a character defect. Most of my fears, he pointed out, were based on self and driven by my demand to either get my way or not lose what I had. The way out of my fear was to stop thinking about myself and what I could get, and instead turn my will and my life over to my Higher Power. Constantly ask yourself, he advised, "What is God's will for me here?"

It was hard to let go of my will, my old ideas, and my self-centered fear. But with constant practice, a sincere desire to be free of fear, and faith in my Higher Power, I began to outgrow fear. In those situations where fear begins to take over today, I stop and ask what God would want for me and others. "How can I best serve Thee?" is my constant mantra. When I start telling my fear how big my God is, I am thinking of Him and not my fears. At that point, I begin to overcome fear, and I am free to be of service to others. And when I'm into you, and into God, I am out of myself and fear.

JUNE 4

"If you spot it, you got it!"

I used to be so self-righteous. I spent a lot of time and energy judging and finding fault in others. I used to enjoy watching and telling you and others what you were doing wrong, but I was largely blind to my own faults. While it was easy to point my finger, I never realized that when I did, there were three fingers pointing back at me.

When I entered the program, I began judging everybody and everything. As I shared some of my observations with my sponsor, he suggested I might want to take my focus off others and place it more on myself. As I did, I became more self-aware, and that's when I learned that the reason it was easy to find specific faults is that I often have the very same faults as well. In other words, *if I can spot it, I got it*. That was quite a revelation.

The longer I'm in recovery, the truer I find this to be. In fact, nowadays if I curse at someone for not using a turn signal, I find that I'm doing the same thing moments later. Ultimately, what I've learned is the lesson of humility. No one, including me, is any better or worse than anyone else. No one is a saint. We're all doing the best we can, and my job is to work on myself, and to spot and correct my own faults—not yours.

JUNE 5

"The worst vice is advice."

Everybody has an opinion. And before recovery, I would readily give you mine. It didn't matter if you asked for it or not; it didn't matter whether I had ever taken the advice myself to see if it worked; and it didn't matter if it made you feel better or worse—I was addicted to giving advice, and if you were nearby, you'd get it. As you can imagine, I was obnoxious to be around, and all my advice didn't seem to help anybody. In fact, most people grew to resent me, and as fewer people called, my circle of friends grew smaller and smaller.

When I entered the program, I still had a lot of advice to give, but my sponsor suggested I listen for a while to what others had to say. When I kept trying to tell him my good ideas, he pointed out that my best thinking got me a seat in a recovery meeting. When I persisted and tried to tell him about relationships, career choices, and investing, he told me people might not be interested given that I was single, unemployed, and broke. That kind of put me in my place.

What I learned by listening is that others didn't share advice. Instead, they offered their experience, strength, and hope. Someone who didn't have direct experience to share would encourage me to find someone who did. Over time, I learned that advice is worthless without compassion, understanding, and experience that comes from a shared point of view. Today, I don't offer advice on things I don't have experience with, and I don't give it unless I'm asked for it.

JUNE 6

"We may be powerless, but we're not helpless."

Accepting that I was powerless over people, places, and things was a concept I rebelled against on almost every level in the beginning. Before recovery, I was driven by the belief that not only could I control others (especially those I loved and cared for), but it was my duty to do so. Despite the fact that it rarely worked, I stubbornly persisted, frustrating myself and irritating and alienating those I was trying to control—err, I mean, help.

When I entered another Twelve Step program for this, I was told that the reason I had been unable to influence, help, or control another was because I was in fact powerless over other people, places, and things. *If that's true, then there is absolutely no hope for this situation!* I thought. Accepting this was contrary to everything I believed, and it meant complete defeat. What was I to do?

By working this wonderful and much-needed program, I soon learned that surrendering to this powerlessness was the gateway to a new freedom. Once the untenable burden of controlling or fixing others was lifted, I was suddenly free to invest my energy where I did have some power and influence—over my own life. And that is when I realized I was no longer helpless to fix my situation and my life. Today, I understand and truly appreciate that I may be powerless, but I'm not helpless to make things better.

JUNE 7

"Going to meetings is like taking aspirin before a headache."

I was reminded of how true this saying is just the other day. I had been really sick for a week—I mean in-bed sick. As such, I hadn't been to a meeting all week. This is unheard of for me, as three meetings a week is my usual minimum, while four to five is more common. So there I was at my local Rite-Aid pharmacy, staring down at the cough syrups, when all of the sudden I saw one that said "Alcohol-free." So that's the one I automatically chose, right? Not at all!

You see, because I hadn't been to a meeting in a week, my keen alcoholic mind was thinking again. And without my conscious permission, it was arguing with me as to why the nonalcoholic version obviously couldn't be as good as the one with alcohol. In a flash it had me convinced that it must be the watered-down version, and that it didn't have as much of the active ingredients in it. And without the alcohol, I wouldn't even get the rest I so desperately needed to get better. I was sold. . . .

As my hand reached down to get the "right cough syrup," a tiny, faraway, twelve-year-sober voice whispered, "That might not be such a good idea." I almost didn't hear it, but its truth was powerful. I snapped out of it, and in a moment of clarity I grabbed the alcohol-free one and quickly got out of there. Now I'm pretty sure that if I had been to my regular meetings that week, the choice would have been much easier. It just goes to show that if you don't want a (major!) headache, then keep taking your aspirin regularly.

JUNE 8

"Anger is one letter away from danger."

When I came into the program, I was so angry, but I didn't realize how much. For years I had used drugs and alcohol to numb my feelings, to manage and hide them. When my temporary solutions were taken away, my anger quickly turned to rage, and I soon found that I had turned much of this rage inward. In fact, today I still believe that a core characteristic of alcoholism is deep self-loathing.

Thank God for recovery. By working the Twelve Steps I learned how to forgive others and myself and take responsibility for my part. I also learned how to surrender to a Power greater than myself. Slowly, I began to release a lot of the regret and resentment that made up a great deal of my rage. And once the rage dissipated, I discovered I had the ability to choose healthier ways of dealing with my feelings.

But I *still* get angry sometimes. These days I've learned that when I do get angry, I'm still in danger of turning it inward and acting in self-destructive ways. I'm quick to isolate and grow depressed, to tell someone off and create resentments, or even to eat too much and go back into self-loathing. Thankfully, I have learned to acknowledge and deal with my anger before it turns into rage. Today, I realize that anger is one letter away from danger, and I use my program to stay out of harm's way.

JUNE 9

"The monkey may be off my back, but the circus hasn't left town yet."

After I had about six months of recovery behind me, I began to feel as if my addiction was finally becoming more manageable. I didn't crave alcohol all the time, it didn't drive me as it once had, and I found myself thinking more about the Steps, my life, and the work ahead. The monkey was off my back!

But that didn't mean the circus of my life had left town. With the monkey gone, and my focus now redirected, I was confronted with the damage, the wreckage, and the circus of my life and my affairs. What a mess! I felt as if the different areas of my life were like separate Big Top tents—each with its own wild circus act going on and all out of control. How was I ever to deal with it all?

One day at a time, that's how. One of the most valuable lessons I learned early on was that I hadn't created this mess in a day. Therefore, I couldn't fix it in a day either. But one day at a time, with God's help, I could be honest and clean house, and sanity would return. And it did. Today, I'm happy to report that the circus, the monkey, and all the ringleaders have left town. It's peaceful here now, and I'm grateful.

JUNE 10

"We go to meetings for relief;
we work the Steps for recovery."

It happens every time: I always feel better after a meeting. Regardless of what's going on or what my mood is, after a meeting I always feel more centered, more connected, and more at peace. The only problem is that this relief doesn't last very long. Once I'm back in the world or in my routine, the effects of the meeting wear off, and I often find myself irritable, restless, or discontented.

I was taught a long time ago that meetings were an important part of my program, but they wouldn't give me the recovery I needed. Only the Twelve Steps would do that. Working the Steps causes the needed transformation of my personality, which leads to a spiritual experience. And it is this spiritual experience that results in the miracle of recovery.

Even though I have recovered from a seemingly hopeless state, I am reminded that I still have a disease. This is where meetings help me. When I become anxious or uncomfortable, I know that my regular meeting schedule provides the relief and the reminders I need. But I also know that I must keep working the Twelve Steps of the program to experience the recovery that saves my life.

JUNE 11

"When I say no *to you, I'm saying* yes *to me."*

B efore recovery, I wasn't very good at setting personal boundaries. When people asked me to do things, I almost always said yes—despite the emotional, physical, or financial costs to me. For years, I blamed and resented people for taking advantage of me, and it took me a long time in recovery to believe that saying "no" was not only my right but often my responsibility to myself as well.

Despite how much practice I've had at it, it is still hard for me sometimes to say no to people. Even though I'm much better at it and do it much more frequently, I still feel like I'm letting someone down, and I often struggle with either feeling guilty for saying no or resentful for saying yes. When I heard today's quote, I finally understood why.

Saying no to others means that I'm saying yes to *myself*, and that concept is still foreign to me. Having been raised to disregard my needs and wants, the idea of honoring and respecting them is something that still takes contrary action for me to reinforce. The good news today is that the more I do it the better I feel, and I know that each time I do, my self-esteem gets a little stronger. Today, it's a little easier to say no to you because it feels better when I say yes to myself.

JUNE 12

"Problems are solutions in training."

This was definitely not the way I used to look at problems before recovery. My problems used to overwhelm me; they had no solutions, and there was a long list of them. I would bounce from one to the other, and as I tried to solve them, I just seemed to create more and more. I once heard that the only thing worse than my problems were my solutions to them!

When I entered the program, I surrendered both my problems and my solutions. My sponsor kept pounding into my head that my best thinking had gotten me here, and with his help, I turned my attention to working the first Three Steps. And once I was able to turn my will and my life over to a Power greater than myself, the real solutions started to appear.

As I stayed sober and worked the other Steps, my problems began to solve themselves. As I became more experienced in turning them over, applying the Steps on them, and using more of the tools in my spiritual tool kit, I found that my problems were really opportunities for me to grow and change. Today, my problems have become my teachers, leading me to spiritual solutions as long as I remain open and willing to learn from them.

JUNE 13

"Half measures do avail us something—
it's just the half we don't want."

Before sobriety, I was a master of "half measuring" in my life, and what I got was the half I didn't want. At work I arrived late, did just enough to get by, and was the first to leave. The result was that I was fired a lot. In relationships, I paid attention just enough to get what I wanted and wasn't very interested in doing what she wanted to do. The result was that my relationships didn't last very long. I half measured my way through school, my family, and my health, and the results I got were always the half I didn't want.

In the beginning of the program, I was half measuring it as well. I showed up late, sat in the back, didn't help clean up, and wouldn't go to fellowship. After complaining to my sponsor that the program wasn't working, he quickly pointed to my half-measure attempts and the half-measure results I was getting. If I wanted to be happy, joyous, and free, he told me, then I would have to give the program everything I had.

Once I became willing to do whatever it took to get and maintain sobriety, things did begin to change. When I arrived early and greeted people, I became known and felt a part of the group. When I started sharing what was really going on, I felt better. And when I really worked the Steps, I began to recover, and the desire to drink and use lessened and finally left me. Today, I no longer half measure my way through life, and because of that, I get to enjoy the full benefits of everything I do.

JUNE 14

"I'll never be all right until it's all right, right now."

I've always lived waiting for some future time or event to make me happy. "When I meet 'her,' then I'll be happy." "As soon as I make enough money, then I'll be all right." "When I finally pay off my house, then I'll feel secure." Happiness, security, and feeling all right were always tied to something I didn't have right now, and that meant that in the present I was always irritable, restless, or discontented. No wonder I drank all the time.

In recovery, I learned a whole new way to live, and I was given tools to help me be present. "One day at a time" was a huge help as I despaired at remaining sober forever. When I started worrying about not having enough money or health or companionship next month or next year, my sponsor would ask me if I had everything I needed *right now*. As we went through it, I admitted I had a roof over my head, money in my pocket, food to eat, and a whole fellowship for support. These and other tools helped me to stay present and appreciate that, right now, I was all right.

I once read a saying by Pascal that really resonated with me: "All man's miseries derive from not being able to sit quietly in a room alone." And that's when I finally understood it all. Being able to be comfortable in my own skin, regardless of what's going on, is the path to the happiness, security, and contentment I always sought in some future event. The miracle is that this feeling is available to me right now, right here. In fact, I already have it. Through working the Steps, I have discovered how to be all right, right now.

JUNE 15

❧

"I have a God-shaped hole."

For most of my life I have felt an emptiness in my core. As a child I tried to fill this emptiness with constant TV watching or pigging out on candy, and so on. When I discovered alcohol and drugs, I devoured both, trying to fill the void I felt. Later, I used money to fill the hole by buying cars, clothes, and other material items. The horrible thing is that nothing worked. No matter how much I ate or drank or bought, the desperate feeling of emptiness never went away.

When I entered recovery, I began hearing others talk about a similar hole they felt as well. I heard familiar tales of obsessive use and abuse of alcohol and other things, all in an attempt to fill that hole. No matter how much or in what combination they tried, nothing worked. Everyone still felt irritable, restless, and discontented. I heard many people say that they felt like others were given the operating manual to life, but they didn't get one. I felt that same way for most of my life, too.

As I worked the Steps, my feeling of emptiness began to subside. The deeper into the journey I ventured, the more my hole seemed to get filled. The closer I got to my Higher Power, the more fulfilled I became. As I talked to others, I was told that I had a God-shaped hole, and that I had been trying to fill it with the wrong things. Only connection to God could ever fill the emptiness I felt. As I poured His love and light into my life, I felt whole for the first time. Today, I know that I have a God-shaped hole, and only continued conscious contact will keep me whole and happy.

JUNE 16

❧

"Life is as bad as I want to make it."

I used to make my life really hard. I'd wake up with a bad attitude and immediately begin searching for all the things that were wrong or that could go wrong. I hated my job but felt stuck in it. If I was in a relationship, I couldn't wait to get out, and if I was single I was sure I always would be. When people tried to point out possibilities and options, I always found the negative. My life was pretty bad, and apparently I was determined to keep it that way.

When I hit bottom and had to enter the program, I was sure my life had descended to a new low. At first, all I focused on were people talking about their problems. As I worked the Steps, though, I began to change. Soon I started listening for and finding solutions, and I began applying them in my life. Over time my life began to improve, but what made the most dramatic difference was that my attitude got better. Hope returned and possibilities appeared, and soon my life got kind of good. In fact, I even began imagining a brighter future.

Before I got sober, I used to think there were a lot of bad days. But I heard in a meeting once that there are no bad days—just bad attitudes about a day. Someone said that on any given day somebody was going to a Beverly Hills dealer to pick up her new Bentley. It was a wonderful day for her, and they said that I lived in that same day. What made the difference was attitude. Today, I have the tools to adjust my attitude and know how to be grateful for all I have and all that can be. I know that today my life can be as good as I want to make it.

JUNE 17

"We weaken what we exaggerate."

I have a habit of exaggerating things to make sure you get the full impact of what I'm trying to say. This was especially bad when I was drinking excessively. On and on I would go, embellishing as I did, on how bad my financial prospects were, or on how badly I had been treated by [fill in the blank]. I would exaggerate everything because I was sure you weren't listening or that you didn't really care anymore. And after years of my lying, making things up, and exaggerating, who could blame you?

When I entered recovery, I continued to exaggerate and elaborate on the stories of what had been done to me. "You just don't understand, my case is different," I would say. After a while, my sponsor had me inventory my experiences, concentrating my attention on the invisible fourth column: "my part." As I did, I found that the exaggerated role I had been assigning to others was actually my responsibility. And as I got honest and began owning my side of the street in things, I found less need to exaggerate my experiences. People began listening to and trusting me again.

These days, I am still inclined to exaggerate to emphasize how people, places, and things still don't go my way. But I've learned something very valuable: When I stay focused on my part and relate my experience honestly and sincerely, I no longer have to weaken my story by exaggerating (much). Today, there is less drama in my life because I no longer try to minimize my role in how my life turns out. And there is no reason to exaggerate, and thereby weaken, my stories to feel okay.

JUNE 18

"If I don't go to meetings, I don't hear
what God wants me to hear."

Before recovery, I kept a lot of lower-companion company. I worked with a bunch of self-serving thieves who wanted the easy way out at the expense of others. My friends were alcoholics or drug addicts who were great to party with but not much help when I needed to move apartments. Eventually I ended up lower than them all and was isolated, angry, and out of options.

When I crawled into the rooms, it was suggested that I go to a lot of meetings and start paying attention to what I heard. When one of my old friends said that I was being brainwashed, I brought this up to my sponsor. He told me that from what he had heard from me so far, my brain could use some washing. As much as I didn't want to admit it, he was right, and over the years I've heard exactly what I've needed to hear from people sharing in meetings.

I've always been in awe of the wisdom that comes from the rooms. Even today, when I think I know it all, I'm amazed by what can come out of a newcomer's mouth. When I'm feeling scared, discouraged, or disconnected, I almost always hear just what I need to change my perspective and find a solution. Today, when I'm feeling too busy or too comfortable to go, I remind myself that if I don't keep going to meetings, I won't keep hearing what God wants me to hear.

JUNE 19

"The two things an alcoholic can't deal with are adversity or prosperity."

I used to think the reason I drank so much was because my life was so hard. There was a time when I barely made enough to pay my bills, my credit cards were maxed out, and I lived in a tiny rental. I had let myself go physically and had no satisfying relationships. Each morning I woke up and thought, *Oh, God, another day!* I lived to drink as this was the only time I felt better, and I thought that if only my life got better, then I wouldn't have to drink so much.

A couple of years later, my life did turn around. I got a really good sales job and started making more money than I could count. I bought a house and got a hip girlfriend. As I got more successful, however, I just drank more. Suddenly I was buying expensive champagne and wine, and I moved on to designer vodka as well. As my drinking swirled out of control, I soon lost most of the things I had, and all I had left was my alcoholism.

One thing I have learned in recovery is that the extremes of adversity or prosperity are dangerous things for a self-aggrandizing alcoholic. When things aren't going my way, I become resentful and demand the things I feel I deserve. When things are going well, I demand even more. The restlessness and discontent I feel as an alcoholic simply can't be sated by money, property, or prestige. Instead, serenity and contentment come from the inside by working a spiritual program and developing a relationship with a Higher Power. Today, I am grateful for what I do have, and when I wake up, I now thank God for another day.

JUNE 20

"When I feed the problem, it grows;
when I feed the solution, it grows."

In the program, I learned I have a magic-magnifying mind. I discovered that I tend to obsessively think about certain things to the exclusion of all else. Before recovery, I focused my magic-magnifying mind on my problems, and as I did, they tended to get bigger and even multiply. Round and round I went, chasing each problem and imagining the worst. The only solution I could think of was to drink more, and that just led me to even darker places.

In recovery, I discovered some solutions. The first was to put the plug in the jug. Next, I learned to share my problems with others and learn from the solutions they found to similar situations. I also learned to develop a relationship with a Power greater than myself. This took away the burden of solving problems on my own and taught me to be open to God's will and direction. During this process, I also learned that what I feed grows, and if I want my life to get better, I have to change what I am feeding.

While this sounds easy, it still takes work even today. The good part is that I am much quicker to recognize when I'm feeding a problem, and when I do, I quickly ask myself what I'm afraid of. Once I know that, I can focus my magic-magnifying mind on the solution. I've gotten much better at turning things over, thinking about more positive outcomes, and feeding solutions. And I'm happy to report that my life is much better for it. I'm now open to God's infinite array of better outcomes, and I choose to feed those today instead of my problems.

JUNE 21

❧

"I cannot think myself into good living, but
I can live myself into good thinking."

Toward the end of my drinking, in late September, I was drinking way too much, so I made a list of the five times left that year I would drink. These were Halloween, Thanksgiving, my birthday, Christmas, and New Year's Eve. My thinking was that I would remain sober in between. I made this list in a bar, and I felt so good about it that I ordered another pitcher of beer for myself. The next day, a Monday, I was drinking by noon. But that day wasn't on the list!

When I got sober, I made more lists. I made a "join a gym and get healthy" list. I made lists on getting a job, getting a girlfriend, and many others. While I was thinking how good my life would be once I did these things, what was missing was taking any action. Thankfully, working the Steps with my sponsor taught me a whole new way to live my life. What I learned was that it wasn't the intention, but rather the action that would lead me to feeling better.

This lesson has been crucial not only to my recovery but my happiness in life in general. I have learned that actions always precede feelings and thinking, not the other way around. It's like the gym. I rarely feel like putting in the action and going, but once I'm done with my workout, my thinking has completely changed, and I'm glad I did. It is the same with recovery. While I usually don't feel like working a Step or helping out at a meeting or extending myself to help another, but once I take the action, my thinking and life improve.

JUNE 22

❧

"When all else fails, follow directions."

I don't know why it is, but many alcoholics don't like to follow directions. I sure didn't. Even if I didn't know how to do something, I would rarely ask for help. "I'll figure it out," was my motto. This philosophy didn't work out very well for me as I struggled in school, in my job, and in my relationships. As my drinking progressed, I still refused help, and even though my best friend was successfully sober, I failed to follow his suggestions or direction either. And then one day I surrendered.

New to the program, I looked at the Twelve Steps and thought I saw twelve directions. I could feel my resistance rising as I read through them. But then my sponsor told me they were simply suggestions that had worked for others in the program. He suggested that if I wanted what they had—a way to stay sober, one day at a time—then I might want to try them. I grudgingly did. After a short while, I did stay sober, and soon thereafter my life began to improve.

What also improved was my willingness to take suggestions and follow directions. What I learned is even though I think I know or think I can come up with a better way, I rarely can. These days, it's much easier to leverage someone else's experience, strength, and hope. Doing so saves me a lot of time, effort, and even heartache. Today, my wife is glad that I'm quick to ask for directions, and now I even read through instruction manuals before I attempt something. Today, I follow directions before all else fails.

JUNE 23

"Just what is it I'm afraid of?"

I've not been sleeping well lately. I've been waking up a little after 4 AM, and I've been thinking about my life. I've been worried about my financial future. I've been worried about how much junk food I've been eating, and about how much weight I've been gaining. I've been stressing about how much I have to do and about how little time in the day there is to do it. During these early mornings, lying awake thinking and worrying, I just go around and around. There doesn't seem to be a solution.

This morning, I got out of bed early and went to my 6:30 AM meditation meeting. I sat next to a couple of regulars and told them what I've been thinking and how much I've been thinking it. They looked at me and said the problem is that I've been thinking about myself. "When was the last time you took a newcomer to a meeting?" they asked. "How about working with your sponsee?" They reminded me that when I'm involved with others, helping them with their spiritual development, then all the things I worried about for myself would disappear.

This was the same message I was given when I was new, when it was all about me. Then, as now, it's only when I get out of myself that I find—or remember—how good I truly have it. If I think about myself only, it's easy to become afraid—afraid that I'll lose something I have or not get something I demand. The solution, as always, is to get into service. Every time I do, I feel better. And if I do this often enough, I not only forget about myself, but I also forget what I'm afraid of.

JUNE 24

"God can't give you anything new
until you let go of the old."

I hate change. For some reason I'm convinced that things will get worse if they change, and even if things aren't so good now, I'd rather they stay the same than risk a change. I was told when I came into the program that I would only have to change one thing, and I was relieved to hear that. But then they told me that one thing was everything! I quickly realized that the first thing I needed to change was my attitude about change.

A good friend of mine in the program has a different view on change. She says that you can't know what you don't know. "How many times do things get better after they change?" she asked me. When I thought about this and looked at my experience, I found that they almost always get better. "Then why not look at change as a chance for improvement and turn the results over to your Higher Power?" she suggested.

The more I follow my friend's advice, the easier it is for me to handle change. A couple of days ago my wireless router went out, and it felt like the end of the world. After I calmed down, it occurred to me that I might get a more powerful router and have improved wireless coverage in my home. Now that was a change! These days when things change, I ask myself how they have improved or how I can make them better. Once I put my focus here, I find it's easier to let go and even look forward to change. What I've learned is that God can't give me anything new until I let go of the old.

JUNE 25

"Develop an 'attitude of gratitude.'"

I have a secret weapon in my recovery tool bag: the gratitude list. Oh, I know, you've heard all about gratitude lists, but when was the last time you made one? Whenever I'm feeling overwhelmed, stressed, or in fear, the fastest way out is for me to make a quick list of twenty-five, or even fifty, things I'm grateful for.

When I mention this to people, their first reaction is *"Fifty?"* If fifty seems like a lot to you, too, it's just because you're not in the habit of making gratitude lists. There are many fundamental things that can get you started, like the gift of sight, hearing, breathing without pain, and so forth. But one helpful secret is to list the things you're grateful for that are centered on what you are feeling anxious or fearful about.

For example, when I'm in financial fear, I list all the things around finances I'm grateful for. These usually include that today I have a place to sleep, my rent is paid, the electricity is working (and it helps when I think of all the people who don't even have electricity!); I have money in my pocket; I've always earned money and did so yesterday or last week/month, and so on. This works for every topic, and after you get started, fifty comes easy. Today, my life is good. I'm appreciative and I know serenity because I know how to develop and live in an attitude of gratitude.

JUNE 26

"My definition of balance is being able to obsess equally in all areas of my life!"

As an alcoholic, I completely understand all-or-nothing thinking. When I was in my disease, I used to obsessively plan out my drinking and using, always making sure I had the right amount available to me, and I would even drink before meeting friends at the bar so that I could pretend to drink like them. In the end, my obsession consumed me and drove me into the rooms.

Once I started working the Steps, I began obsessing on other things. For a while I was consumed with dying, sure I had done irreparable damage to myself during my years of abuse. Next I became obsessed with the fear of financial insecurity, this time convinced I had ruined my professional future. And then I got into a relationship, and that obsession nearly drove me to drink. During my Sixth Step, I realized that I had to surrender my obsessive thinking if I wanted to stay sober.

For me, turning over my obsessive thinking and other character defects came down to a question of faith: Did I or didn't I trust that my Higher Power would take care of me? As I began to obsess on that, my sponsor told me that faith wasn't a thought but rather an action. He suggested I begin letting go and letting God, and each time I did, my life got a little better. Today, I know that obsessing isn't the answer. Turning it over is.

JUNE 27

"Bring the body, the mind will follow."

This is a quote I heard early on in my recovery, and it has served me well over the years. Over and over again, when I haven't wanted to go to a meeting, I went anyway, and once my body was there, my mind ended up being glad it went along, too. Like much of the wisdom in the program, I can apply the truth in this quote to many other areas of my life as well.

What I've learned is that taking action is almost always the gateway into feeling better. Rarely have I been able to think my way into different behavior or results or attitudes. Instead, it's only when I take action (especially when I don't want to) that things begin to shift, and I begin feeling better. The program, like life, doesn't work when I'm into thinking, only when I'm into action.

It's interesting how, even with this knowledge and experience, my mind still tells me not to do the things that will make me feel better. Often I'd rather watch TV than go to a meeting, rest after work than go to the gym, procrastinate rather than take action. The good news, though, is that it always works out for the best when I go ahead and take action anyway. Whenever I bring my body, my mind always follows.

JUNE 28

*"Behaviors are like tennis rackets;
if yours is broken, get a new one."*

A woman at a meeting shared that behaviors are like tennis rackets. While a tennis racket works for a while—years, even—eventually the strings wear out, the grip comes apart, and after a while you have to get a new one. She said that for years she was using rackets of behavior long after they had stopped working. It was only after she "got a new racket" that her life improved.

When I was new to recovery, I had a lot of old, worn-out behaviors, too. What I didn't realize was that the reason my life wasn't working was that I kept trying to use them—isolating instead of joining in, being selfish instead of giving, and so on—to achieve different results. When I spoke with my sponsor about it, he told me that unless I worked the Steps and changed the way I thought and acted, the results in my life would stay the same.

Today, I'm much better at recognizing my old rackets of behaviors, and thankfully, I'm more willing to try something different. Today, when areas of my life aren't working, I know to look at my behavior, talk to someone in the program, and pray for guidance. Today, when my racket isn't working, I'm quick to get a new one. I know that I can't win in the game of life if I continue playing with an old racket.

ww .

JUNE 29

***"A mistake is only a mistake when
I don't learn from it."***

It was hard making the same mistakes over and over. Each new relationship ended just like the last one, and after a while I just resigned myself to being single the rest of my life. Same thing with jobs. Each new, exciting opportunity ended like the last disappointment, and soon I was unemployed again, searching through the Sunday classified ads. As each area of my life crashed and burned, I finally had to admit the unmanageability of it all, and I surrendered.

When I reached Step Four of the program and learned about the first three columns of the Fourth Step inventory, I finally thought I would be vindicated. Now I could list what others had done to me and assign the proper blame for the failure of my life. And that is when my sponsor sprung the mysterious fourth column on me—my part. What at first seemed a gross insult—"What do you mean my part? Look at what they've done to me!"—soon turned out to be the key to my freedom and recovery.

What I learned is that it was my character defects that were truly the cause of my repeated suffering. For as long as I was unwilling to change how I behaved, my life would remain unmanageable. I learned that when I finally admitted and corrected my part, I could begin learning from the mistakes I was making and move past them. Today, when something doesn't go my way, I am quick to look at my part and to see where I have been at fault. Doing so allows me not only to learn from it but also to avoid repeating it in the future.

JUNE 30

"You can blame others for the way you are;
you can only blame yourself
for staying that way."

I had a rotten childhood. Torn away from my father when I was five, I never saw him again. Torn away from my older brothers and sister when I was seven, I rarely saw them when I was growing up. Like itinerant farm workers, my mom, stepdad, and I moved constantly. I attended four different fifth grades and was always the outcast through my school years. It's no wonder I started drinking so much.

When I entered recovery, I kept to myself. I had no interest in fellowship, and I was guarded when speaking to my sponsor. Revealing myself through sharing at meetings, inventories, and Twelve Step work was terrifying. I was going to keep to myself, and secretly I was going to keep blaming others. During my Fourth Step, my mom and stepdad topped the list of resentments, and I laid the responsibility squarely on them for the way I turned out. And that's when my sponsor explained today's quote to me.

He told me that while my parents certainly had a huge impact over the first half of my life, it was now my choice as to how the second half would go. I could either choose to remain shut down or I could have faith, clean house, and join the human race. Sure, there would be times when I felt let down, hurt, or disrespected, but by working the Twelve Steps I would make it through and grow stronger. He told me that my future was up to me now, and that with God's help, I could live a useful, fulfilling, and even joyous life. He was right!

JULY 1

"I could drink, or I could do everything else."

By the end of my drinking, my world had become very small. I lost my job, again, but this time I didn't get a new one. Most of my friends and family didn't want to hang out with me much because I was usually drunk, or well on my way there. I had long ago abandoned my hobbies like photography and reading; they tended to get in the way of my drinking. In the end, I was alone on my couch with my booze.

I'll never forget my first meeting—on a Tuesday night in Westwood, California. It was a large, hip speaker meeting at a church. There were probably a couple of hundred people there, and it was like I had arrived at a concert. People were talking, laughing, racing in and out of the room at the break. Wow! For a brief instant I felt part of the human race again. Later, after I had joined the program, I learned that the path back to life was through the Twelve Steps, and I committed to taking them.

As I got sober, my life did open up. There were lots of meetings, sober parties, fellowship, and more. I got a job again, learned how to be of service, and started sponsoring others. In sobriety I've traveled the world, gotten married, started businesses, written and published books. And each morning I greet the new day with joy and optimism. These days whenever I think of a drink, I think of everything else I would have to give up. Nothing, especially a drink, is worth all I've been blessed with in recovery.

JULY 2

"Willingness is the key."

I was one big Gordian knot of self-will when I got to the program. I bristled at others' suggestions to attend meetings every day and took offense at many of my sponsor's directions. I was too good to sweep the floors and had no interest in shaking people's hands as a greeter. I was going to do the program my way, and when I did, I was drunk a short time later.

When I worked Step One again, my sponsor asked me if I was willing to try things the A.A. way. I grudgingly admitted that I was. Secretly, however, I didn't think I could do Step Three—you know, the "God" Step. As I vacillated between avoidance and outright resistance, my sponsor asked me if I was willing to believe in a Power greater than myself. I said I was, and that was all it took. As the Big Book says, with the door to faith opened only slightly, God would help me open it more and more.

As I made my way through the Steps, I repeatedly had to call upon the tool of willingness. At Steps Six and Seven, there were some character defects I was not going to let go of. Gently, my sponsor listened to my resistance and then asked me, "Are you at least willing to be willing?" I admitted I was. "Then simply pray on that." As I prayed, I felt the door open just slightly, and as it did, my Higher Power opened it some more. Eventually, I walked through those open doors to freedom and to a new life. Willingness was the key to my recovery, and it remains the key to my happiness today.

JULY 3

*"Seven days without God
makes one weak."*

I don't know how or why God seems to disappear from my life, but He does. Monday morning I'll be running late and not have time to pray, and the next thing I know it's Wednesday. I'll go to my meeting that night, but Thursday and Friday rush by, and before I can catch my breath, suddenly it's Sunday afternoon. By then I find myself alone and not feeling very well, and that's when I make the connection.

Early on in recovery, I was taught that the first Three Steps could be summarized as, "I can't, He can, let Him." The problem is that I quickly forget the "I can't" part. Once I'm under the illusion that I'm in charge, I'm off trying to control life to get everything I think I need. The only good news is that it takes less time these days for me to feel the effects of this self-will run riot.

Happily, it's easy for me to get reconnected to my Higher Power, and the positive effects I feel are immediate. Once I practice the "He can" and the "let Him" part, I'm restored to sanity and to my proper role in life. My job isn't to rush around like a crazy person trying to accomplish and control everything; rather, my role is to seek God's will and to be of service. And when I stay connected to the Steps and to God, I'm as strong as can be.

JULY 4

"How do you know when you've hit bottom?
When you stop digging."

For years, I was driven by an obsession to drink. In the beginning I tried to control it, but after a while it had complete control over me. My drinking led me to a deep emotional, spiritual, and physical bottom, and only when I could admit to my innermost self that I was an alcoholic could I find the willingness to surrender and try a different way of living. And for me, that was working the Twelve Steps of Alcoholics Anonymous.

I have found sobriety to be a process. When I put the drink down, I found my obsessive thinking was woven into many other areas of my life: eating, shopping, sex, and so forth. Just about anything I wanted, I wanted more of, and soon my behavior led to new bottoms. It was hard to surrender things I wasn't ready to let go of yet, and I quickly learned what they meant by the saying, "Anything an alcoholic finally lets go of has deep claw marks on it."

One of the gifts of my recovery is that I can choose today when to stop digging. When my obsessive thinking starts, and my actions begin to make my life unmanageable, I now have tools I can use to be restored to sanity. By turning my thinking over to my Higher Power, or sharing my crazy thoughts in meetings or with my sponsor and others, I avoid new bottoms and can live a much happier life. How do I know when I've hit bottom today? When I stop digging.

JULY 5

*"Those who leave everything in God's hands will
eventually see God's hand in everything."*

I was many years sober when I first heard this quote. It reminded me of how I had turned my recovery over to God, and how everything had worked out. I got through my Fourth Step—when I thought it was going to tear me apart—and God helped me make all those terrifying amends as well. I can now see God's hand in every part of my recovery, but what about the rest of my life?

Lately, I've been back in a lot of financial fear. I've been worrying about my work and stressing about the future, and the old thoughts of *What is going to become of me?* have crept back in. The difference between this and recovery is that I've kept God out of it lately, thinking instead that I have to handle this part of my life by myself. This has made my life unmanageable again.

Last week, I hit an emotional bottom. My wife finally sat me down and said, "Enough is enough." I knew it was time to surrender. When I did, a wave of relief washed over me, and I have been free of fear since I left it all in God's hands. I was given the perspective to see that He has been handling my financial future all along, and that I'm a lot better off than I think I am. Once again, I see God's hands in everything, and—as long as I leave things there—I'll be just fine.

JULY 6

"I would love to, but I need to talk to my sponsor first."

While I was in my disease, I listened to my own best thinking, and you can imagine where that got me. Time and time again I'd follow one "good idea" with another, until I was in so much trouble I didn't know what to do. And that's when I'd think of the best idea ever, and I'd act on it. After a while, the only thing worse than my problems were my solutions to them!

When I entered the program, my sponsor constantly asked me if I had any good ideas left. Plenty, I told him. "Make sure and run your thinking by me first then," he said. When I objected to this, he reminded me that my best thinking and good ideas had led me to a bottom. As I followed his direction, and as he walked me through the inevitable consequences of my thinking, I began to see the wisdom of his advice.

What is so interesting to me now is that even with years in recovery, my thinking remains much the same. It is still driven by the disease of alcoholism and automatically defaults to self-will and self-seeking. Because of this, I've found that the same advice I was given in the beginning of sobriety remains true for me today. I should still run my "good ideas" by my sponsor first.

JULY 7

"A.A. = Altered Attitudes."

When I came into the program, I was self-centered and self-seeking in the extreme. Everything I did was focused on feeding my own insatiable needs and demands. My sponsor told me that the Twelve Steps would enable me to alter my attitude and allow me to be focused more on others. This, he said, would be like the difference between living in heaven or hell. When I asked what he meant, he told me this story:

Hell, he said, is a huge buffet where endless, large halls are filled with an infinite selection of delicious foods all prepared to perfection. All your favorites are there: Italian, French, comfort foods, the most scrumptious desserts, and more. The only problem is that instead of hands, everyone has a three-foot spoon at the end of one arm, and a fork on the other. The utensils are too long to feed themselves, so they starve while surrounded by all this mouthwatering food.

Heaven is exactly the same: hall after hall of deliciously prepared and presented foods, the aroma of which is intoxicating and mouth-watering. Here, too, everyone has three-foot spoons and forks too long to feed themselves. The difference in heaven, though, is that the people have figured out that the utensils are perfect for feeding one another. My sponsor then told me that the same altered attitude is what we learn in the program as well. I've now learned that what separates people from living in heaven or hell is whether we're focused on ourselves or others.

JULY 8

❧

"Advice that is not asked for is criticism."

I have someone in my life who, after asking me how I'm doing and I begin to tell her, immediately starts telling me the things I need to change or start doing. Until this quote, I didn't realize that the reason her unasked-for advice made me feel so bad was that it was thinly veiled criticism of the way I was living my life.

Thank God the program doesn't work that way. If people in the program, or my sponsor, started giving me unsolicited advice or telling me what to do, I would have left long ago. Instead, people give me suggestions (when I ask for them) based on their own experience. If they had a similar situation as mine and they did something that worked for them, then they may suggest that it might work for me as well. It's up to me at that point to try it or not.

Because of the program, I have learned to apply this wisdom in my other relationships also. In fact, people now call me a good listener, and it's because I know that all people really want is to be heard and understood. If asked, the best I can do is share my experience with a similar situation—if I have it. Otherwise, it's best to just listen, empathize, and help them process their experience. That's always better than giving advice that's not asked for.

JULY 9

❧

"The difference between me and God is that God doesn't want to be me."

I can't tell you how many times I've tried to arrange all of life to suit my needs. I've planned and schemed, worked and manipulated, hoped and dreamed, and then manipulated some more, all in an attempt to get the world to behave the way I wanted it to. When my sponsor told me I was trying to play God, I took it as a compliment and secretly thought I was doing a pretty good job at it.

When I started working the program, I began looking more closely at my behavior and at the consequences of my unchecked ambition and ego. I had hurt a lot of people, including myself, and I was forced to admit that my way wasn't the right way after all. Once I surrendered to this, I became right-sized, and I began to let God assume His proper role in my life.

Today, it's a relief not to have to play God. It's so much easier to just suit up and show up, and let God determine the results that are the best for all concerned. Because I am still tempted to try to control things, I continue to pray to be relieved of the bondage of self. As I get out of the way, God does more in and through my life. Today, the difference between God and me is clear.

JULY 10

"It's not old behavior if I'm still doing it."

I often don't let go of things until they are causing more pain than pleasure. When my drinking was killing me, I stopped, and even though it was really hard at first, I found that being sober was actually the easier, softer way. But I had a lot of old ideas and behaviors that still worked for me sometimes. Letting go of these was not so easy.

As I sat in meeting after meeting, I heard that "The result was nil until we let go absolutely," but I never really understood the full impact of this statement. I mean, I was still getting results—I was clean and sober, I got my job back, and I began repairing broken relationships. But there were also times when I was intensely unhappy and irritable, and I needed and wanted a drink. It took a long while for me to see that these feelings were almost always caused by old ways of thinking and behaving.

The longer I'm in recovery, the more I understand the value of Steps Six and Seven. My old behaviors will continue just as long as I remain unwilling to give up the character defects that cause them. But when I do become willing, something wonderful happens: my Higher Power does for me what I can't do for myself. He relieves me of my old ways of thinking and acting, which allows more joy and freedom to flow into my life. Today, I continue to pray for my old behavior to be removed, even if I'm still doing it.

JULY 11

*"Try praying. Nothing pleases God more
than hearing a strange voice."*

This quote hit me on several levels. First, it reminded me of how often I forget to use one of the most powerful tools in my spiritual tool kit: prayer. I was taught early on that praying is simply talking to God, and my repeated experience is that it works in so many ways. Each time I use it, I receive the peace, guidance, and strength I need to live life with grace and serenity.

This quote also reminds me that no matter how long it has been since I reached out to God, He is always waiting and happy to hear from me. I remember I learned this lesson early on in my recovery when I was angry with God and felt guilty as I blamed and cursed Him. My sponsor told me that it didn't matter *what* I said to God; He was big enough to handle it. The important thing was that I was finally talking *to* God.

What this taught me is that God's love for me is unconditional. Knowing this enabled me to develop an open and honest dialogue that led to a loving and trusting relationship with my Higher Power. I grow and benefit from this relationship each time I remember to pray, and this quote reminds me that no matter how long it has been, God is always ready and happy to hear from me.

JULY 12

"Our neighbor's window looks much cleaner if we first wash our own."

Now that it's hot again, I've begun sleeping with the windows open to let in some of the cooler evening air. My neighbor must have the same idea because her window is open as well, and the sound of her TV carries in the still summer air, sometimes making it hard to go to sleep. Even though she's eighty-two years old and probably hard of hearing—and is the perfect neighbor otherwise—I easily become indignant and start with the "How dare she!" ranting. How soon I tend to forget. . . .

For years while drinking, I carried on like a madman. I played my music as loud as I could stand it, late into the night, and often partied with friends and family on the patio next to my neighbor's living room. I had no awareness or concern for anyone but myself, and through it all, my neighbor remained calm and respectful and never said a word. You'd think that now that I'm in recovery, I'd have more empathy and understanding, but that's not always my first reaction.

What I've found is that I have little initial tolerance for behaviors I used to practice with abandon. As an ex-smoker, for example, I'm an antismoker now and am irritated and resentful if someone smokes within twenty feet of me. Through it all, I have learned to continually ask for understanding and tolerance from my Higher Power, and I've learned that it's up to me to take the high road and set the example with my behavior. When I do, everything works out for the best. I find that my neighbor's window looks much cleaner when I wash my own first.

JULY 13

"The problem with isolating is that
you get such bad advice."

By the end of my drinking, I was all alone. Unlike some of the stories I hear about people drinking in bars, I preferred to drink alone in my home. My friends were gone, my family wasn't inviting me over, and it was just me and my alcohol. After months of listening to my own best thinking, I had run out of options and was at the end of my rope. By some miracle, I was able to reach out for help, and my journey in recovery began.

While I have worked the Twelve Steps several times over the years and labored hard to turn my character defects over to God, I still find that my default mode is to isolate. I stay in, turn off my phone, and binge-watch movies I've seen a hundred times. When I do, I am cut off from others and from my Higher Power, and that's when my best alcoholic thinking starts again. What I've learned is that it never has anything good to say.

Today, I try to do the things I learned early in sobriety to keep from isolating: I have a sponsor, I get commitments at meetings, and I say yes when asked to participate. I also answer the phone these days and am willing to help another. In other words, I continue to take contrary action because, as they say, "An alcoholic's best thinking treats loneliness with isolating." And when I'm isolating, the advice I get is all bad.

JULY 14

❧

"If you want to make God laugh, tell Him your plans."

When I was drinking, I had a lot of plans. I was going to do this and accomplish that, and when things didn't work out, I'd use alcohol to fuel my self-will and strengthen my resolve. It was during these drinking sessions that I made lists of things I was going to accomplish—tomorrow. In the end, when I got sober, I had a lot of lists, but I hadn't accomplished much.

When I entered the program, I told my sponsor all the things I was going to accomplish now that I was sober. I pulled out my lists and proudly told him that finally I was going to get this and achieve that. He asked me if that was all I wanted, and after I said yes, he told me to write it all down and give it to him. After I did, he said that we would review it all after I got more time in the program.

Years later, long after I had forgotten about it, my sponsor pulled out that list and we went over it. All the things I was sure I needed to be happy—the home on the beach, the Academy Award–winning screenplay, and so on—had not materialized, but as we sat and talked, I realized I had received much more. I was comfortable in my own skin, and I knew peace and even serenity at times. I realized then that I was finally happy and that my life had meaning. And that's when my sponsor told me that if I wanted to make God laugh again, just tell Him my plans.

JULY 15

"Have you prayed about it as much as you've talked about it?"

This quote could easily have said "thought" or "worried" about it as much as "talked" about it. Before recovery, that's all I did with my problems. Around and around I'd go, rehashing problems, painting the same unworkable scenarios, and obsessing myself into depression. And if others were around, I'd drag them down with me. Because I didn't have a Higher Power in my life, there was never the thought of turning it over. Instead, it was just me and my problems—or worse—my solutions to my problems!

When I entered recovery, I was taught that I no longer had to be alone. First, I discovered a fellowship of other alcoholics who had overcome the same problems I had, and they offered suggestions and solutions that had worked for them. Next, I was introduced to the Twelve Steps, which offered a way out of my old self and my old thinking. Finally, I found my Higher Power, and through much practice I came to believe that He could do for me what I couldn't do for myself.

Through prayer and meditation, I have learned how to strengthen my conscious contact with God, and I have been given the gift of a transformed life and way of living. Today, I know that I am no longer alone, and that I no longer have to carry a burden or problem by myself. My Higher Power is always there and ready to help if I am willing to turn my will and life over to Him. Today, when I find myself talking or thinking or worrying too much, I remember to start praying. The right solutions always come when I do.

JULY 16

"I want to be a doctor, but I don't want to become a doctor."

I used to be driven by a huge sense of entitlement. Rather than be a good partner in a relationship, I just did what I wanted and expected my girlfriends to put up with me. At work, I felt my employer was lucky to have me show up, and I didn't understand when they got angry when I was late. In college, I expected good grades because I paid my tuition and even took notes sometimes. In everything I did, I expected the top-end result even if I wasn't willing to work for it. My attitude was, "Don't you know who I am?"

Early in the program, I persisted in self-righteous, selfish thinking, complaining to my sponsor that I didn't want to get sober, I already wanted to be sober. He said that like everything else, there were no shortcuts—that if I wanted to have the sense of ease and comfort that comes from being recovered, then I had to do what everyone else did. He told me that if I was willing to do the work, then I would experience the miracle of the program.

By following my sponsor's direction and working the Steps—writing inventories, making amends, turning things over, and so on—I learned the value of putting in the work. Today, I know that if I want to attain something or become something, then I can, as long as I'm willing to work for it. By breaking down seemingly impossible goals into the next indicated actions, by suiting up and showing up, and by turning the results over to my Higher Power, I've been able to build an amazing life—all one day at a time.

JULY 17

❧

"If I just had more, better, different, I'd be okay."

Before I had a program, I was always searching for something outside myself to make me feel okay. I was sure that if I could only get more money, a better job, a different relationship, or if I lived in a different house in a different neighborhood, then I would finally feel better about myself. When none of these things worked, I concentrated on drinking more, getting better quality wines, or trying different types of premium alcohol. In the end, this didn't work either.

When I entered the rooms of recovery in Hollywood, California, I suddenly saw a group of people who seemed to have more, better, and different things than me. As I watched famous actors, successful businesspeople, and movers and shakers mingle in seemingly exclusive groups and then drive away in their Mercedes and BMWs, I felt distinctly less than. When I told my sponsor this, he told me I would never be happy as long as I compared my insides with someone else's outsides.

What I have learned over the years is that sobriety, serenity, and recovery are truly an inside job. Only by working the Steps will I find the true peace and contentment I've always searched for in outside things. I now know that believing more or better or different will make me feel okay is a lie that my alcoholism still tells me. It is a lie that will always lead me to a drink. Today, I know that the path to feeling comfortable in my own skin starts with being grateful for what I have and with trying to give away what I have found. When I remember that, I realize I'm more than just okay; I'm blessed.

JULY 18

"Even God can't fill a cup that's already full."

I had a lot of opinions before I got sober. I knew I didn't have stable employment because the companies I worked for were so screwed up. The reason I didn't have a significant other was because the women I dated had too many demands (like I should call them regularly, etc.). And there were many reasons why I drank: I blamed the family I was raised in; the education I didn't get; the IRS who wanted my money. . . . You would drink, too, if you were me.

When I entered the program, I had a lot of opinions about that, too. Even though I knew nothing about it, I was sure it wouldn't work for me. Heck, I couldn't stay sober for two or three months, let alone a year. When I heard the Lord's Prayer, I knew that a religious group could never help me. And when I read about a fearless and thorough moral inventory, I knew that was a waste of time. When I gathered the courage to tell my sponsor all this, he told me to remain open. He suggested that perhaps I didn't know what I didn't know.

For me, getting sober was more about letting go of old ideas than it was about forming more opinions. My recovery started when I learned to admit that perhaps I had been wrong about things, and that maybe I didn't know everything after all. By peeling back the onion layers of self and discarding my character defects, I became open to the light and love of a Higher Power. Even today, though, it is easy to get full of myself again. When I find myself in judgment these days, I remember to pray for humility because I know that even God can't fill a cup that is already full.

JULY 19

"If a drink solved problems, I would have solved a lot of problems."

I seriously used to think that drinking helped me manage my problems and my life better. When I got too stressed to think straight, a drink or two would immediately relax me and enable me to think differently. In my creative life, I always wrote or drew much better after a few drinks. And after a few more drinks, I sometimes had epiphanies that I was sure could change the world. Unfortunately, when I sobered up, my problems were still there, plus some additional ones caused by my drinking.

When my sponsor told me I wasn't going to drink alcohol anymore —not even beer!—I was shocked. *But how was I going to make it through all my problems and stress?* I wondered. And what about all those deep, creative insights? As we talked through things, he helped me see that those "creative moments" I had while loaded, those that I wrote down at least, made almost no sense when I sobered up. Also, after inventories centered on my drinking, it was clear that alcohol didn't solve any of my problems.

It took many years of journaling, meetings, and Step work, but today I know that I am much more creative and disciplined now that I'm not drinking. Today, I don't just think of things, I do them. I've also found that I handle my problems and stress so much better with a clear head and a Higher Power in my life. Plus, I create a lot less mayhem! Sobriety has given me the life that alcohol promised but never delivered. And that's why I begin each day with gratitude.

JULY 20

"Each morning if I don't address my alcoholism,
then alcoholism will address me."

It is so easy for me to forget I have alcoholism. I can go along for a few days not attending meetings and not praying or meditating each morning, but if I do, alcoholism quickly takes over. Soon I am irritable, restless, and discontented. Sometimes I don't make the connection right away, but then I remember that I haven't done anything to address my alcoholism. And I remember what I once heard in a meeting: Day and night, alcoholism is getting stronger, and it is just waiting for me to relax so it can take control again.

One of the most important things I learned in the program is that it is alcohol*ism*, not alcohol*wasim*. Regardless of how much distance I have put between my last drink and today, alcoholism is alive and well and is still whispering in my ear. My sobriety is still a daily reprieve from this devastating disease based on my spiritual condition in any given moment. What I need to do today, even after years of continuous sobriety, is the same thing I had to do on day one—treat my disease.

I have learned many ways of treating my alcoholism, but one of the most important is to start my day by practicing prayer and meditation. By spending some time in the morning with my Higher Power, I'm able to feed my spirit, turn my will and my life over, and establish conscious contact with God. By doing so, I maintain my spiritual condition and gain the strength I need to resist the subtle yet steady current of my disease. Today, I continue to address alcoholism each morning before it addresses me.

JULY 21

"Help me to see the crazy today."

Looking back on it, I can't believe how crazy my life was before recovery. Not only was I doing really stupid things, but many of them were illegal and dangerous as well. As my drinking increased, I no longer cared about the consequences of my actions, and it didn't matter who or what I hurt. In the end I was driven by resentments, self-pity, and self-loathing, and I think I was certifiably insane. I'm surprised I survived.

When I crawled into the program and stopped drinking, what didn't stop was my insane thinking. I was already making crazy plans for what I was going to do if the program didn't work for me. Thankfully, my sponsor encouraged me to share them with him. When he heard them, he suggested that from that point on, I should share my plans with someone in the program before I acted on them. While this sounded a bit controlling and intrusive, it also made sense to me on a gut-level survival sort of way. I agreed.

Running my crazy thinking by someone else before acting on it has saved me a lot of pain, remorse, and amends. Because I still have alcoholism, I still have the same self-centered, ego-demanding crazy thinking as before—even when sober. As if my crazy thinking isn't enough, even crazier is that by myself I still don't recognize it. I often still think I have some pretty good ideas! And that's why I need to share them with others. I need other people to help me see the crazy today.

JULY 22

"Discomfort is required for change."

I don't like to be uncomfortable, and for a long time I drank a lot to avoid feeling that way. When I had stress at work, I'd drink as soon as I got off. When relationships got complicated, I drank before, during, and after interactions. After a while, my solution—drinking—made my life unmanageable, so I drank even more. Finally, when I was forced to admit my solution was no longer working, I grew so unhappy that I was willing to change. And that's when I entered recovery.

Once in the program, I was very uncomfortable again. I wasn't familiar with how meetings went, didn't know anyone, and the feelings that were bubbling to the surface made staying sober nearly impossible. Plus, my sponsor was suggesting many actions that made me even more uncomfortable, like sitting in the front of the room. He said, "Sit up front in recovery row, instead of at the back in denial aisle." He also suggested I take commitments, go out to fellowship, and write a First Step inventory. What had I gotten myself into?

Because I couldn't imagine a life of drinking anymore, I was willing to follow his direction. As I did, something magical happened: I began to feel better. I soon learned that feeling uncomfortable doesn't last, so long as I'm willing to take action. I also learned that I wouldn't be willing to take the actions unless I was motivated by discomfort. In this way, I have come to see anxious feelings, negative thoughts, and old fears as merely signals that change is needed. I honor these feelings today and get into action to make the changes required for my life to get better.

JULY 23

"Getting stuck means you are in between surrenders."

Before recovery, I felt stuck in many areas of my life. I was stuck in an unfulfilling career, unhealthy relationships I didn't know how to get out of, and an endless cycle of drinking and using. With no tools to help me, my life continued to spin out of control. Once I reached my bottom, though, I finally surrendered, and my recovery began.

When I started the Twelve Steps, I was introduced to a whole new life. I learned new ways of thinking and new ways of acting, and I also learned new ways to be stuck. Because of my old ideas and my resistance, I soon became stuck on the Third Step, and it was a long time before I surrendered to God's will. Then I was stuck on the Fourth Step, and once again it took a while to surrender to the process of an inventory. Oddly, even though the tool of surrender always worked, I usually insisted on being stuck for a while before I would use it.

Today, I'm much quicker to recognize when I'm stuck and to do something about it. Today, my tolerance for pain is small, and whenever I'm feeling uncomfortable, I immediately ask myself what I'm afraid of or what I'm resisting. As soon as I'm clear on what it is, I surrender and ask for God's will and direction. As always, this restores me to sanity and to the serenity I've come to cherish in my life. Today, I know that when I'm stuck, it just means I'm in between surrenders.

JULY 24

"Anything an alcoholic lets go of has claw marks all over it."

In the past, I tried to control everything. I would lie in bed at night planning my days and weeks, and I would make endless lists of activities I could follow that would lead to specific results. I played and replayed conversations that were sure to take place to make sure they came out the way I wanted them to. When the last thing I tried to control—my alcohol use—spun out of control, I finally surrendered.

When I got sober, I had to let go of all my plans and schemes for controlling my drinking and drug use. Because I was at a bottom, it was easy for me to abandon my old ideas and to ask God to restore me to sanity. Just because this worked for my alcoholism, though, didn't mean I was willing to turn the rest of my life over. "God, you can have my drinking, but I'll handle the rest," was my attitude. You can imagine how that went.

What I've learned over the years is that my life gets better in direct proportion to my willingness to trust God with the other areas of it. It continues to be hard to let go and act with faith, especially when I'm in fear, but each time I do, I'm rewarded with a freedom and a joy that could never have come as long as I continued to try to control things. Today, if I'm not willing to let go, then I pray for the willingness to be willing. And once I withdraw my claws, God takes over and the healing begins.

JULY 25

"I wanted to be famous,
but God made me anonymous."

I had some pretty big plans when I entered the program. Even though my sponsor told me it wasn't about money, property, and prestige, I knew better. I was convinced that, by being sober, I would finally write the books and create the products that would get me the recognition and riches I deserved. I even told my sponsor how good of a circuit speaker I would be and asked what I needed to do that. He smiled and suggested that a year of sobriety might be a good start.

As I began working the program, I made some startling revelations. In doing inventories, I found that there was a time when I had a lot of money, property, and prestige, but I was still miserable. As I did more work, I discovered that the hole I felt inside could never be filled with anything outside me, and the more I chased that, the emptier I felt. It was only when I surrendered the character defect of feeling terminally unique that I began to feel better.

One of the truest things I've learned in the program is that I will always feel less than when I compare my insides with someone else's outsides. It has taken years, but I now understand why character building and my spiritual connection must come before any outside success if I'm to be happy. And I now appreciate the powerful role anonymity has played in helping me develop these essential qualities. Today, I understand the folly of wanting to be famous, and the wisdom of God's anonymity.

JULY 26

"It's a simple program for complicated people."

They say that this is a simple program, but that it's very hard to follow. I heard this in the beginning of my recovery, but when I read the Twelve Steps I didn't see why. In fact, the program seemed simple, and I confidently told my sponsor that I could get through the Steps in a couple of weeks. I can still see his smile as he told me, "Let's take it one day at a time." When I finally started, I saw what he meant.

How can such a simple program be so hard to work? I quickly began asking myself. What I found was that each Step asked me to do something I had never done before: uncover my beliefs, discover how I had twisted them to serve my own selfish ends, and then discard them for God's will rather than my own. Simple, yes, but not easy to do!

Over the years, I've found that this program is much easier to work if and when I quit making it so complicated. And the way I do that is to stop trying to force my will on things. I now know it's much simpler when I evaluate my motives, seek truly to be of service, and ask for God's will, not mine, to be done. This truly is the easier, softer way. Today, I understand when they say that this is a simple program for complicated people!

JULY 27

"It is the mosquitoes that will chase me out of the woods, not the bears!"

It's amazing how I intuitively know how to handle the big things. A few weeks ago, my brother and his wife, who live right around the corner from me, came home from vacation to find their home had been robbed. At 2 AM they pounded on my door, waking me up from a dead sleep. I sprang into action, getting them access to the Internet to check their accounts, calming them down, and helping in any way I could. If only I could handle the little things as easily . . .

Last week, I noticed my kitchen faucet had come loose from the sink. Each time I turned it on, it wiggled back and forth, and I couldn't decide what to do about it. I looked underneath and there didn't seem to be any way to tighten it, and I didn't want to spend $200 on a plumber to fix it. I quickly began to obsess on it, and as soon as it started dripping, I was at my wit's end!

Even though the little things can still paralyze me and leave me feeling helpless, thank God I have a program that has taught me what to do. I've learned to reach out to others and find someone who has experience with what I'm going through. I now know that I don't have to fix everything at once; rather, I just have to take the next indicated action. And most of all, I've learned how to ask for help. Today, with the guidance of the program, I know how to handle both the big *and* the little things.

JULY 28

"Anxiety is the difference between now and then."

Prior to having a program of recovery, I had a hard time staying in the present. Without permission, my mind would race into the future, where it was quickly mired in anxiety and the dread of "What's going to happen then?" What I didn't realize was that I was using alcohol because drinking always brought me back to the now, and in the present, everything was (and always is) okay.

But then drinking stopped working for me, and what a dark time in my life that was. Without the immediate ability to be present, my mind galloped into the future like a pack of wild horses. At times, it was all I could do to hang on. In recovery, though, I learned new ways to get present and, as a sponsor often said, to "be where your feet are."

What I've learned over the years is that my serenity today is directly related to how much time I spend in the present. Oh sure, I still set goals and plan ahead, but I've learned that after I do, it's important to put the tool of my mind down and return to the now. And once I'm back here, in the present, where my feet are, I find that I already have everything I need, and I'm relieved of worry. Today, I use my level of anxiety to determine if I'm truly present or lost in the past or future.

JULY 29

"I don't like things changing without my permission."

I used to spend a lot of time and energy trying to arrange life to suit myself. I would lie in bed at night planning not only *my* every move, but yours, too. I even used to think I could manipulate places and things, and I burned up a lot of energy foolishly trying to bend life to my will. Then I would wake up and things would change, so I started all over again trying to twist the changes to suit my will. I was exhausted when I entered the rooms.

Once I had attended my first week of meetings, I started planning how my recovery would go. I lay awake at night thinking about where I would sit at meetings, who would sit next to me, what I would share, and more. I planned out the first year of my sobriety, including the new job I would get, the perfect sober woman I would marry, and the circuit speaking I was sure they were going to ask me to do. But then I woke up and found that the meeting location had changed, and my sponsor told me no relationships in the first year, and that I should hold off on changing jobs until I had more time in the program. I started feeling exhausted again.

That's when he told me I might want to "let go and let God." My sponsor suggested that I begin taking my life one day at a time, and that I begin asking for God's will instead of trying to have things my own way. He told me I would be much more open to the changes that constantly happen in all our lives once I turned things over. It took a lot of practice, but when I started going with the flow and welcoming change, that's when I began seeing the miracles and opportunities that come with it.

217

JULY 30

"A.A. = A program of 1,000 surrenders."

I was taught to never give in and never give up. To surrender was to lose, and I was to avoid it at all costs. As such, I led with my ego and thought that I could bully, cajole, or manipulate my way into getting just about anything I wanted. And for the most part it worked—until my alcoholism took over. After years of trying to control my drinking, I had reached the bitter end. It was either surrender or die.

In the program, the first thing I heard about was surrender. It was something I was still very resistant to. My sponsor told me that if I wanted to recover from my alcoholism, then I would have to surrender my will and my life to a Power greater than myself. When I asked him how in the world I was going to do that, he told me he would show me by helping me work the Twelve Steps. He also told me that I would find that it was the easier and softer way to live. When I asked him what else I had to surrender and how often, he told me, "Everything, all the time."

It has taken me years to see the wisdom in this seemingly impossible statement. But the more I follow it, the better my life goes. When getting sober, I turned my drinking, my career, my relationships, and so on over to my Higher Power, and they all improved. Today, I find that the answer remains the same: Whenever my ego is pushing and I'm feeling anxious, depressed, or fearful, I ask myself what I need to surrender. As soon as I let go, the situation gets better, and I discover the easier, softer way to live again.

JULY 31

"You'll never have it altogether.
That's like eating once and for all."

I've wasted a lot of time and energy waiting for everything to be just right, but it's never turned out that way. I felt if only I could get that perfect job and make a certain amount of money, then I'd finally stop worrying. I did get the job, and I made even more money, yet I still had financial insecurity. I hoped that when I met the right woman, then I'd be complete. Turned out that was a complete mess. Finally, I knew that if I could only control and enjoy my drinking, then everything would be okay. Instead, I ended up in A.A.

As I sat in meetings for the first few months, I was sure that if I could only get ninety days, then I'd be okay. Then, at the nine-month mark, I hoped I'd feel a lot better at a year. Then I waited to complete my Steps—for the second time! My experience has been that parts of my life get better, but there are always other areas that need work. And sometimes, areas that I thought were fixed need some attention again. As I struggled to accept this, my sponsor reminded me of today's quote.

When I remember that I'll never have it altogether, I can finally let go of the illusion of control. What a relief I feel as I turn my will and my life, once again, over to a God of my understanding. As soon as I empty myself of my demands for the way I think things should be, I am able to accept and appreciate the way things are. As I set to work on a current gratitude list, I'm able to reflect on everything I've already been given. And that's when I realize that by not having it altogether, I can remain open to the unexpected gifts yet to come.

AUGUST 1

"Faith is spelled a-c-t-i-o-n."

I did a lot of thinking when I was drinking. I'd think about how bad my life was and how things weren't going to get any better. As I kept drinking, I thought about all the things I could do, and after a few more drinks, I thought about how good I'd feel if I did them. After a while, I stopped thinking, couldn't remember where I was, and I entered oblivion. Finally, I had some peace from thinking—until I came to. Then it all started again.

When I got sober, I started to wear my sponsor out with all the things I was thinking. They say early recovery is a roller-coaster ride: first up with newfound hope and possibility, then down with regret and remorse. I took along for the ride anyone who would listen to me. After a while, my sponsor directed me to the Big Book and showed me there was a chapter called "Into Action," not "Into Thinking."

What I discovered about my thinking was that the majority of it was based on fear. My sponsor showed me that the way out of fear was through faith in a Higher Power, and the way to cultivate that was by taking action. "Fake it until you make it," I heard over and over again. "Do the things you would do if you had faith, and suddenly you will find that you do," was another. So I got into action, and my life changed. Even today, I remember to feel the fear, but to take the action anyway. And every time I do, things get better, opportunities open up, and my Higher Power shows me the way.

AUGUST 2

*"If you want to be secure, you have to
give up the need to be secure."*

I have spent so much of my life stressing and worrying about being secure. I've never felt like I've had enough money, or will ever have enough. In relationships, my insecurity has ruined many promising starts. I've lain awake at night worrying about my health, ruminating on the "what ifs." It's no wonder I drank so much; it was one of the few ways I had to quiet my mind.

When drinking stopped working for me, I entered recovery. At first I thought I'd get immediate relief from my worry, but with alcohol gone, I just grew more insecure. I overwhelmed my sponsor with all my "what ifs," and he always asked the same thing: "Are you all right, right now?" "Yes, but . . . ," I'd begin. "Right now, God has led you into recovery and has taken care of everything for you, right?" I admitted that was true. "Then let go and let Him take care of you," he suggested.

I never thought it could be that easy, and I still tend to forget it. Today, while I still may not have all the money I want, I have all I need—and then some. I have love, health, hope, and long-term recovery. As soon as I gave up the need to be secure, I realized I already *was* secure. Today, I realize that my *wants* are what keep me from appreciating my *haves*. And today, I have all the security I need.

AUGUST 3

*"If God leads you to it,
He will lead you through it."*

I came into the program with so much fear. I didn't even know how much fear dominated my life because I used drugs, alcohol, food, sex, and people—anything I could—to hide from it. As I began to get clean and sober, the suffocating fear bubbled to the surface and quickly manifested itself as anger, rage, irritability, discomfort, and depression. Needless to say, I was not a happy camper in early recovery.

I was amazed when people shared in meetings about how they walked through real life, and real scary stuff, without drinking. They had experienced the deaths of those near to them, they lost jobs, houses, spouses, their own health, and more. I felt like these things would have devastated me. I wondered how they could deal with all this and still stay sober. And where did they get the strength to face all this with peace, courage, and even grace?

Today, I know this courage comes from God. Now my near constant fear has been replaced with consistent faith in my Higher Power. I've discovered from watching others, and through my own experience of letting God lead me through my own difficulties, that I can also face life on life's terms and go through my own challenges with serenity and courage. Today, I rely on God to lead me through the things He leads me to.

AUGUST 4

"A Big Book that's falling apart is usually carried by a person who isn't."

I have heard so many times in meetings that the answers to my disease, and to the problems in my life, are to be found in the Big Book. The question I have to ask myself is how often do I go there to find them? And the answer, these days, is not often enough.

When I was new, I spent a lot of time reading the Big Book. My sponsor and I went through it page by page, and we discussed each sentence I underlined or highlighted. I also attended book study meetings where I would break it down even more. And as my book began falling apart, I realized that my life no longer was.

Recently I've made a commitment to get back to basics and read the Big Book again. There are areas of my life that aren't where I want them to be, and I know that I'll find the answers I need in the Big Book. I've got the latest edition, a new yellow highlighter, and I'm going to read and study it until it begins to fall apart. As it does, I'm confident those areas of my life will once again get back on track.

AUGUST 5

❧

"The answer is not in the problem;
the answer is in the solution."

Before recovery, I lived in the problem. If things weren't going right, or if something went wrong, that's all I thought about. I would dwell on it, talk to my friends about it, and think about all the ways it could get worse. It was as if I was addicted to the dark outcomes of my problems. Soon I couldn't see—and didn't even want—a way out.

Once I began working the Steps and seeking outside help, I became aware of my negative thinking and I learned the way out. My therapist taught me that I couldn't solve my problems using the same mind that created them. She told me that I had to source deeper and turn to my Higher Power. And sure enough, as soon as I stopped thinking about the problem and started thinking about God, the solutions began to appear.

Today, I live in the solution much more than in the problem. Even though I can occasionally still go to the dark side, my program, my sponsor, and my friends in the fellowship are all focused on finding solutions. When I turn to them, they are quick to help me find the answers I need. I am also quick to rely on my Higher Power, asking many times each day for inspiration and a new perspective. Today, I know the answer is not in the problem; the answer is in the solution.

AUGUST 6

*"The only thing an alcoholic does in
moderation is work the Steps."*

Whenever someone mentions this quote in a meeting, it brings the house down with a chorus of identifying laughter. We certainly know how to go to any lengths when it comes to a new relationship, a hobby or project, going to the gym, avoiding the gym, and so on. But when it comes to something that may restore us to sanity, give us a deep sense of meaning and serenity, well, we wouldn't want to rush into anything. . . .

This sure can get us into trouble. For instance, just this week I worked myself into a frenzy with my business, and then I put a tremendous amount of pressure on myself to complete a creative project until I reached a breaking point. I made everyone around me crazy, including myself. Completely spun out, I went to my Friday night meeting, and a friend suggested I might be into self-will. And that's when I surrendered.

I am so grateful to have other people in my life who understand the obsessiveness of this disease, and who remind me to let go and let God. While I may not obsessively pursue recovery (and I'm not sure that would be such a good idea anyway), whenever I do work my program, it works on me by restoring balance, perspective, and sanity to my life. Working the Steps may be the only thing I do in moderation, but thank God I do it consistently enough to keep me sober and to keep me coming back.

AUGUST 7

❦

"Nothing, absolutely nothing, happens in God's world by mistake."

L ately, things haven't been going my way. Small things as well as big, scary health-related issues have come up that are definitely not what I wanted and can't be good for me. As I climbed up on my pity pot and started collecting even more evidence why and how the world had it in for me, I heard today's quote and things began to shift.

In the past, *Poor me, poor me* soon led to pour me another drink. In recovery, however, I am able to shift my perception and ask, "What might God's will be for me here?" This almost always leads me to ask how what I'm going through can benefit or help another. No matter how far I've fallen, or how rough my road has been, each experience I've had enables me to be of service to others.

As I looked at my current set of challenges through the lens of service, I suddenly felt lighter. I realized I wasn't alone, and that by involving others I could benefit from their experience, strength, and hope. I also realized that together we would grow from this experience and we would learn new ways to help others through common difficulties. As I reframed what was going on in my life as opportunities for growth, I realized the wisdom in the saying, "Nothing, absolutely nothing, happens in God's world by mistake."

AUGUST 8

"I'm glad that what's going on in my head isn't happening in my life."

I don't know why, but my perception of my life is always different —and worse—than the reality of what is happening in my life. I can simply be in line at Starbucks, but my head is elsewhere and it's all bad. I'm thinking the line is so slow, and I'll be late to work; the coffee won't be hot enough, and the traffic afterward will be horrible, and I'll miss that big deal, and then I'll lose my job and join the rest of the world of the unemployed in the Second Great Depression. And this is all happening while in line getting coffee!

When I heard today's quote, I began to understand what they mean when they say that alcoholism is a disease of perception. My best thinking used to get me into trouble, and even in recovery the distortion of my thoughts can easily make me restless, irritable, and discontented. That's why I must rely on my Higher Power and the program to constantly restore me to sanity.

These days, I've learned to run my thinking by others in the fellowship and to turn my fears over to God. I now listen less to my thoughts, and instead I pay attention to the reality of my life in the present moment. When I do this, I'm able to appreciate the miracle my life is today, and I'm able to enjoy the serenity I have access to, no matter where my thoughts are or what I'm doing. Today, I'm grateful that what's going on in my head isn't happening in my life.

AUGUST 9

❧

"Improve your memory—tell the truth."

Toward the end of my drinking, my memory got worse and worse. To start with, my mind was a big blur from being constantly loaded, or from recovering from a blackout. In addition, it got harder and harder to remember what story or excuse I had recently made up or told to different people. Because my drinking had become the most important thing in my life, I had begun lying to protect it, and because most of the lies and stories I made up were followed by a drinking binge, I couldn't keep anything straight. It's no wonder people stopped hanging around me.

When I got sober and my head began to clear, I went right on lying and telling stories. As I worked the Steps, I realized that I was lying to protect my ego and get my own way. I quickly found the truth in the statement that "self-centeredness and self-seeking" was my natural state as an untreated alcoholic. It took a lot of inventories and conversations with my sponsor before I was ready to get honest. I also had to uncover, discover, and discard a lot of character defects that were keeping me sick before I could fully recover.

These days, my life is much easier now that my default is to just tell the truth. I no longer feel the need to defend or construct a big story because today I've learned how to be responsible and honest. Now I go through life looking for ways to be of service rather than to cheat or deceive. It's a wonderful feeling being able to look someone in the eye again and feel a part of the human race. And best of all, my memory has improved because today, I tell the truth.

AUGUST 10

❧

"The three most dangerous words for an alcoholic: 'I've been thinking.'"

It took me a long time to learn that my head isn't my friend. For years in the program, I heard it was best to run my thinking by others, but I secretly never believed it. My head would always convince me it had a better idea, and time and time again I followed its advice. It almost always turned out badly because what I always forgot was that my thinking was usually centered on me.

After many more bottoms, in many different areas, I finally became willing to check in more often with others. It was hard at first because I was sure I wouldn't like what I heard, or they wouldn't let me have my way, but once again contrary action saved the day. After listening to and following other's suggestions, things turned out better, and my life began to get better, too.

What's so interesting is that today, even with years of experience of checking in with others, my head still tries to convince me to follow its advice. The voice in my head is subtle, and, like alcoholism, it can be cunning, baffling, and powerful. I know better than to listen to it (most of the time), and I will forever be grateful for my sober experience and the loving support and direction I get from my friends in the fellowship. Today, though, those three words, "I've been thinking," still remain dangerous.

AUGUST 11

*"God didn't save me from drowning so He
could club me to death on the shore."*

When I crawled into recovery, I was as desperate as a drowning man. My life had been overwhelmed by the tidal wave of addiction and despair, and the lifeboat I was clinging to was rapidly filling with water. In the final moment, I reached out for help, and God pulled me to safety.

Once I was on shore and drying out in the rooms of recovery, I found myself drowning again, this time in the wreckage and unmanageability of my life. I constantly worried about how I would repair relationships and repay debts, and what would become of me. Sometimes, I was so convinced things wouldn't work for me that a drink looked pretty good. And that's when I heard today's quote.

For me, this quote is all about faith. Today, just like in early recovery, when I get overwhelmed with fear that things won't work out, I remember that I have been pulled out from the ocean of alcoholism, restored to sanity, and that my job now is to trust that the "next right thing" will manifest when the time is right. It always has, and my living faith tells me it always will. Today, when I'm in fear, I remember that God didn't save me just to disappoint me later.

AUGUST 12

*"The way to make a mountain out of
a molehill is to add dirt."*

I t used to be that anything that went wrong—or didn't go my way—
easily became an impending disaster. Toothache? Must be a root
canal. Boss not smiling? Probably going to get fired. Left to myself,
my incessant negative thinking was quick to add dirt to any molehill
until the mountain of imaginary evidence overwhelmed me.

When I entered recovery, my sponsor was quick to point out a few
tools I might find useful for my distorted thinking. The first was, "One
day at a time." He asked me, "You're not having a root canal, and you
aren't being fired today, are you?" "No," I grudgingly replied. "Then
take it easy," he suggested. Next, he taught me, "Take the next indicated action." Calling my dentist was a manageable action, whereas
worrying endlessly about an imagined root canal wasn't. Using these
and other tools of recovery helped restore me to sanity.

Today, I'm quick to recognize a molehill when one comes up, and
I have the tools to keep it from becoming a mountain. My three favorites to remember are (1) there is a solution, (2) whatever is happening
is temporary, and (3) God is in charge. By focusing on God, and not
the problem, I get to experience serenity while the situation sorts itself
out—as it always does. And by not adding dirt to the molehill, I avoid
the imaginary mountain that used to make my life unmanageable.

AUGUST 13

❧

*"Never look down on someone, unless
you're helping them up."*

I used to love taking other people's inventory. My fragile ego thrived on looking down on others—reveling in those who had less, made less, or weren't as smart as I thought I was. By constantly comparing myself to others, I could always justify my behavior, and regardless of how bad I did, I was always doing better than most of the people I looked down on. By denigrating and devaluing other people and their experiences, I became numb not only to them but to myself as well.

In recovery, I brought my twisted perspective with me. I began judging and looking down on others, disregarding their experience and unique challenges. Soon I was alone, bitter, and nearly went out. My sponsor helped me see the inferiorities and fears I had that caused me to put others down so that I could feel better. By working the Steps, I realized that everyone's path is different, and that if I was dealing with what they had to go through, I might have done much worse. It was a revelation that truly humbled me.

I have now learned to step back and view others with empathy. Because my ego is more right-sized—I am no better or worse than you—I no longer have to look down on you to feel better. At any moment, I can look you in the eyes and understand we are the same. Now, I look to help you, because when I do I am helping myself and all others in the program get better.

AUGUST 14

❧

"Keep it simple; get stupid."

I'm a pretty complicated person. I not only tend to think about things, I like to overthink them. "What if this or that happens?" is one of my favorite thoughts. "What will he or she do and what will or can I do if they do?" On and on my obsessive thinking goes, questioning, worrying, doubting, and always trying to manipulate situations to get what I think I want. And it's not only this way with problems. I'll question and think my way out of good solutions also. I am too smart for my own good, and I seemingly have little interest in simple suggestions.

When I entered the program, I saw a sign on the meeting room walls that said, "Keep it simple." I didn't agree and started arguing with people as I tried to think my way around the Steps. And that's when someone suggested that I "get stupid." At first I was offended, but then he said that by keeping my focus on the simple things like attending meetings, not drinking one day at a time, and reading the literature, I would discover an easier, softer way and my life would get better.

It took a lot of work to "get stupid," but I found that the simpler I made things, the easier my life became. The more I "let go and let God," the less I had to try to control, manipulate, and force my will on things. By resigning from the committee in my head and becoming humble enough to admit that perhaps I didn't know better after all, I became more comfortable in my own skin. Today, I can still complicate any problem or situation, but then I remember the wisdom of "getting stupid," and I realize how simple the solutions really are.

AUGUST 15

❦

"I usually want justice only for myself."

When I was a newcomer, I was filled with self-pity and was resentful at how I had been treated in life. I used to point at all the people, places, and things that had done me wrong and ask where the justice was. "Why aren't people making amends to me?" I wanted to know. "What about all the hard times I have endured through the years?" I bemoaned to anyone who would listen. "There is no justice in the world," I said. "If life were fair, then things would be better." I truly believed this.

As I sat in meetings, I expected to hear a lot of self-righteous indignation. I mean, from the sharing I had already heard, a lot of people had been through hell, including years of emotional and physical abuse, financial ruin, loss of families, and even suffering through prison and homelessness. I expected to hear tales of these people finally getting even, but instead I was hearing about gratitude, amends, and turning their lives over to a Higher Power. *But where is the justice?* I wondered.

What I've come to realize now is that none of us are saints. We've all acted the best we could, given our awareness and where we stood at the time. And I've learned that there is something more important than justice, and that is forgiveness. It's much easier to be self-righteous than it is to practice love and tolerance, but that is the path to freedom and serenity. I now recognize the selfishness in wanting justice for myself, and instead I pray for forgiveness, understanding, and acceptance. And when I do, I get much more than justice. I get serenity.

AUGUST 16

"Reality is always so much kinder than the story I tell myself about it."

As my life was unraveling at the end of my drinking, the story I told myself about it was worse than what was happening. I thought most people hated me—almost as much as I hated myself—but I found out later they just felt bad for me. I also thought I had ruined my career and would never be hired again. And as far as ever having a relationship, the story I painted proved that I would be alone forever. At the end of my drinking, the reality of my life seemed quite dark indeed.

In recovery, I brought my dark stories with me. I was consumed with negative thoughts about the damage I had done. I obsessed about my health and worried I had cancer or some other horrible disease. I feared my financial wreckage and could feel the IRS closing in. When I shared these stories with my sponsor, he simply told me to look at my feet. He said, "Right here, where your feet are, are you okay?" I admitted I was. "Then if you stay in today and out of your head, one day at a time, you will be fine."

It wasn't always easy to stay in today, and I still struggle with it sometimes, but when I do I find the reality of my life is much different than the stories I tell myself about it. I not only have everything I need to be happy, joyous, and free, but I have more than I could ask for. I have a God of my own understanding that continues to perform miracles in my life. And I now have the awareness to know that the reality of my life is much better than any story I make up about it.

AUGUST 17

"You grow, or you go."

Years ago, when I was new to the program, I heard someone say that if you got a horse thief sober, all you had was a sober horse thief. I couldn't for the life of me understand what that meant. At the time, I thought that if someone got sober, then everything else would change, too. All the problems would go away, situations would get better, and life would improve in general. How wrong I was.

When I got sober, I still had a lot of old ideas that I acted on. I still felt like I deserved more than most people, and now that I wasn't drinking anymore, I felt that the world owed me even more. Getting a normal job still seemed beneath me, so I used that as a rationalization to continue my illegal activities. My sense of entitlement led me to keep cheating in other ways as well, and soon I was even more miserable than I had been while drinking.

When I confronted my sponsor and asked why I wasn't feeling better now that I was sober, he said it was because I was refusing to recover. He said just putting the plug in the jug but not changing anything else meant I was just another sober horse thief. He explained that recovery meant working the Twelve Steps and growing past my old self. Only by discarding the old and having a spiritual experience would I change and feel better. As I watched others refuse to do this and go back out, I realized the wisdom in the saying: "You grow, or you go."

AUGUST 18

"If you're going to worry, don't pray.
If you're going to pray, don't worry."

When I was running with my disease, I had a lot to worry about. During a night of drinking and clubbing, I worried about getting pulled over while driving drunk. When I came to the next day, I worried about the things I couldn't remember doing and saying. When I lost a job because of my behavior, I worried about paying my bills and if I'd get another one. If I prayed at all during this time, it was to get out of trouble, but soon I'd just worry some more.

In the program, I found that everyone seemed to be doing a lot of praying. I joined right in. I prayed my past wouldn't catch up with me, that I'd get what I wanted, and so on. Finally, my sponsor taught me the right way to pray. He said the only thing I should pray for was the knowledge of God's will for me and the power to carry that out. He told me that after I had prayed and turned the results over, that I should then stop worrying and focus on developing faith instead. This was hard to do at first, but in time I got better at it.

Today, I have refined my technique of prayer. Whenever I am in fear or doubt or worry, I immediately stop thinking about the problem or situation and shift my thoughts to God instead. I think about the qualities God has, like "God is infinite love," or "God has unlimited resources," or "I am surrounded by the peace and love of God." By withdrawing my attention from worry and focusing it instead on faith in God, I get to know peace. Today, I understand the wisdom in, "If you're going to worry, don't pray, and if you're going to pray, don't worry."

AUGUST 19

"A.A. is the only place I can hang out with sick people and get better."

I remember sitting in meetings in early recovery and hearing speakers share some of the most appalling stories. There were stories of robberies, prison, infidelity, and other assorted and demoralizing activities. What was as surprising to me as the stories was the reaction of the people in the meetings. Rather than be scared of, repulsed by, or even indignant over these stories so openly shared, they laughed and nodded their heads in understanding. *What's wrong with these people?* I thought.

When I shared with my sponsor about how I didn't understand how people could share such embarrassing and private things so openly, he told me that's how we get better. He said we have all done stupid, selfish, and sometimes utterly incomprehensible things when we were drinking. This was part of the sickness of alcoholism. He told me that the way we recover is to share with one another these shameful secrets, and in this way, they lose their power over us. He said as long as we aren't doing these things any longer, then they remain old behavior, and the Twelve Steps teach us how to get better.

Listening to the sick things people did while in their disease gave me the courage to look at and admit my own dark secrets as well. Suddenly I realized that I wasn't a bad person after all. Rather, I had just done bad things when immersed in my disease. By hanging out with other people who had the same sickness of alcoholism as I had, I was able to draw on their experience, strength, and hope to recover.

AUGUST 20

"This, too, will change."

Before I had a program of recovery, I didn't have much perspective on my problems. In fact, many of my problems seemed insurmountable to me, and I spent weeks and even months obsessing over them. It never occurred to me that things would get better, let alone change. No, for me, I seemed to go from one problem to another, and soon I was convinced that even if things did change, they would probably change for the worse.

I thought the worst did happen for me when I ended up in A.A. I was now sure that any and all good times I might have were over. And as I began working the Twelve Steps, acknowledging the wreckage of my past and confronting my defects of character, I was convinced that my life was only going to go from bad to worse. And that's when my sponsor reminded me that things would indeed change, and that for those who stayed sober and worked the Steps, things often changed in miraculous ways.

It took a lot of faith for me to believe him and stay sober long enough to see for myself. But gradually things did change, and all of the changes were good. Today, whenever I have a problem or worry that I begin obsessing over, I remind myself of how hopeless I once felt, and how everything turned out for the better. When I do this, I am able to stay sane and even serene while things work themselves out. One thing I know for sure today is that "this, too, will change."

AUGUST 21

❧

"You can always restart your day."

The first time I heard this quote, it was a revelation to me. I could start my day over? This was so unlike the way I had lived my life, I could barely comprehend it. My usual way of living was to wake up and wait for something negative to set the tone for my day. An angry or hurt look from my girlfriend, a driver cutting me off, or just not getting what I wanted, and that was it—the whole day was ruined. And with this attitude, I'd ruin everyone else's day as well.

Early into recovery, I looked for negative events to once again launch me into my day, and I found plenty. Many days I woke up with a new sense of shame or hopelessness as I struggled to put my life back together or stay sober. I walked around as if a dark cloud was over me—until I got to a meeting. And then, as if miraculously, I discovered hope again as I drank in the laughter and warmth from the fellowship. That's when I heard this quote.

While it was hard to practice in the beginning, I got better at it as I persevered. And I had many occasions to practice it. The first thing I had to do, however, was recognize that I had slipped into a funk because I was so used to feeling bad all the time. But once I did, I remembered I could start over. I needed help to do this, of course, and that's when a quick prayer to my Higher Power helped. Even today, I often get quiet and ask God to reset my attitude, and it always works. It saves me from ruining my and other people's day. Knowing I can always restart my day is another precious gift of recovery.

AUGUST 22

❧

"Pain is necessary; misery is optional."

For years, I used alcohol to try to avoid the pain in my life. Whether it was emotional pain caused by relationships, financial pain caused by poor job choices, physical pain, or spiritual or even mental anguish, drinking was my way out. The problem was that when I came to the next day, my problems were still there, and now I also had misery as well. Not only did I fret and worry about my problems all over again, but I had new ones because of the actions I had taken while loaded.

When I came into the program, I thought the Steps might somehow teach me how to avoid pain in my life. I magically thought that because I was now being good and trying to get spiritual, that somehow my life would be free of pain. Delusional, I know, but we alcoholics are a grandiose lot. Besides dealing with all the pain I had and had caused, I also found that life was still in session. And a part of life includes pain. Somehow this revelation shocked me a bit.

What I also learned, however, is that there is a huge difference between pain and misery. While pain is inevitable, misery—caused by how much I dwell on the pain, what I choose to do about it, how I decide to handle it—is optional. The program and the Steps have given me many ways to release the misery I used to hold on to, and they gave me so much more. They taught me the true purpose of pain: that pain is the touchstone of growth, and that after pain there is recovery. Today, I recognize pain as an opportunity to grow, and that creating misery is optional.

AUGUST 23

"Happiness isn't out there, it's in here."

One glorious, sunny day, I was driving my big, beautiful, black Mercedes through Malibu canyon on my way to do some shopping at the high-end galleries on Pacific Coast Highway. As the car snaked around the mountains, I caught glimpses of the shimmering, blue ocean. It was a Sunday morning, and I seemed to have it all: money, property, and prestige. I pulled over to an outlook and stood gazing at the incredible beauty around me, and I wondered why I felt so bad that I wanted to die. This was what my bottom felt like.

In recovery, I started to see life from a completely different point of view. When I read in the literature that character building and spiritual values had to come before trying to acquire and gain satisfaction from material things, I could really relate. It was hard, at first, to turn away from what I had been taught to pursue almost my entire life, but I had evidence that happiness and contentment definitely weren't "out there." And so I set to work the Twelve Steps.

It has been explained to me, over and over, that the Steps are written in the specific order that you should take or work them. And what I have found is that the foundation of the Steps is in developing a relationship with my Higher Power first. I now have vast experience that He can do for me what I can't do for myself. And that includes giving me the feelings of serenity, peace, and purpose that I never got from outside things. Today, I strive to acquire greater knowledge of His will for me and the power to carry that out. And when I do, I find that happiness has always been available inside me.

AUGUST 24

❧

*"I may not know how to make it better, but
I sure know how to make it worse."*

I remember how bad things were before recovery, and how easy
it was for me to make them worse. If my job wasn't going well,
I'd cop an attitude, show up late, or start slacking off (more than I
already was). If my relationship wasn't going the way I thought it
should, I'd shut down and withhold—all with the justified thought,
I'll show her. No matter what was going wrong, I always found a way
to make it worse.

When I entered recovery, my sponsor taught me that what
happened in my life was my responsibility. He showed me how I had
a part in everything that happened to me and how my solutions often
became worse than the original problem. It took many years for me
to accept this and many more to learn how to make better choices.
Thank God I had the Twelve Steps to teach me how.

I have often heard people say that the program was the life manual
they wish they would have had when growing up. I completely relate
to this, because now I, too, know how to handle situations that used
to baffle me. Best of all, though, by staying focused on my part, I know
how to make things better. Today, I have a choice between making
the situations in my life better or worse, and most of the time I make
the right choice.

AUGUST 25

*"It all works out in the end. If it hasn't
worked out yet, it's not the end."*

This is one of the truest quotes I've heard yet. I can't tell you how many times I've stressed and worried about something I was sure wasn't going to work out, only to eventually realize that in the end it all worked out just fine. Sometimes it took months, other times years, but of all the things I've obsessed about, nearly all of them worked out in the end. The key is waiting for the end.

Before recovery, I was more focused on the middle than the end. I was addicted to drama and was sure that all the negative things in my life would only get worse. I secretly liked being a victim and when something started to work out, I quickly pointed to other awful things that were, or could be, happening. As you might imagine, my life rarely got any better.

When I entered the program, I was sure that it, too, wouldn't work out. I spent many months trying to convince anyone who would listen why my life would end in disaster. Their answer was always the same: Keep coming back. What I eventually learned was that with the right thought and action, and with a faith in a Higher Power, things did work out in the end. And now when I'm in fear, I remind myself: If it hasn't worked out yet, then it's not the end.

AUGUST 26

"You're exactly where you're supposed to be."

For as long as I can remember, I've been unhappy where I was and wished I was somewhere else. In school I always wanted to be in the next grade; at work I wanted a more senior position making more money; when I bought my first home, I quickly wanted one with a pool. When I entered recovery, I brought this same impatience and discontent into the rooms with me.

I remember complaining to my sponsor after a few months that things hadn't gotten better, and that I even felt worse. He listened patiently and then said, "You're exactly where you're supposed to be." This didn't make any sense to me, and as my life continued to unravel and as I grew more frustrated, irritated, and angry, I kept complaining. His answer remained the same, and it took years before I finally understood what he meant.

One of the most important things I've learned in recovery is that accepting where I am physically, emotionally, and spiritually is the necessary key to changing it. Once I stop resenting how things are or wishing they were different, I can begin working with God to make them better. But it all begins with acceptance of where I am right now. Today, I know that I'm exactly where I should be, and because of this, I know how to make it better.

AUGUST 27

"God's message to me is:
'Stay out of the way but be ready!'"

This quote made no sense to me for many years. I mean, in the beginning the whole concept of "turn it over" and "surrender" was as foreign to me as speaking another language. I fought every step of the way to control every aspect of my life and was sure I could do it, too. As I worked the Steps, though, I was confronted with the unmanageability and wreckage of my life, and I finally admitted that perhaps I didn't have all the answers.

As I began to surrender to the program, I felt like I was getting a lot of mixed messages. On the one hand I was told to "Let go and let God," yet then I was told to "Suit up and show up." *Which is it?* I wondered. *When do I need to use my will versus when do I turn it all over?* This was all very confusing to me for a long time.

Over the years, I've finally learned the difference. Today, I know that it's my job to prepare to take the next indicated action to the best of my ability and to remain willing. The results, the actions and reactions of others, and many other things, however, are all in God's hands. Today, I understand God's message to me is "Stay out of the way but be ready." And by continuing to work the program one day at a time, I am.

AUGUST 28

"Drinking gave me the feeling of a job well done
without having done a thing."

I remember a restaurant/bar in the rich neighborhood of Brentwood, California, where I used to go to after work. I'd sidle up to the long, swank bar and order cocktails while I watched the successful people with money come in to have $200 dinners. I was struggling financially at the time and in the beginning I felt out of place, but after a few drinks I had goal-planned my first million and was soon feeling as if I belonged.

Years later in recovery while working on my Eighth Step—making a list of all the people I had harmed—I was surprised when my sponsor told me to put my name on it. When I asked why, he told me to list all the things I had wanted to do and what I had wanted to make out of my life, and then write about how alcohol and drugs had taken them away. I thought about that bar in Brentwood, and many more like it, and of all the plans and goals I had drank and used away.

When they say that alcohol is cunning, baffling, and powerful, they mean it in so many insidious ways. When I think of the potential, the future, the life I drank away, I'm sorry to my core. It's hard to forgive myself sometimes. But when I think of all I have accomplished since I got sober, and of the lifetime of dreams still ahead, I'm filled with hope and gratitude. Today, I live in and appreciate the miracle of my recovery.

AUGUST 29

"Don't take yourself so damn seriously!"

When I came into the program, everything was a big deal, and I was very serious. My finances, my future, and my wrecked relationships—everything was overwhelming. I remember attending meetings and hearing the laughter and thinking, *What's so damn funny? The only reason we're here is because our lives suck!* It took me quite a while before I could join in with that laughter, and the moment I did, my life began to change.

As I got further into the program, that sense of impending doom began to dissipate, and I felt like I could breathe again. The secrets and shame I had hidden for so long began to come out, and as I shared with others what was inside me, I began to feel lighter. I began to laugh more at myself and with others, and I finally began to feel human and a part of life again. Most of all, I started to realize what was truly important.

Today, I know that the future will take care of itself if I take care of today. I now have faith that there is a God working in my life, and that even if things don't go my way, it's not only okay; it often turns out for the better. Today, money isn't as important as relationships, and the only things that really matter are health and sobriety. I've learned to live life on life's terms and, most of all, not to take myself so damn seriously.

AUGUST 30

*"We cannot do everything at once, but
we can do something at once."*

I tend to get overwhelmed by all the things I want to do. The perfect career, the best relationship, get into top physical shape, write a bestseller, and have time left to read, hike, vacation in Europe—the list is endless. When I was drinking and crashing toward my bottom, all these goals were like ripped pieces of a parachute trailing me from above. When I finally hit the ground, the scattered bits of my goals lay around me.

As I began working the program and developed some clarity, I picked those pieces back up. I wanted to do everything again—and even more! It didn't take long for me to be overwhelmed again, and that's when I had to surrender once more. As I discussed this with my sponsor, I realized my number-one goal was to get through the Steps and establish a firm foundation in recovery. He assured me there would be plenty of time for all the rest if I made sobriety my priority.

While it was hard to put other things on hold, I now see the wisdom in that advice. I realized I couldn't do everything at once, but I could concentrate on the most important thing, my recovery, and I could take definite action toward that at once. I made it a priority to go to meetings, to get commitments, and to work the Steps. By doing so, my life improved immeasurably. Today, when I once again get overwhelmed by my dreams, goals, and wants, I remember I can't do them all. But I can pick the most important thing for today, and I can do something at once.

AUGUST 31

"Do the next 'right thing.'"

W hile I was drinking, I had a knack for making bad decisions. I chose inappropriate partners in relationships, cheated in my job, and made other shortsighted choices that didn't end well. What I didn't know at the time was that the majority of the decisions I was making were based on selfish and self-seeking motives. By the end of my drinking, the consequences of these choices surrounded me, and I had to surrender.

When I was new in the program, I once again had many choices to make. How many meetings a week should I go to? Should I get a sponsor right away or wait for the perfect one? When should I get serious about working the Twelve Steps? I learned early on that I should never say no to an A.A. request, and I found that by taking suggestions, my life improved. I also found out the difference between my will (usually based on self) versus God's will (based on service to others), and this helped me identify the next "right thing" to do.

Now that I've been sober a while, I still have a lot of decisions and choices to make. Whether it is business, relationships, or any other part of my life, I still have to choose between self-will (what I want) or God's will (what would be best for others or the situation). When I stop to think about it, I always know what the "right thing" to do is, and when I choose this, my life and those of others run more smoothly. I've learned, often through trial and error, that this is always the easier, softer way.

SEPTEMBER 1

"God bless you—God change me."

I was at a speaker meeting one night where the speaker began his share this way: "If I say something tonight that you don't agree with or that angers you, then say a prayer for me. God knows I could use the prayers, and you could probably use the practice." Well, that got everyone's attention! I fumed in my seat for a while and could barely hear what he was sharing. After the meeting, I grabbed a bite to eat with my sponsor and we talked about it.

As I dumped my anger and indignation onto my sponsor while dipping my French fries into ranch dressing, he listened quietly and nodded his head. When I started repeating myself for the third time, he held up his hand to stop me. "I see what he said in a very different way," he began. "While it may have sounded disrespectful, what he was saying is the fundamental truth. Everyone has a different opinion, and if you don't agree with it, that's your problem, and not theirs. In other words, it's up to you to change or accept."

I've often thought of that night, and that share, and it has taken me years to appreciate the deep wisdom in it. What I've found is that people are indeed very different; all our perspectives are uniquely ours, forged by heritages, families, and environments we can barely fathom. If I want to get along with people, then it is up to me to accept them for their differences. If I have a problem with that, then it's probably best for me to say a prayer. It's up to me at that point to ask God to change me so that I can be okay with who they are—and who I am as well.

SEPTEMBER 2

"It's not going to get easier, but it's going to get better."

When I got sober, I thought my life would get easier. I mean, I wasn't drinking to black out any longer, and now that I was sober, everyone should be happy for me. I even thought I deserved some kind of an award. I was sure my money troubles would disappear, my health would get better, and all the people I hurt would forgive me and life would get back to normal. None of that happened right away.

In early sobriety, the only thing that changed was that I wasn't getting loaded any longer. I still had all the same problems as before, and in addition, I was now also racked with feelings: feelings of remorse, resentment, fear, anger, and more. And as I struggled to work the Steps, things got worse as I lost job after job, found I was unfit for most relationships, and was in constant fear. I didn't think recovery was for me.

I told my sponsor that if this was what sobriety was like, I'd rather start drinking again. He told me this was what *getting* sober was like, but it wasn't what *being* sober was like. He said if this was how we were going to feel all the time, then none of us would have remained in recovery. Each year, my life did get better and better. Even though it wasn't easy in the beginning, I found that overall, I had discovered the easier, softer way. Today, I can't imagine not being sober and living in recovery.

SEPTEMBER 3

"Act as though, until it becomes so."

W hat a wonderful lesson this was for me to learn early on in recovery. At first, I didn't think I could make it through the day or week sober, and my sponsor would tell me to *act as if* I were going to make it. He told me to go to meetings, take commitments, and share honestly about what was going on. He also told me not to drink between meetings, and to suit up and show up.

I did, and soon my actions became reality, and I got sixty days, ninety days, six months, and then a year. It had become so. As my life got better, I began to want other things and to have my life change in other ways as well. "Act as if," my sponsor told me again. If I wanted a job in an office, he instructed me to wake up and put on a suit as I looked for work. Soon, I was wearing that suit in the new company that hired me.

As I continue to grow my awareness in recovery, I realize that "acting as though, until it becomes so" is one of humanity's universal spiritual truths. Books like *The Secret* and others on the law of attraction explain why this is so, and I know, through experience, that this universal law is true. Today, if I want my reality to change, I simply begin acting as if, and it soon becomes so.

SEPTEMBER 4

"The degree of my anxiety is a measure of my distance from God."

Anxiety used to be the master of my life. Without a relationship with God, I faced life alone and was in constant fear of not getting my needs met or of losing something I had so desperately fought to get. The past was a constant source of regret and shame, and the future was filled with countless unknown dangers that would surely overwhelm me. All of this made the present intolerable.

When I entered recovery, I brought my constant obsession with the past and future into the rooms with me. Thankfully, my sponsor taught me about living one day at a time, and he showed me that this was where I would find God—today, right here, right now. He told me that if I could get present, and thus *be* in the presence of God, my anxiety would go away.

This was simple advice, but not so easy to follow. The more I worked at practicing it, though, the more I found it to be true. Over the years, I've discovered that the more I use the tools of the program—prayer and meditation, pausing and asking for God's guidance, and acknowledging in the moment that God is here—the more I find myself in the peace and serenity of God's presence. Today, I use the degree of my anxiety to measure my distance from God.

SEPTEMBER 5

*"If you're looking for an easier, softer way,
there are no other directions."*

In the past, there was only one way to do things—my way. I was convinced I had all the answers, knew the right way, and thought that because I did, life would be easy. I believed I would be happy if everybody would just obey my commands. After years of bullying my way through life and manipulating others to get what I wanted, I was finally brought to my knees and admitted defeat.

When I began working the program, I was told it was the easier, softer way, but it sure didn't feel like it at first. There were Steps, commitments, honest inventories, lots of feelings, and new ways of acting and interacting with others. In the beginning, I rebelled mightily against this new way of life and often longed to, and sometimes did, revert back to old ways of thinking and acting. And each time I did, my life became unmanageable once again.

As I persevered and worked the Steps, something miraculous happened: I changed. As I changed, this new way of life began working for me. After a while, the Twelve Steps and the principles of the program became the life manual I had always wanted but had been unsuccessful in writing for myself. One day I realized that I had found the easier, softer way, and now I had the directions I had always longed for.

SEPTEMBER 6

"When you're going through hell,
keep going!"

Hell often seemed like a destination rather than a passing part of the overall journey before I had a program. Whenever I found myself in an insufferable situation, I often convinced myself that this was my new lot in life and that it would never get better. Rather than try to figure ways out of it, I usually wallowed in self-pity and waited for things to get worse. And they usually did.

When I started working with my sponsor, I argued, debated, and tried hard to convince him that I was different, and that I could never recover. After listening to me for weeks, he asked if I was willing to try a different way. "But it won't work," I whined. "Are you at least willing to try?" he repeated. When I finally said yes, my life began to change.

The freedom and recovery I have found through working the Steps has shown me the way out of the hell I used to put myself through. Today, I look for solutions to situations that used to baffle me, and I have learned through experience that "this, too, shall pass." Today, I ask my Higher Power for guidance and am shown the next indicated action. Doing so allows me to look for ways to move through times that seem unbearable. Today, I know that when I'm going through hell, it's important that I keep going!

SEPTEMBER 7

"Worry is a terrible waste of the imagination."

I used to be addicted to so many things—alcohol, drugs, food, sex, anything I could use to escape—and I abused them as I sought a way out of the impending doom I often felt. When I entered the program and began putting these vices and distractions down in my Fourth Step, I found I had been addicted to something else as well: worry.

It took a long time for my emotions to become stable and for my thoughts to become clear, but once they did, I was amazed at how much time and energy I spent worrying. I worried about my health, my job, my relationships, my future, and even my past. When I shared this with my sponsor, he explained that worry was caused by excessive self-will, and it meant that I hadn't fully surrendered to my Higher Power.

After years of working the Twelve Steps, turning my will and life over to God, and spending more and more time looking for and trying to follow His will, I find that I worry less and less. Today, my mind is focused on what God would have me do and be, and from that place I've learned to take the next indicated action and to turn the results over to Him. These days, I use my imagination in a positive way: to envision my life and world as God intends it to be. And once I set about trying to make that happen, I become much happier.

SEPTEMBER 8

*"You need to spend some time with God this
morning and then let your day go."*

N ow that I'm in recovery, I find that I can start my day in two
different ways. The first is the old way, which means rushing
through my morning, preparing for work and thinking (or worrying) about how I'm going to control everything to get what I want.
The second is the new way the program taught me, which is sitting
quietly in meditation and prayer and turning my will and life over to
my Higher Power.

You can imagine how the first way goes. I swear my way through
traffic, enter work defensive and resentful, and find that I am at odds
with others and myself throughout the day. After work I fight my
way through traffic again and arrive home exhausted and on edge. If
I don't go to a meeting, I take these feelings to bed with me and wake
up in an uneasy mood. This is what living in self-will is like.

The second way is definitely the easier, softer way, and it's amazing how differently the same day goes when I begin it with God. By
starting with prayer and meditation, I connect to God and turn over
my will, life, and day to His care. Relieved of the bondage of self, I
now go about my day from the perspective of service, and suddenly
my day (and life) takes on a deeper meaning. The result of starting
my day this way is fulfillment, serenity, and true purpose. And it all
begins by making the right choice to begin my day with God.

SEPTEMBER 9

*"My sanity today is directly
proportional to my honesty."*

In the old days, it was hard to keep my story straight. As my drinking increased, my omissions turned into half-truths, and these turned into little white lies. After a while, I couldn't recognize the truth anymore. As I became disconnected from people and myself, my very reality changed and my sanity disappeared. After living in this dark abyss, I finally surrendered and entered the program.

As I began to get sober, I started in on the overwhelming task of unraveling the massive knot of lies, stories, and deceptive behavior I had engaged in. I felt shame, anger, and remorse as I painfully made my way back to my true self, which had been buried beneath the disease of alcoholism. I used the tools of "uncover, discover, and discard," and after many inventories, I finally saw the light ahead.

The road back to sanity began with the words "rigorous honesty." Although seemingly straightforward, the challenge I had was in coming to believe that, of myself, I was enough—that if I spoke my truth, I would be accepted. The miracle is that the truth really did set me free, and the more honest I was, the more peaceful and serene I became. Today, if I'm feeling uncomfortable, I look to where my honesty may be lacking. As soon as I become genuine again, my sanity is restored.

SEPTEMBER 10

"Friends are God's apology for your relatives."

When I was new, I had very few healthy boundaries. I especially had little defense against the observations, suggestions, judgments, and criticisms of my family members. Someone once said that your relatives know how to push your buttons because they were the ones who put them there. I quickly found out how true that was.

At first, my reaction to their views on recovery was to try to explain what the program was, how the meetings worked, and why I needed them. After that didn't work, I severely limited my contact and involvement with them, instead focusing on the new friends I was meeting in the rooms. What a blessing not to have to travel the road alone, and the bonds I formed literally saved my life.

As the years passed and I discovered a sense of who I really was, I began to reengage with my relatives and found that while I had changed, they basically had remained the same. Accepting the limits of those relationships was hard at first, but over time the unconditional love and understanding of my new family of friends helped provide me with the close connections I had always craved. Today, I am learning to improve my relationships with my relatives, and my friends are showing me how.

SEPTEMBER 11

"Don't ruin an apology with an excuse."

I used to be full of excuses: "I didn't do this because. . . . I acted this way because she did. . . . He deserved it, so I gave it to him." On the rare occasion when I was cornered and couldn't justify my behavior, I'd make an apology, but I'd always qualify it with an excuse or, at the very least, a justified reason. The bottom line was that I could always place the blame outside myself.

As I worked through the Twelve Steps of the program, I discovered a fourth column in the Fourth Step called "my part." While I at first resented having to look at my side of the street, I found that this column soon made up my Eighth Step list of amends. This column also made it clear what the proper definition of an apology was supposed to look like during my Ninth Step.

My sponsor told me that we don't make apologies any longer, we make amends. And knowing this made the direction clear. Rather than reverting back to old behavior and trying to hide behind excuses and reasons, I was to focus strictly on my part, ask if there were any other wrongs I was unaware of, and then ask what I could do to make things better. "You've done enough damage," I can still hear my sponsor tell me. "Whatever you do, don't ruin your amends with a bunch of excuses."

SEPTEMBER 12

***"We never know the difference between
a tragedy and a blessing."***

When I got sober, I thought it was the worst tragedy ever. First, I thought, I could never go to Europe again. Who could enjoy England without going into a pub and having a pint? And can you imagine a café in Paris without a glass of wine? And how about all those special times, like New Year's Eve, weddings, weekend parties? Everybody would be drinking and enjoying themselves, and I would be hating it. Tragedy? The enjoyment of the rest of my life seemed gone for good.

In recovery, I began taking inventories of my career of drinking and using. What emerged wasn't a pattern of drinking like other people and enjoying parties, but of getting drunk, blacking out, and engaging in humiliating behaviors. During my last trip to Paris, I realized all I wanted to do was drink red wine, not visit museums or monuments. I should have just stayed home.

What started out as a tragedy—getting sober—has turned into the greatest blessing of my life. My life today is indescribably better than I could have ever hoped for. And what it all comes down to is that, today, I try to do God's will rather than my own. When something doesn't work out the way I think it should, I now ask, "Is that a bad thing?" Now I wait to see what God has planned, and many times it's much better than what I had in mind. Today, I have the wisdom to look beyond a seeming tragedy and look for the blessing instead.

SEPTEMBER 13

"I've never regretted something bad I didn't say."

Restraint of pen and tongue was a foreign concept to me before recovery. I used to speak my mind, even when my mind wasn't made up. I was quick to retaliate for perceived wrongs, quick to take your inventory when I was feeling less than, and quick to tear you down to make myself feel better. And if I had been drinking, the insults, judgments, and condemnations flowed even more. Afterward, regret was heavy, and the familiar feeling of shame would descend, forcing me to retreat into the bottle once again.

When I got sober, I heard the saying that feelings aren't facts. As such, I was told that I didn't have to act on every feeling I had. Instead, I could write about them, pray about them, and share them with other people. I could restrain from acting on them and wait until I had clear direction as to how to react. Nine times out of ten the feelings would pass, and I was glad I hadn't acted on them. I was also relieved that I had less regrets because I hadn't said hurtful things.

Now that I'm sober a while I still have to be vigilant about acting on or saying things I might regret later. For instance, a neighbor's dog barks pretty much constantly, and I'm pretty annoyed. I've written an anonymous letter expressing how irritating it is, but I haven't delivered it yet. As time passes, I've been very relieved as I know I've avoided the guilt and shame that I would feel if the neighborhood discovered I was the letter writer. And besides, when I'm in my house, I don't even hear the dog! Today, I remember "I've never regretted something bad I didn't say."

SEPTEMBER 14

"I suffer from 'terminal uniqueness.'"

I used to think I was so special. Wherever I went and whatever I did, inside I'd constantly be thinking, *Look at me! Look how special I am!* I used to think the world revolved around me and that I was too important to extend myself and help somebody. *Someone else can be kind and save the world,* I'd think. *I'm way too busy for that.* Because of this self-absorption, people avoided me, and I ended up being ignored and alone.

When I entered recovery, I brought my self-centered point of view with me. I secretly felt that as soon as people saw how *I* did the Steps, there would be a revolution within all of A.A. As I began working them, however, my ego began breaking down, and I had to confront the fact that I was no more special than anyone else. My sponsor told me I suffered from "terminal uniqueness," and the sooner I let go of that delusion, the better off I'd be. He suggested I get humble and help someone.

I used to think there were too many people and situations that needed help, so what was the point of extending myself? But then one day at a meeting, I heard a story. Two people were walking on a beach where a hundred starfish had washed up and were stranded on the shore. One of the guys picked one up and threw it back into the sea. The other guy said, "With all the other starfish lying on the beach dying, throwing one back isn't going to make a difference." "It made a difference to that one," the first guy replied. And so it is with putting aside my feelings of terminal uniqueness. If I help just one person today, then I've made a big difference.

SEPTEMBER 15

"Yesterday was the deadline for complaints."

When I was drinking, I had a lot of complaints. I complained that I had to work a crummy job; people didn't do what I wanted them to do; the world was out to get me. As my drinking progressed, other people began complaining as well. They complained that I was out of control at parties, that I was selfish and didn't care about their feelings, and that I had become a danger to be around. These complaints doubled my own, and soon I was consumed by resentments.

When I crawled into the program, I found more things to complain about. I complained about having to go to ninety meetings in ninety days. I complained about people talking during meetings. But mostly I complained about doing the work: the inventories, readings, and commitments that my sponsor suggested. It was a slow process but eventually I learned to replace my complaints with prayers, and once I developed an attitude of gratitude, my life was transformed.

Today, I still have a tendency to complain and look at all the things that I still don't have or that might go wrong. But I also have a full spiritual tool kit and proven ways to be restored to sanity and serenity. Gratitude lists are still my favorite tool, and anytime I'm in fear or feel like complaining, I make a list of twenty-five things I'm grateful for. By the time I'm done, my perspective has completely shifted and I'm back on my spiritual beam. I realize now that yesterday was the deadline for complaints, because today is the day for living happy, joyous, and free.

SEPTEMBER 16

"I'm in the action business,
and God is in the results business."

I was at my local coffee shop last week, and I ran into a friend who is in the program. He asked me how I was doing, and I told him how overwhelmed and scared I felt about some upcoming medical tests. He reminded me that there are some things I can control, and some things I can't. As soon as he said this, I felt a great relief because I realized immediately that I had been trying to control everything again.

Before recovery, that is how I lived my life. I planned everything, took massive action, and then I tried to control all the results. It was exhausting living that way, but without a Higher Power in my life, I didn't dare let go of anything. What a gift (and relief!) it was to learn that my real role in life is to just suit up and show up, and then let God take care of the results.

As we kept talking, he reminded me that all I had to do was take the next indicated action, and then turn it over. When I looked at it this way, I was comforted because I knew I could control setting the next appointment, or taking the next test, and as I released the results I released the tension and worry as well. What a gift it is to live this way, and when I worry these days, I remind myself that I am in the action business, and God is in the results business.

SEPTEMBER 17

"That's fine, but what would you do if you wanted to be helpful?"

It was easy for me to criticize, judge, and complain before I had a program of recovery. People at work never did things right, and my manager always wanted me to do things I thought were beneath me. My roommates were slobs, and I was constantly amazed at their lack of cleanliness or common sense. At family gatherings, I grew annoyed at how things were run and would talk endlessly behind my family's back after the party was over. Never once did it occur to me to help.

When I got into the rooms, I was quick to judge how the meetings were run and would selfishly not volunteer to help there either. When someone suggested I empty the ashtrays outside, I indignantly responded that I didn't smoke. After sitting and seething in meetings, I developed many resentments over how things were run. When I finally told my sponsor how I felt, he listened carefully and then repeated each point, following it with, "That's fine, but what would you do if you wanted to be helpful?"

Things changed once I stopped judging and started helping. For one, my mind shut off once I got into action and started contributing. For another, as I got to know people, I found that I could identify with what they shared. As I became helpful, others in my apartment and family and even at work became more helpful as well. Today, when I find myself criticizing or judging a situation, I silently say, "That's fine, but what would you do if you wanted to be helpful?" Things get better when I do.

SEPTEMBER 18

"Become willing."

I wanted a lot of things before recovery, but I wasn't willing to do much to get them. Instead, I had an inflated opinion of myself and what I thought I deserved. When I started a new job, within a couple of weeks I thought I knew enough to be running the company. In school, I felt I should be teaching the class, not taking notes. And in most social situations, I was better than and knew more than you. To say I was difficult to be around is putting it mildly.

When I started attending meetings, I felt I should have been given an award for staying sober for a week. When I read the Twelve Steps, I didn't think Step Four really applied to me, and Step Nine was out of the question. My new sponsor suggested I stay focused on the First Step. When I started whining about following direction, he asked me if I could become willing. In those situations where I couldn't, he recommended I pray for the willingness to become willing.

It took many years to shed my sense of entitlement, but now I've gained an important tool: willingness. Today, I know that if I want something—a more fulfilling career, more serene relationships, and a more spiritual perspective on my life—then I can have them as long as I become willing to put in the time and effort to work toward them. And even today, if I balk at what it might take, I can still pray for the willingness to become willing.

SEPTEMBER 19

"Prayer might not change things for you,
but it changes you for things."

One of the things I love about the program of recovery are God shots. God shots are when things happen—consequences, chance meetings, happenings, or hearing the right things—just when you need them most. The magical thing is that they often fulfill a need you had but weren't even aware of. Working a spiritual program tunes you in to these wonderful moments, and the more you open yourself up to them, the more they appear. They are one of the ongoing gifts of sobriety.

I heard this quote the night before I was to have surgery, and it couldn't have come at a better time. I had been managing my anxiety pretty well, but when it came to the night before, I was starting to imagine the worst. For some reason, I had forgotten to pray about it that day, and so fear had pushed upon me the responsibility for how the surgery would go and what the recovery would be like. The scenarios I was painting were pretty black.

And then I checked my email and got this God shot. Someone had sent this quote to me, and suddenly everything was in perspective again. I immediately prayed and asked God to restore me to sanity around my surgery, and I turned the results over to Him. As soon as I was done, I felt the familiar peace I've come to know from talking to God. Nothing had changed about the surgery, but everything had changed in me. As I went to sleep that night, I said another prayer of thanks: for my recovery, for my relationship with my Higher Power, and for the God shot I received just when I needed it.

SEPTEMBER 20

*"Don't let your expectations exceed
your acceptance."*

Through recovery, I have discovered a wonderful way to avoid disappointment, anxiety, and resentment. I simply check my level of expectation about any upcoming—or current—event, interaction, or situation. Because I find that my expectations are invariably driven by my selfish needs or desires, and because situations or interactions rarely go the way *I* want them to, my solution is to monitor my expectations first and ask myself if I'm okay with whatever unfolds. If not, then that's my problem.

Before recovery, I had neither the awareness nor the tools to access or deal with my often unconscious need to have things go my way. As such, my expectations—of myself and others—often exceeded not only how things went, but blew past my ability to accept things as they were. In fact, I had little to no acceptance at all. As such, I regularly had resentments, often formed negative opinions in advance, and was generally not pleasant to be around.

Today, thankfully, I have some tools. I know enough to recognize in advance that I am not in control of people, places, or things. The best thing I can do is focus on the part I can control: my level of acceptance. This is easier if I remember the saying "Everything happens in God's time." When I do, I find I can let go and relax. Developing the proper level of acceptance around all the situations in my life allows me to watch God's will, and not mine, unfold. Today, I'm much happier because I don't let my expectations exceed my acceptance.

SEPTEMBER 21

"The best escape from a problem is to solve it."

When I got sober, I was still running from my problems. Besides not picking up a drink, my behavior was just the same as before. My job was the same, and I still had all the problems from that; my shaky and shady relationships were the same, and the problems that came with them persisted as well. In meetings I had some relief from the wreckage of my life, but once they were over, my problems descended like a thick fog.

When I started working with my sponsor, he encouraged me to reveal my back-pocket plans for fixing my problems. These were the self-centered and selfish ideas I had to either evade responsibility or escape the consequences of my actions. As we worked through Step Five, though, I finally accepted my part in things and realized that the only way to truly escape my problems was to attempt to solve them. And that meant making amends.

Steps Eight and Nine were terrifying for me on many levels. In addition to the shame and embarrassment I felt, I was also worried about the very real possibility of going to jail. I put many conditions on who I would approach and what I would reveal, and the back-and-forth started to drive me crazy. My sponsor finally told me there was only one way out of my fear: I had to make a decision and take an action. By becoming humble and making amends, I discovered the one true way to escape my problems, and that was to solve them.

SEPTEMBER 22

"If you've still got it, you haven't given it to God."

Seeing this quote today was an example of another God shot. My wife and I are going back home for the holidays, and there are some family members I'm not looking forward to seeing. Old resentments, past and current hurts, and the overriding belief and feeling that any interactions will be the opposite of nourishing and healthy have me playing negative scenarios over and over. When I least expect it, I find myself rehearsing caustic conversations that will never happen. As the date gets closer, my mood becomes bleaker.

When I entered recovery, I had these kinds of thoughts and feelings about virtually everyone and everything in my life. When I finally did a Fourth Step inventory, I uncovered this deep vault of fear, shame, anger, and remorse. I never realized how hurt and resentful I was, and getting it all on paper helped a tremendous amount. And seeing my role in it all opened the door to my healing. Recognizing and acknowledging my part meant that I didn't have to stay a victim. I could and did make amends, and I also changed a lot of my behavior.

I couldn't have healed so deeply by myself, though. The real miracle was being able to turn it all over to my Higher Power. Through the actions I took, and through His healing love, I was able to repair and let go of most of the hurt and resentment in my life. Not all the amends went how I wanted them to go, and not everything was forgiven. Family, especially, has deep roots, and not everyone changes. Today, when these kinds of feelings come up, I remember to turn them over to God, and I try to keep the focus on my part—past and present.

SEPTEMBER 23

*"We are responsible for the effort,
not the outcome."*

W hen I entered sobriety, I didn't know how I was ever going to fix everything in my life. All the relationships I had ruined, all the bridges to jobs and opportunities I had burned—there didn't seem any way I could control and manipulate everything back into place. How was I going to get all the people I had stolen from to forgive me? How was I going to get healthy after all the abuse I'd inflicted on myself? How was I going to get my family to trust me again? I didn't think I could pull it off.

Luckily, my sponsor assured me that I didn't have to. In fact, he told me I could never be responsible for other people's attitudes and reactions to me. That wasn't my job. Instead, he told me my job was to stay sober, clean house, and take the next indicated action. In doing my Ninth Step, he told me I was responsible for admitting my faults and making sincere amends. Whether someone forgave me or not wasn't up to me. I was responsible for the effort, not the outcome.

Learning to let go of outcomes wasn't easy for me. After a lifetime of trying to arrange life—including other's reactions and opinions—to suit myself, simply taking the right actions and leaving the results up to God seemed impossible. But the miracle is that every time I follow God's will and not my own, wondrous and unexpected outcomes flow into my and other people's lives. Plus, now that I know I'm not responsible for all the outcomes in the world, I'm able to live a life that can be happy, joyous, and even free.

SEPTEMBER 24

"It's the first drink that gets you drunk."

For years, this saying made no sense to me. It wasn't the first drink, I argued, but rather the seventh or tenth drink that got me drunk. I'd been able to control my drinking for a long time, and with a lot of willpower I'd been able to limit my drinking to a few glasses. Toward the end though, I'd inevitably have that sixth or seventh or umpteenth drink and end up roaring drunk. *If only I could regain control*, I thought, and when I entered the program, I secretly hoped I'd learn how.

I remember sharing with my sponsor my desire to once again control and enjoy my drinking. He said, "Heck, when I controlled my drinking, I didn't enjoy it, and when I enjoyed it, I couldn't control it." That was my experience, too. He then told me that, for him, one drink was too much and a thousand was never enough, because once he started, he could no longer stop. And that's when I began to understand.

Today, I know very well that if I began drinking again, even one drink, it would soon enough lead to ten, and I'd be drunk. I don't know when I crossed the line into full-blown alcoholism, but I did. I now know there is no going back. Thankfully, I no longer fantasize about being able to control my drinking, because I know that if I tried, I wouldn't enjoy it. I also know that it's the first drink that will get me drunk.

SEPTEMBER 25

❧

"CALM: Care about life's moments."

They say that one of the gifts of recovery is the sense of peace and calm that you get. I have heard it described as feeling comfortable in your own skin. That concept was totally foreign to me before I got sober; in fact, I felt the opposite way. My solution was a drink, and for brief moments I could relax and feel okay with myself. But by the end of my drinking, I was uncomfortable both drunk and sober, and that's when I knew I had hit bottom.

I remember being amazed by how happy and easygoing everyone seemed in meetings. They could look me in the eye, smile, and offer me their phone numbers. They didn't seem driven by the anxiety that was my constant companion, and I soon wanted what they had. I could have that, my sponsor assured me, if I was willing to do the things they did. And that meant working the Twelve Steps and developing a relationship with a Power greater than myself. I was willing.

It took years for me to work though the layers of my old self, but today I have the feelings of serenity and peace I sought. I even like and respect myself. I am so very grateful to not feel that restlessness and discontent any longer. Today, I know calm and am able to take in and appreciate life's precious moments. The gifts of sobriety go far beyond just not drinking, and these gifts are available to anyone who is willing to honestly work the program.

SEPTEMBER 26

*"The only thing worse than my problems
are my solutions to them."*

I used to think I had all the answers when I was drinking, so I couldn't understand why my life wasn't getting better despite what I did to fix it. If my boss was a jerk, I'd quit. If my girlfriend wasn't paying attention to me, I'd go out with someone else. If my landlord didn't like it when I was late with the rent, I'd move. No matter what I tried, things only seemed to get worse.

When I began working the program, I told my sponsor all about my problems. He listened for a while and then asked me how good of an employee, boyfriend, and renter I had been. At first, I was insulted, but then he told me to carefully write about each problem focusing only on my part. Well . . . that certainly opened my eyes.

After many thorough inventories, what I've found is that all my problems start with me. And I've come to see that the reason my solutions make them worse is that they are driven by the same selfishness and self-centered fear that caused them to begin with. Now, the only solutions that work start by acknowledging where I've been at fault, and end with a sincere desire and offer to make amends. Because of this, I have solutions that make my life better today.

SEPTEMBER 27

❧

"The reason the program works is because we're not all crazy on the same day."

A fter I was in the program for a few years, I remember hearing some people sharing and thinking they were still clearly out of their minds. This scared me because I realized I relied on them to save my life. A week later, I remember sharing some of my own stuff and realized that I probably sounded kind of crazy as well. That's when I heard today's quote.

This quote means many things to me. To start with, it reminds me I still have the disease of alcoholism, and that my thinking will always be affected by it. It also reminds me that in the rooms I have the freedom to be myself—whatever that happens to be that day. In fact, the saying "You can't save your ass and your face at the same time" has literally saved my life on a number of occasions. It also reminds me, "The reason we're all here is because we're not all there."

The hope and strength I take from these sayings is that alone I can't, but together *we* can. Together we make up the mosaic that is recovery, and despite those times when I still feel a little crazy, I am comforted as I see the miracle still taking place in others' lives. Somebody once said that he only needs one meeting a week but he went to five because he never knew which one it was going to be. Thank God the voice of recovery speaks through us all, one day at a time.

SEPTEMBER 28

❧

"Everyone wants to feel better, but no one wants to change."

Before I had a program, I did a lot of things to feel better. I moved; changed jobs, girlfriends, and cars; tried different combinations of drugs and alcohol; took up yoga; joined a gym—the list is endless. While these things worked briefly, inevitably I would be left feeling that giant hole inside me, a hole that I could never fill and that always made me miserable.

When I entered recovery, I had the same initial relief as when I tried other new ways to distract myself. After a while, though, that relief also began to wear off, and I could sense the emptiness returning. I met with my sponsor, and he told me I was feeling this way because I was resisting and refusing to change. "But I'm sober!" I told him. "Yeah, but you're still trying to do things your way. Until you surrender and really work the Steps, you'll just be the same old you—only you'll be miserable *and* sober this time."

Thank God my sponsor was willing to tell me the truth, and thank God I was ready to hear it. Deep down, I knew I was the common denominator in all the things I had tried that didn't work, and once I got to Step Four and honestly looked at my part in things, I finally realized what had to change: me. While thoroughly working all the Steps, the promises began coming true for me, and today I am not the same man who entered the rooms all those years ago. Today, I am happy, joyous, and free. And that was worth changing for.

SEPTEMBER 29

"Humility is our acceptance of ourselves."

I used to think that humility was for the weak. In school, in business, and in life, I was taught to be competitive and to always strive to win. When I drank, I took this to the next level and became aggressive and looked for ways to dominate others, even if that meant cheating, stealing, or lying. Money, property, and prestige, regardless of how I got them, were my goals, and humility was not something that interested me. This relentless pursuit of "outside" stuff, fueled by the disease of alcoholism, brought me to my knees and drove me into the rooms of recovery.

When I got sober, there was a lot of talk about surrender, willingness, and humility. My ego fought against it all, and as I tried to acquire these character traits, rebellion dogged my every step. Thankfully, I learned new ways of framing these concepts. I was taught that surrendering means people "stop fighting, lay down their arms, and join the winning side." And that's when I learned the true definition of humility.

I was taught that humility isn't thinking less about yourself, but rather thinking *about* yourself less. As I worked the Steps, helped others, and got closer to my Higher Power, I began feeling better about myself. By doing a Fourth Step inventory, and then working my Eighth and Ninth Steps, I finally forgave myself for my past transgressions. I was given the gift of empathy and acceptance of myself. Today, I feel comfortable in my own skin, and I appreciate the gift that humility truly is.

SEPTEMBER 30

"Easy does it, but do it."

I was quite a procrastinator before recovery. I had a lot of good ideas, but I didn't want to act on them until I had thought things through and the time was right. For example, I wanted to go back to college, but I thought I should have my house paid off first. I wanted to get married but thought I should actually have a better career first. Regarding drinking, I thought I would be able to stop once I had that good job that allowed me to get a better house, a wife, go to school, and so on. I didn't get much done.

In sobriety, there seemed like a lot of things I could do. I could get commitments, get a sponsor, work the Steps, and, oh yeah, stay sober. When I saw the saying on the wall that said, "Easy does it," I relaxed and thought I'd just keep thinking about it all. And that's when my new sponsor told me there is a chapter in the Big Book called "Into Action," not "Into Thinking." He suggested I get busy.

I'm so thankful he directed me to jump in and become part of the program. He told me I should take contrary action even if I didn't feel like taking action, and that if I brought the body, the mind would follow. He told me that "Easy does it" refers to my tendency to obsess and overdo things, and that the "But do it" part refers to overcoming my resistance to change. I learned that I can't think myself sober—or into any of the things I want in life—but if I take action, I can live the life of my dreams.

OCTOBER 1

❦

"We didn't get here because we
sang too loud in church."

After a weekend of hard drinking, I would commit to sobriety on Monday. By Tuesday, I began to feel better, and by Thursday night I'd allow myself a couple of beers. By the weekend, I'd be hard at it again, and Monday morning I'd swear off drinking all over. This pattern continued until the Thursdays became Tuesdays, and after a while I just gave up and gave in to my disease. Somehow I survived the abuse, and when I committed again it was to the program of Alcoholics Anonymous.

During my First Step, I surrendered when I admitted to my innermost self that I was an alcoholic and that my life had become unmanageable. After a few weeks, though, when I started feeling better, I began second-guessing whether it had been that bad. Same thing happened with Steps Two and Three. I'd surrender my will and my life, but midway through the day, I'd take it all back. In discussing this with my sponsor, I learned that surrender is not an event, but rather a process.

There have been many surrenders in my recovery. Each day, I surrender my disease to my Higher Power, and I turn my will and my life over to His care. Sometimes this lasts ten minutes, sometimes several hours. But whenever I find myself uncomfortable or at odds with people, places, or things, I know it's time for another surrender. Thankfully, I have the tools and the willingness to do this. Surrender is indeed a process, not a one-time thing. And the better I get at it, the better my life becomes.

OCTOBER 2

"Be all right with being all right."

I was generally irritable, restless, and discontented before recovery. As a kid I was anxious and afraid of things. When I found alcohol, I finally found a way to be comfortable—hopeful even. Drinking gave me that sense of ease and confidence I saw in other people. Suddenly, I could dance better, talk to girls, and be one of the guys. Unfortunately, the solution soon became the problem, and I had to quit drinking.

In recovery, I felt very vulnerable without my solution. Soon all the feelings I used to drown out with alcohol were front and center. At times I thought I would be overwhelmed by them, so I did what was suggested: I took them to meetings, I shared them in fellowship, I inventoried them, and I worked the Steps on them. Sometimes it worked, but when it didn't, my sponsor would always bring me back to the present. He'd ask, "Are you all right, right now?" "Do you have enough food, gas, money, right now?"

It took a lot to corral my galloping mind and rope it back into the now. But each time I'd have to admit that, yes, right now I'm all right. Right now, everything *is* taken care of. After years of going through this exercise, I have the perspective to know that I really am all right. Problems come and go, but I've always survived them and have usually done just fine. What I've learned is that the key to my serenity is truly being all right with being all right. And when I can remember that, my serenity returns, and I can live happy, joyous, and free.

OCTOBER 3

"Take the mess to your sponsor,
take the message to the meeting."

A friend in recovery shared something once that I've never forgotten. He was newly married and struggling with the transition from living alone for many years as a bachelor. His therapist suggested that rather than trying to process his uncomfortable emotions with his new bride, he should, instead, bring his problems into therapy, and then bring the solutions back to the relationship. I thought that was just brilliant advice.

And it was definitely not how I was used to living my life. Before recovery, if I had a problem (and I had many), everyone heard about it. I would bemoan the state of my life to anyone within earshot, and if I thought you were the cause of my stress, I talked endlessly behind your back. My ultimate solution was to get drunk, but when I came to, none of these problems had gone away. Instead, I often had just made it worse. I needed a better solution.

When I entered the rooms, I thought I had found one. In each meeting I went to, I began sharing how bad my life was, how it was everyone else's fault, and how the Twelve Steps probably wouldn't help me. My new sponsor pulled me aside early on and suggested I share this mess with him, one on one, and then bring any solutions I found back to the meetings. That worked much better. Today, I go to meetings and listen to other people's solutions to the problems I may be struggling with. I always hear them if I'm willing to listen.

OCTOBER 4

"You're only as sick as your secrets."

When I first entered the program, I was filled with guilt and shame over some of the things I had done. When I sat in meetings and heard others share openly about some of their past behaviors, I was shocked by how honest they were. Even more baffling was how they and everyone else could laugh at their dark secrets. I didn't know it then, but this was the beginning of hope and recovery for me.

"You're only as sick as your secrets" was a saying I heard early on in the program. At first there were things I swore I would and could never reveal. After hundreds of meetings, though, the openness, forgiveness, and recovery of others created the safe place I needed to come clean. As I began to uncover, discover, and discard those parts of myself I was ashamed of, I experienced the freedom and forgiveness I needed to fully recover.

As I completed my Fourth and Ninth Steps and cleared away the wreckage of my past, I was reborn into a new man who is sober and recovered. Now I can laugh at myself, along with others, over some of the things I used to do. Moreover, I realize how the shame I felt about my dark past is the very key I need to help connect with and help others heal. Today, I use the Tenth Step to guard against keeping secrets, and to stay free of shame, so that I can be available to work with others.

OCTOBER 5

*"Would you rather be right, or would
you rather be happy?"*

Now that was a hard one to answer when I was new. In fact,
my answer back then was, "But I *was* right! He/she/they were
wrong! It has nothing to do with being happy!" How wrong I was. By
clinging to my self-righteous pride and ego, I fought a lot of people
and a lot of things to maintain my right to be right. In the end, I was
right about one thing: There was little happiness in my life.

In addition, I paid a steep price for this stubbornness. Living in
opposition to people, places, and institutions takes a lot of energy,
and it constantly creates resentments. And resentments will kill me.
In order to stay alive, I've had to learn to forget about who is right or
wrong, and instead to focus on my part. Mine is the only part I can
control, and if my side of the street is clean, then I become open to
the only real solution to any situation: forgiveness, surrender, and
acceptance.

Today, I know that while I may not always have the opportunity to
be right, I always have the choice to be happy. By doing a Tenth Step
each day, and looking at and correcting my part, I get to forget about
who is right, and I get to be happy and free instead. I have found that
it is a lot easier to live in harmony with people, places, and things
today. And I'd rather be happy than right.

OCTOBER 6

"Keep the lesson, but throw away the experience."

This quote gave me a jolt when I first heard it. For years I'd been so wrapped up in the drama of my life, I never stopped to look at what I could have learned from it. Events seemed to descend on me, each like the one before it, but because I wasn't learning the lessons, I didn't know I was destined to keep repeating the experiences. And because I wasn't learning, the experiences just kept getting worse.

When I was new in recovery, I used to complain to my sponsor all the time. "And then this happened to me, and she didn't do this, and they told me this . . . ," and on and on. He would listen very patiently (bless the guy), then ask, "And what is your part again?" After I'd figure out where I was at fault, I'd find the solution—and that always led to the lesson. At first, the lessons were painful to learn, but after a while I welcomed what they had to teach me.

Today, I don't have to keep reliving similar experiences, and so I don't have to drag the past into the future either. Because of the Tenth Step, each night I can review the experiences of the day, look at my part, and discover and grow from the lessons they hold. They are always there if I'm willing to be open and honest. Today, I look for and learn from the lesson, so I don't have to repeat the experience.

OCTOBER 7

*"When all the little things really bug me,
it's because there's a big thing
I'm not facing."*

Irritable, restless, and discontented—that is my normal state as an alcoholic. Going to meetings, working the Steps, praying, and relying on my Higher Power are the ways I get restored to sanity. By doing so, I'm able to achieve some peace and serenity. But even when I am in a calm space, if little things still bother me, I now know to look beyond my alcoholism.

It's amazing how my first instinct these days, even with considerable time in the program, is to deny or ignore things that are uncomfortable in my life. It's been my experience that not facing what at first appears to be no big deal often turns it into one and quickly makes my life unmanageable. And the first warning I've done this is when all the little things (stuck in traffic, misplacing my keys, a line at the market) start to really bother me.

Today, I've learned to acknowledge these things and recognize them for what they are: indications that there is something bigger that I'm not facing. As soon as I take the time to look at what's really going on, I immediately begin to feel better. And once I begin to apply the tools I've been given in this program to deal with whatever is going on, I find that it really isn't such a big deal after all. Today, I use the little things to help me become aware of and deal with the big things.

OCTOBER 8

"I don't have a rewind button in my life, but I do have a pause. . . ."

I can't tell you how many times, in the heat of the moment, I have said or done things that I've later regretted. But, when angry or hurt, I felt I needed to defend or justify myself, and I have acted in ways that hurt not only others but myself as well. Later, after things had settled down, I was left with regret and shame, and these feelings drove me to seek relief in a drink.

When I entered recovery, my sponsor told me that just because I was sober it didn't mean that I would never be hurt or angry again. He said there would still be plenty of times I would want to strike out. But in order to recover, I had to become responsible for my actions. "You don't have a rewind button, but you do have a pause," he told me. Then he taught me how to use it.

Practicing restraint of pen and tongue has been one of the most practical things I have learned in recovery. I was taught not to react when upset, but rather to call someone and run my feelings by them first. I can still write that email, text, or letter, but I have to show it to my sponsor before I send it. Pausing and praying to my Higher Power always restores my power of choice and allows me to check in with others before I react. Today, I pause, and that often saves me from later wishing I had a rewind button.

OCTOBER 9

*"When you get to your wit's end, you'll
find that God lives there."*

In the past, whenever I got to a bottom I just moved over and started digging another hole. I would leave jobs, relationships, and even states looking for a different solution. I didn't have a God in my life, so there was no turning it over. It wasn't until I had broken my shovel and hit my final bottom that I was ready to admit complete defeat.

When I came into the rooms, I heard a lot about God. I didn't like it. I had given up on Him a long time ago, and I was sure He had deserted me. What I came to find out was that God was always there to help me when I hit bottom. What I also learned, years later, was that He was there for me all along. I just had to ask for help sooner.

What I now know is that I don't have to wait until I'm at my wit's end to reach out and get help from God. He lives in me and is with me every step of the way. The key that opens the lock is and always has been willingness. And today, I'm much more willing to be willing. Today, I know I don't have to reach my wit's end to find out where God lives. I just have to ask for help.

OCTOBER 10

"Am I interfering in the experience
God wants others to have?"

Before I entered our sister program of Al-Anon, I always thought I knew what was best for everyone. I spent a lot of time working behind the scenes trying to control and manipulate situations and people. I was sure that if only I could get you to do what was right, then I could help you avoid getting hurt, and both your life and mine would be better.

After years of this exhausting strategy, I dragged myself into the program and surrendered. Not only were others not taking my advice, but I was growing even more miserable than I was making them. When I asked my sponsor what was wrong with trying to protect those I loved, he told me that denying people the dignity of learning and growing from their own experience never helped anyone. Furthermore, all I was really doing was interfering in the experience God wanted them to have.

It took me many years to understand the truth and wisdom in those words. I now know that we each have our own path and our own Higher Power. I realize that my job is to try to improve my own life, set a healthy example, and love others unconditionally. Today, I've learned that all experiences are teachers and that it's up to each of us to learn our own lessons. My job is to share my own experience and support if and when I am asked.

OCTOBER 11

"The program does for us slowly what alcohol did for us quickly."

I clearly remember what I felt like before recovery. I was anxious, on edge, and so uncomfortable with my life that I wanted and needed to escape from it. Each morning I awoke with the terror of a new day, and making it through that day was a real struggle. I can also remember the immediate sense of ease and comfort that came from that first drink. Suddenly everything was okay; I had a new plan, and there was some hope for the future.

Drinking and escaping like this were my solution for a long time, but it stopped working. I reached a point where I couldn't imagine life with alcohol, and I couldn't imagine my life without it either. I was at a jumping-off point. In the beginning of my recovery, meetings and fellowship offered me temporary relief from the near constant dread and anxiety I felt. The problem was how to survive between meetings, and it was very rough going for quite a while.

And that's when I heard someone share, "We go to meetings for relief, but we work the Steps for recovery." And as I worked my program, I found this to be true. The relief and sense of ease and comfort I used to get from drinking now became a part of my everyday experience. After a while, I experienced moments of peace and serenity, and much of the time I even felt comfortable in my own skin. One day I realized that the program had done for me slowly what alcohol used to do for me quickly.

OCTOBER 12

*"Life is tough because you get the
test first and then the lesson."*

When I was in school we would spend weeks, and sometimes even whole semesters, preparing to take tests. I remember studying lesson plans and course outlines, reading and highlighting books, taking chapter quizzes, and attending lectures and taking copious notes. I studied this material all in preparation for midterms and finals. How I did on these tests depended on how well I studied the lessons beforehand.

In life, it's quite a different story. We get the test first, and then it's up to us to learn the lesson. And while this may be tough, what's worse is that if we don't learn the lesson, we get another test, then another, and another, until we learn the lesson. This is something I never understood while I was in the fog of my drinking, and because of it, I seemed to end up in the same bad situations over and over again.

One of the things I love about recovery is that I've been taught to look for and learn the lesson. Today, when I get a test I immediately look for my part, examine my motives, and look for how I can either make amends or act better the next time. This is called a daily Tenth Step inventory, and it ensures that I learn the lesson quickly. Life may still be tough sometimes, and the test may still come first, but now I know how to learn the lesson to avoid having to take the test again.

OCTOBER 13

*"If you want to feel rich, just count all the things
you have that money can't buy."*

Gratitude lists have been an important tool in my spiritual tool kit for a long time. Whenever I feel the old self-pity creep back in, I get out a piece of paper, number it from one to twenty-five, and start making a list of all the things I'm grateful for. While this always makes me feel better, there have been times when I still wished for a bigger house, more money in the bank, and so on. That is why today's quote means so much to me.

No matter how much money, property, or prestige I have, there will always be those who have more. By reviewing my gratitude list, what I am reminded of is that the real riches I have today come from within. For example, today I feel comfortable in my own skin, and that feeling of peace and comfort that I used to seek outside myself now comes from the things money can't buy.

I've learned to keep material things to a minimum on my gratitude list. The true riches in my life start with the gifts of my recovery: the meaningful relationships I have, my connection with my Higher Power, and a true appreciation for all the opportunities I have to be useful to other people. This kind of gratitude list is endless, and when I finish it, I feel alive and vital. Today, the real riches in my life come from counting and appreciating the things I have that money can't buy.

OCTOBER 14

*"The **only** thing that can ever make me drink
again is untreated alcoholism."*

There is a lot in this quote. First, it reminds me that no matter how much time I have in the program, I still have the disease of alcoholism. I used to think, and hope, that one day I would outgrow my addiction. But like someone once said, after each day I stay sober, at night alcoholism is exercising and doing push-ups, and by morning it has grown stronger. In other words, it's never going away.

And this is why, each day, I have to do something to strengthen my recovery and treat my alcoholism. I can go to a meeting, work the Steps, talk to another alcoholic, or be of service in some other way. Each of these activities helps to keep me spiritually fit, and only by developing, maintaining, and growing my spiritual life can I effectively treat my alcoholism and stay comfortable in my own skin.

Second, this quote reminds me that other people's untreated alcoholism is a danger to me as well. If I'm *not* spiritually fit, then I am vulnerable to the influence, the resentment, the lure, and the romance of others' alcoholism. In these and many other ways, alcoholism truly is cunning, baffling, and powerful. Only by constant vigilance and treatment of it can I remain safe, sober, and recovered.

OCTOBER 15

"Don't count the days; make the days count."

C an you remember counting the days in early recovery? I sure can. I remember how difficult it sometimes was to make it through the weekend, or even the evening, and I can still feel how grateful I was to have made it through another day. Those thirty-day, sixty-day, and ninety-day chips were a *big* deal to me, and with each chip I felt a growing relief—as if I had escaped from prison and was still free.

As the months turned into years, my focus shifted, and I began to wonder what I wanted to do with my life. This was new thinking for me, and it was difficult at first to overcome years of self-loathing and low self-esteem. But after a while, I began to dream of what I might become and what my Higher Power had in store for me. Once I settled on a direction, I began living my life with purpose.

Today, my days are filled with the joy of living. My focus is no longer on survival and thoughts of myself; instead, I now focus on what I can pack into the stream of life. I no longer wake up and say, "Oh, God, not another day!" But rather, "Thank God, I have another day!" I'm grateful that I no longer count the days, but rather, I look for new and exciting ways to make the days count. Today, I'm fully alive and living the miracle of recovery.

OCTOBER 16

❧

"I don't react to the present the way I reacted to the past."

L ast week I had a God shot that revealed the miracle of recovery in my life. An emotionally charged situation came up that used to trigger a wounded, withdrawn, and resentful reaction, but as it unfolded I noticed something wonderful happening inside me. For the first time, I was aware that I could choose a different, healthier way of responding. What a welcome change that was!

Before recovery, I was a slave to the old, hurtful wounds of my past. I was like one of Pavlov's dogs: As soon as a stimulus was presented, I reacted automatically. And predictably, my reactions almost always made the situation worse. Not only was I unaware that I had a choice, I also had no idea there might be a better, more appropriate way of responding. And that's what the miracle of recovery has given me.

Through years of working the program, running my thinking and ideas by my sponsor before I acted, praying for an intuitive thought and then waiting for inspiration, I have developed the space to consider my options before responding. And in that space, newer, more appropriate choices are available to me. This new way of reacting has freed me, and allowed me to live a happier, healthier, and more fulfilled life. Today, I don't react to the present the way I reacted to the past.

OCTOBER 17

"If God had made today perfect, there would be no tomorrow."

As an alcoholic, I have a lot of black-and-white thinking. Things are either all right or they are all wrong—there is very little in between. Before I got sober, this kind of thinking was a big handicap in my life. If I didn't do something perfectly, then I considered myself a failure that day, and for all the days in the future as well. If something didn't go right, I just gave up and became resentful. By the end of my drinking, I learned to not even try anymore.

When I entered recovery and looked at the Twelve Steps for the first time, I secretly gave myself thirty days to do them. If they didn't work, then I was going back out. When I finally got a sponsor, he told me we would work a Step a month. "*What?*" was my reaction. He asked me how long I had been drinking, and I told him years. He told me I didn't get to my bottom in thirty days and that I wouldn't recover that quickly either. He told me to consider sobriety as "slow-briety."

As I worked through the Steps, one of the defects of character I discovered I had was perfectionism. As I slowly wrote a fearless and thorough Fourth Step inventory, I realized I hid behind the unrealistic ideal of perfection to escape the messy and difficult work of progress. When my sponsor pointed out that in the program we strive for "progress not perfection," it released me from my obsession and allowed me to grow, to keep trying, and to value and appreciate the progress I was making. I finally learned that if I failed today, I could learn from it and try again tomorrow. I'm glad God didn't make today perfect, and I'm grateful for all the tomorrows I still have.

OCTOBER 18

"I can't get drunk on yesterday's booze, and I can't get sober on yesterday's sobriety."

During the early part of my recovery, I had frequent "slip dreams." I would wake up scared that the drinking I had done in my dreams really happened, and that I had lost the sober time I had managed to scrape together. Lying half awake, terrified, it slowly came to me that it had only been a dream and a wave of gratitude passed over me. In those moments, I realized that no matter how much I had drank in the past, none of that mattered as long as I didn't drink today.

Over the first few years of recovery, I went to hundreds of meetings. I almost always felt better when I did, and I heard people say that going to a lot of meetings was like putting sobriety in the bank. They said on those days you didn't go, or when life suddenly got tough, you could draw on that sobriety bank account to get you through. After many more years in the program, I felt like my bank account of recovery was pretty large, so I went to fewer and fewer meetings. Then one day at a beach bar in Honolulu, Hawaii, I almost made the ultimate withdrawal by nearly going out.

Thank God I didn't! I went right to a meeting that night and shared what had almost happened. Some people in the rooms shared similar experiences, and that is when I heard today's quote. I suddenly remembered that alcoholism never goes away, and all I have is a daily reprieve based on my spiritual condition. And that condition is directly related to my current program and today's sobriety. Today, I go to meetings regularly because I know I can't stay sober on yesterday's sobriety.

OCTOBER 19

"Quitting is easy;
staying quit is a bit more tricky."

For the longest time, I didn't think I had a problem with my drinking; I had quit many times. And at first the real problem didn't appear to be staying quit either, because I had done that for over a year one time. No, the problem for me was that the period of staying quit got shorter and shorter. After a while, not drinking for two days in a row was out of the question, and toward the end, quitting was just as impossible as staying quit. I finally had to surrender.

When I entered recovery, I heard something that didn't quite make sense. Someone told me that alcoholics didn't have a problem with drinking, they had a problem with not drinking. He said that's why quitting is easy, and he admitted he had done it hundreds of times. The trick, he said, is staying quit. And to do that, we need the Twelve Steps. As I began to work the Steps, I started to discover many of the reasons I struggled to stay quit, and I learned tools to help me figure out the tricky part of staying sober.

What I've learned in recovery is that I had a problem with living and that alcohol seemed to fix that problem. When I drank, I was suddenly confident, unafraid, good-looking, and hopeful. When I was sober, I was just the opposite. The gift I've found by working the Twelve Steps is that I'm finally comfortable in my own skin. It is now easy to stay quit because life sober is no longer tricky. The answer, I have found, is that today I know how to live life on life's terms.

OCTOBER 20

❧

"You'd drink, too, if you had my life."

It was a revelation to me when I read the story in the Big Book about the blind woman who was an alcoholic. Like her, I had many excuses for why I drank so much, including my upbringing, my alcoholic father, the missed opportunities in my life, and so on. I read with wonder as she recounted the reasons she drank so much. She drank because her marriage was bad, because she was part German, because she was legally blind. As I read her excuses, I inserted my own and felt justified as to why I drank too much. And that's when the other ladies told her the real reason she drank as she did.

They listened patiently to her reasons, and after each one they patted her hand and simply said, "That's not why you drink." By the end, they told her that she drank because she had the disease of alcoholism. I remember reading this and feeling a huge load lifted from my shoulders. If alcoholism was truly the reason I drank as well, then it meant I didn't have to fix all the other reasons—which was impossible anyway. Now I only had to deal with one reason, my disease.

By working the Twelve Steps and arresting my disease, I have recovered from a hopeless state of mind and body. I have also received the promises of the program and so much more. Regarding my childhood, I no longer dwell on it, nor do I wish to shut the door on it. Instead, I take the lessons I have learned and use them to help another. I've also found that most of the other problems in my life were of my own making, fueled by alcoholism. Today, I'm grateful for my life and accepting of my past, and I know I no longer have to drink over it.

OCTOBER 21

"We come to A.A. to get a life, not for A.A. to be our life."

After I got over my old ideas about getting sober and fully surrendered to the program, all I wanted to do was hang out in recovery. I felt comfortable and safe going to two meetings a day, seven days a week, and because I was unemployed, I had the time to do so. After meetings, I loved going to fellowship, and some of my fondest memories to date have been late dinners with a group of other sober people. I lived in the pink cloud of early recovery and never wanted to leave.

After a while, my sponsor suggested I look for work. He said we become self-supporting through our own contributions once we get sober. At first, I thought the stresses of the real world would be too much, and cutting down on meetings made me pretty anxious. I resisted until I couldn't borrow enough to live any longer, and so I finally got a job. I hated it. I grew resentful that I had to get up early, drive in traffic, and do something I thought was beneath me. I kept going to my evening meetings, though, and the succor I found there helped me deal with these feelings.

After changing jobs a few times and settling into a more balanced work/recovery life, I realized what the answer was. The key to feeling the same sense of comfort and safety outside of A.A. was to apply the principles of the program in all of my affairs. And chief among these is to be of service. Today, when I am engaged in any activity, I find the same feelings of fulfillment I get in the rooms as long as I seek to help others. I now know that I was given a life in A.A. so that I can have a meaningful life outside of A.A. as well.

OCTOBER 22

"There is no chemical solution to a spiritual problem."

I used to love the immediate effects of alcohol and drugs. Whenever I was feeling low or defeated, I knew I could count on a few drinks to immediately change my mood. I spent many afternoons after work in various bars and restaurants abusing happy hour. I would enter feeling depressed over my slumping sales and career that I was convinced was going nowhere, and after the second drink my outlook improved. After a few more drinks, I was sure a promotion was coming, or even part ownership of the company!

While the initial effects of alcohol were positive, the aftereffects were positively terrible. I soon lost that job—and the next several after it. All other areas I drank over ended poorly as well, and when I finally surrendered, I found myself in sobriety. When I wanted a quick fix in recovery, my sponsor told me to relax and take it easy. He told me they called it "slow-briety" for a reason. My life would get better, he assured me, but I had to put in the time first and work the program.

And so I went to work. It took me eighteen months to work the Twelve Steps (the first time), and it took over two and a half years before the obsession to drink was completely removed. It took seven years for me to find the right career, and another six years after that (thirteen total) before I met the right woman and got married. All the promises of the program did come true for me, and I now have a life that is beyond my wildest dreams. And it all happened when I found a spiritual solution to my spiritual problem.

OCTOBER 23

"Decide what kind of day you're going to have, then start it."

I used to let circumstances dictate my mood and how my day was going to go. I'd wake up, quickly survey all the bad things in my life, and then decide how bad the day was going to be. As I went through the morning, and then the day, it was easy to find evidence supporting how awful the day and my life were. Toward the end of the day, I couldn't wait to start drinking to get some relief. And often that only made the day worse.

I'll never forget sitting in a meeting in early recovery and hearing someone share a solution to this kind of thinking. She said simply that if you found yourself having a bad morning, or even a bad day, you could start your day over. She said that what you do is stop and get quiet, and say a prayer asking your Higher Power to restore you to sanity. After that, it helps to either write or mentally make a quick gratitude list. Finally, you spend the rest of that day looking for opportunities to be of service.

Like most things in the program, this sounded too simple to work for me, but I was willing to try it. With a little practice—meaning sometimes I had to restart my day five or six times—I got better and better at it. And again, like most things in the program, it works when I work it. Today, I realize that I don't have to let circumstances dictate what kind of day or life I'm going to have. Instead, I can decide to have a good day, and when I do, I always find or create the evidence to support it.

OCTOBER 24

"If I'm okay with me, I have no need to make you wrong."

One of the biggest gifts I've been given in recovery is the ability to pause when I'm feeling anxious, angry, or judgmental and ask myself what I'm afraid of. Just today as I was driving, I found that I was taking all the other drivers' inventories. That guy was driving too fast; she was making an illegal U-turn; that guy was driving like an idiot and should be locked up. Suddenly a wonderful awareness came over me, and I stopped and did a quick fear inventory. Within minutes I was restored to sanity, and once again my focus was where it should have been—on my own driving.

It didn't always used to be this way. For years, whenever I was feeling out of sorts, I looked outside of myself for the cause. There was always someone not doing things my way, or someone acting worse than I was, and it was easy to point out their faults to make myself feel better. Needless to say, I had more resentments than friends, and when I entered the program I was angry and alone.

What I've learned in recovery is that whenever I'm feeling irritable, restless, or discontented, it is always because I'm in self-centered fear and spiritually disconnected from my Higher Power. The ability to recognize this has literally changed my life, and today I use the tools of the program to self-soothe and to live comfortably in my own skin. Today, if I'm okay with me, I have no need to make you wrong.

OCTOBER 25

"I've learned to say, 'You may be right.'"

I used to think I knew it all. When someone disagreed with me, I'd argue and go out of my way to set them straight. I loved the saying "Those people who think they know it all are especially annoying to those of us who do." In the end I was self-righteous and smug. It's no wonder I didn't have many people to argue with by the end of my drinking.

When I began working with my sponsor, I started arguing with him, too. At first, he listened to me, but after a while he'd had enough. "Why don't you take the cotton out of your ears and put it in your mouth?" he suggested. I was too desperate to be indignant, so I followed his advice and began listening to what others were sharing in meetings. And that's when the miracle began for me.

Through listening to the experience, strength, and hope of others, I not only learned that my way was not the only way; I learned that it was almost certainly not the right way for you. I learned that others had their own path, made their own mistakes, and grew from their own experiences. By coming to understand this, I came to see that your opinions were just as valuable as mine. Most of all, I learned to stop arguing because I learned how to say, "You may be right," and actually mean it.

OCTOBER 26

❧

"It's progress, not perfection.
We are not saints."

I had some friends over the other night for dinner, and we started talking about road rage. We each had a story to tell about how we had participated in an escalating episode of honking, cutting off, or giving the finger to another angry driver. Being generally centered in other areas of my life, I was a little disappointed in myself when I realized that I, too, can become a complete jerk in about five seconds.

When I entered the program, I was used to acting this way. In general, I had a low regard for other people's feelings, and one of the problems I had with the Twelve Steps was that I thought if I didn't become a saint, I wouldn't stay sober. I remember telling my sponsor this and him saying four words that I still repeat to this day: "It's progress, not perfection."

I've made a lot of progress over the years, and I've come a long way from where I used to be. For the most part, I'm comfortable in my own skin, I'm truly grateful for what I have, and I sincerely try to add to people's lives. And yet every now and then, sometimes even without my being aware of it, something will provoke me into a state of fear and I'll resort temporarily to an old behavior. Thankfully, I'm able to recover my serenity pretty quickly, and when I do I remind myself, "It's progress, not perfection. We are not saints."

OCTOBER 27

"Honesty got me sober; tolerance keeps me sober."

I didn't realize how dishonest I was before I entered recovery. I had half-truths and misleading by omission down to a fine art, and by the end of my drinking, I was even good at deceiving myself. I didn't know it then, but the practice of being rigorously honest was to become the cornerstone of my recovery, and without it, I never would have gotten sober.

Another thing I didn't realize before recovery was how intolerant I was of other people, places, and things. Once I began looking at myself, I found that my first reactions were to judge, reject, and condemn others. What I discovered was that my intolerance was a defense mechanism covering my deep feelings of inferiority and shame, and it wasn't until I discarded these that I began to live comfortably in my own skin.

What I've learned over the years is that if I want to remain comfortable and sober, I've got to continue to practice tolerance. Now when I feel like judging or condemning others, I quickly look within and ask if I'm scared or if I'm feeling less than. Once I'm honest with myself, I'm able to deal with these feelings, and this always restores me to a state of tolerance for myself and others. Today, I realize that honesty got me sober, but tolerance keeps me that way.

OCTOBER 28

"I don't believe in miracles.
I depend on them!"

If you had asked me before recovery if I believed in miracles, I would have laughed in your face. "Look at my life!" I would have said. "There are certainly no miracles happening here." In hindsight, I wasn't aware of how miraculous it was I hadn't, through drunk driving alone, killed myself or anybody else yet, or how the miracle of recovery was about to happen for me.

During the first few years of recovery, the occurrence of miracles was subtle, and I sometimes missed them. My physical sobriety was something I struggled with and then eventually took for granted, but it was surely my first miracle. Later, the grace of emotional recovery and the emerging awareness of and appreciation for my spiritual self were also examples of the miracles taking place in my life. And, of course, I was always surrounded by the many miracles happening for others in the rooms as well.

These days, I have plenty of experience and evidence in my life, and in the lives around me, to believe in the existence of miracles. They may not always look like I expect them to, but they are unfolding in and around me constantly. Today, I realize it's enough to just believe in their occurrence, then suit up, show up, and work hard for them. After that I let God do the rest, and I watch in wonderment as the miracles happen. Today, I not only believe in miracles, but I realize I am one.

OCTOBER 29

"Surrender is not a one-time thing."

It's amazing how self-righteous we alcoholics can sometimes be. Before recovery, many of us acted in destructive, demoralizing, and often illegal ways, regularly hurting ourselves and others in the process. Rather than being remorseful when confronted with our behaviors, we usually became resentful and acted even more inappropriately. In the end, many of us were alone, and the only people who were glad to see us were the people who welcomed us into recovery.

At first, it's hard to confront the damage we've done, but after a while many of us do recover the positions and self-respect we had lost. What also returns, though, is our ego, and sometimes a new sense of entitlement can make us hard to be around again. I have sat and seethed in meetings while people shared how they thought things should be run, all the while harboring my own self-righteous views.

My favorite saying of Bill W's is, "Honesty with ourselves and others gets us sober, but it is tolerance that keeps us that way." When I catch myself feeling mightier than thou, I ask God to remind me of this, and to remind me of where I came from. When I do, I'm humbled by the miracle that has taken place in my life, and once again I become right-sized. I am instantly reminded that we didn't get here because we sang too loud in church.

OCTOBER 30

"Watch out; I still have a self-destruct button."

I used to be the master of self-sabotage and self-destruct. If things were going well, or might go well, I had the knack for ruining them. Surprise party for someone close to me? I would get tight at the party and spoil it. Great job interview in the morning? I would sleep in because I had celebrated too hard the night before. I foiled countless opportunities and thought my punishment was Alcoholics Anonymous.

When I was ninety days sober, at my regular Wednesday night meeting to take a chip, I left because they were out of them. I went home and drank. I beat myself up for weeks over that and finally crawled back four months later. As I worked through the Steps, I continued to make mistakes, and my anger grew into rage. To my surprise, I found my rage was mainly directed inward, and that's when I discovered that the core characteristic of alcoholism is a deep self-loathing. That is why we can ruin so many lives and drink ourselves to death.

It has taken many years to move beyond the illusion of alcoholic hatred. What I found is that in the core of each of us is not loathing but rather love—God's love. Recovery means that we find this love and learn to act from it, and to share it with others. We rely on the Steps to help us grow past the destructive impulse of the disease, but we must remain vigilant because the disease never goes away. Today, I still have a self-destruct button, but I also have the path to healing and love. And because of recovery, I have the power to choose God's love.

OCTOBER 31

"Does it feel sober?"

When I first got sober, the only thing that changed for me was that I no longer drank. Most everything else, though, remained the same. I still stole money at my job, cheated in my relationships, and lied to my family and myself. I still remember when I heard at a meeting, "How do you know when a newcomer is lying? When his lips are moving." That hit home in a very uncomfortable way.

As I began navigating the new world of the program, I kept running into the phrase "rigorous honesty." At first, I kept looking for ways around that, but as I did my various inventories—a fear inventory, a resentment inventory, a relationship inventory—I realized I had to finally get honest with myself if I was to have any chance at this recovery thing. It took a long time for me to overcome my tendency to be dishonest, but each time I told the truth, I felt much better.

In recovery, they say that you "grow a conscience." I sure did. After a while, it got harder and harder to live with even little white lies, and I soon saw and felt the wisdom of being rigorously honest. Today, I know the path to freedom isn't in getting what I want by lying; it's in speaking my truth and being accepted for who I am. These days when I have a decision to make, I just ask myself, "Does it feel sober?" The answer that resonates most with my conscience is the right one.

NOVEMBER 1

"When did [. . .] become your Higher Power?"

I used to believe that people, places, or things would fix me. I was sure that if only I could get the perfect relationship or career, or finally have enough money to be set for life, or whatever, then I would be happy or secure or comfortable. But it never worked. Each time I got it, or close enough to it, I would once again feel empty and would set my sights on the next thing I was sure was going to make me all right. I used alcohol in this way for years, but it, too, let me down.

As I started working the Steps, I learned about a Higher Power. I was taught that I have a God-shaped hole in me that I was trying to fill with other, outside things. Through prayer and meditation, I experienced glimpses of the peace and serenity I had been looking for. Then each time I turned my will and my life over to His care, and took the next indicated action, my life got better. But there was a catch. . . .

The catch was that I constantly defaulted back to my will and my old ideas of what I thought would make me happy. Even after years of recovery and experience, I still get sidetracked into thinking that more money or something else will finally complete me. And that's when I go back to the source—back to my Higher Power. Today, whenever I feel anxious, restless, or unhappy, I ask myself, *What has become my Higher Power?* It's easy to figure out, and even easier to turn my will and life back over. When I do, I am restored to the peace and security I was looking for.

NOVEMBER 2

*"Give all your problems to God.
He'll be up all night anyway!"*

When I first heard this saying, I instantly thought of all the nights I used to lie in bed worrying, rehashing, or trying to solve all my problems. In fact, before early recovery it was actually easier to sleep because I used alcohol to numb me, and then I could fall asleep or drift into unconsciousness. But when I entered the program, it seemed like it was just me and my problems. I didn't get a lot of sleep in the beginning of recovery!

It took a long time for me to develop enough faith to turn my will and my life (and problems) over to my Higher Power. The idea of it sounded good, but it proved very difficult to do in practice. Oh, I could turn it over in my morning meditation, but by noon I had usually taken it all back. And by night? Whew! It was just me and my problems again.

As I progressed in my recovery, I learned that the definition of faith is believing what you cannot see, and the reward of faith is seeing what you believe. Through faith and a developing practice of turning situations, people, and problems over to God, I've been rewarded with a life that is happy, joyous, and free. And now when I go to sleep, I give all my problems to God because my faith tells me He will be up all night anyway!

NOVEMBER 3

"Happiness is not having what I want,
but wanting what I have."

I spent many years trying to get things to make me happy. If only I could get my college degree, then I'd be happy. As soon as I move to the right city, then I'll feel fulfilled. When I meet "the one," then I will be complete and happy. If only I could write that bestseller, then I'd feel accomplished. With each package UPS delivered (from mindless shopping), I'd feel excited for about ten minutes, then I'd feel empty again.

When I entered the program, I was hoping that sobriety would fix not only my drinking but also my steady state of unhappiness. I was sure that if only I could get a thirty-day chip, then a six-month chip, or finally a whole year, then I'd be happy. It was certainly a shock to me to be five and even seven years sober and still find I had days when I was sure the next UPS delivery would fix me. Thankfully, I learned an enduring truth that always works when I work it.

My sponsor taught me, over and over, that things will never bring me that sense of completeness or happiness I seek. He told me that true fulfillment is in the giving, not the getting. I rediscover the wisdom of this when I work with others. They always give me more than I give them. In addition, my sponsor taught me how to feel grateful for all the wonderful things I already do have: my health, sobriety, a roof over my head, money to buy food, a job, and more. He told me that when I want what I already have, that's when I will realize I already have everything I need to be as happy as I choose to be.

NOVEMBER 4

"After five years of sobriety you get your brains back,
after ten you learn how to use them, and
after fifteen years you realize you
never needed them anyway."

What a cord of recognition this struck when I first heard it at ten years sober. I remember the first five years and how I seemed to be in a haze in the beginning. I spent these years learning how to make sense of and deal with my feelings, my life, relationships, and so on. Everything was so new to me. My focus was on recovery and learning how to live life on life's terms.

Once I passed this phase, I did feel as if I had my brains back, and I began thinking and planning. What career did I want? How about a future with a family? How could I use my new clarity and focus to twist life to suit my needs and wants? If other people had things, why couldn't I get them, too? And off I went, trying to arrange life to meet my new expectations.

At fifteen years, things shifted for me again. Today, when I get centered and connected to my Higher Power, I see clearly and simply, and I know that my only real purpose is to do God's work and be of service. It doesn't take a lot of brains to do that. Instead it takes a continuing willingness to listen to my heart and to follow what I know is right. When I'm "into action" and not "into thinking," things generally turn out the best for all concerned.

NOVEMBER 5

*"God has only three answers to your prayers:
'Yes,' 'Yes, but not now,' and 'No, because
I have something better for you.'"*

While the Eleventh Step teaches us to pray only for the knowledge of God's will for us and the power to carry that out, there will invariably be times when we are sure we know what's best and will pray for a desired result or circumstance instead. Surely someone should recover from an illness or get back something they lost, we think. This is the moment when self-will has crept back in.

Momentarily, we have forgotten that we had rarely been happy when we got what we thought we wanted. After careful reflection, we find that once we truly let go of a desired outcome, invariably we find that something grander and more satisfying has taken its place. To arrive at that level of willingness, what we need is a way to get back to the wisdom of the Eleventh Step. And this quote provides that direction.

By beginning my day with the Eleventh Step reading in the Big Book (p. 86: "On awakening..."), I am able to remember the three answers contained in this quote. Doing this allows me to release expectations from my prayers and truly surrender myself to God's will. Through surrender I find faith, and faith leads me to the sure knowledge that God's will for me and others is always better than my own.

NOVEMBER 6

"The key to my serenity today is directly linked to
my ability to stay in the moment—to be in the present."

Before sobriety, I was rarely able to stay in the moment and instead spent most of my energy dwelling on other times. I was either thinking about the past and regretting what I did or didn't do or obsessing about the future and about what will or won't happen. The past and the future both filled me with anxiety, so I filled the present with as much alcohol as I could. After a while, my present became intolerable as well, and I admitted that my life had become unmanageable.

In recovery, I learned the true wisdom in this quote. My sponsor told me that the reason the past and future filled me with anxiety is that when I go there, I go there alone, without God. God only exists in the present, he said, and that is the only place I can find true peace and serenity. And the way to be content with the present is to work the Steps, clear away the wreckage of my past, and develop an ongoing relationship with my Higher Power.

It took a lot of work to achieve recovery in the program, but the result has been life-changing. Through the Twelve Steps, I am able to live in the present and in the presence of my Higher Power. But alcoholism is a tricky disease, and it still tries to lead me into the dark past or an uncertain future. If I go there, I find myself again alone. My solution is to get back to "where my feet are"—to the present. Once I come back to the now, I come back to God, and my ability to be serene returns.

NOVEMBER 7

"God cannot do for you what He cannot do through you."

I used to have the God thing all mixed up. My conception of God was that if I was good and behaved myself, then good things would happen for me. When I prayed, I prayed for the things I wanted, and then I waited for God to deliver. Toward the end of my drinking, I was usually praying to get out of one mess or another, and then promising to be better the next time. It never worked.

When I first heard this saying, I was several years in the program and I already understood the power of action. I knew from years of sober experience that I couldn't just pray to have my life get better, but rather I had to add action and the right thought to my prayers. The old saying "When you pray, move your feet" took on a whole new meaning for me. I became much more efficient, and my life started to get better.

As the years go by, I live even more in the Eleventh Step, and as such I have discovered the deeper wisdom in this quote. Today, I understand and embrace God's will for me: to be of maximum service to others. In this way, God can do for me what I could never do alone—and that is to heal and enrich both my life and the lives of others. Today, I truly know that God cannot do for you what He cannot do through you.

NOVEMBER 8

"It works if you work it."

I t happens every time—when I get too busy, too stressed, or too tired, I slow down on the things that make me feel better. Before long, I'm a little bit irritable and slightly discontented, and I feel a growing restlessness within all areas of my life. What I've been taught in the program is that when I'm feeling this way, it's time to go back to basics.

Lately, I've begun my days by reading pages 86–88 of the Big Book. I sit down and take a few deep breaths, and I ask God to come back into my life. I then pray and ask my Higher Power to direct my thinking, reminding myself that it is His will that will guide my decisions today. I end my meditation asking to be shown throughout the day what my next thoughts or actions are to be.

And it works. It really does. Without exception, my days are measurably better when I begin them by working the program and asking for the guidance and support of my Higher Power. While this is simple, it is also easy to forget, especially when I get busy. Thank God I don't have to start my entire program over—by going out—to remember how to feel better. All I have to do is work the program I have, because it always works when I become willing to work it.

NOVEMBER 9

"Worrying is praying for things you don't want to happen."

I don't know where my tendency to worry came from. Perhaps I learned it from my mother, the queen of fretting, but I'm sure good at it. Before the program, I would worry and stress over most areas of my life. Even if something good happened, my automatic thought was, *This isn't going to last*. Little did I know that my tendency to worry was driven by something far darker and more pervasive than just my upbringing: the disease of alcoholism.

I used to read motivational books that teach that thoughts are things, and that what you think about most you attract into your life. These books tell us that the law of attraction is neutral, and it responds to your deeply felt beliefs and desires, both good and bad. In recovery, I learned that the disease of alcoholism negatively affects my thinking, and the disease was happy when I attracted more pain and suffering into my life. What a shock that was to learn.

When I got sober, I thought the solution was to instead just think of all the good things I wanted. What I soon learned, however, was that even praying for what I think I want (my will) still brought unwanted situations and negative people into my life. Today, I've found a better way. The Eleventh Step teaches me to pray for the knowledge of God's will and the power to carry that out. This not only removes worry from my life but also attracts the best outcomes for all concerned. This is my solution today.

NOVEMBER 10

*"If you are struggling to make a decision,
do the right thing."*

All my decisions used to be easy because they were all based on self. I choose the job that paid me the most with the least amount of effort. I chose relationships where I could get all my selfish needs met, regardless of the other person's feelings or wants. I chose to spend my money on whatever my ego wanted, without a thought for savings, prudence, or retirement. All those decisions based on self-centeredness didn't get me what I thought I wanted, though; instead, they resulted in me hitting a bottom and driving me into the program.

The Steps taught me to look at my character defects and examine the causes and conditions that led to the wreckage of my life. I learned that self-seeking and self-centeredness were the natural states of an alcoholic, and that I would go on making poor choices and decisions unless I was willing to humble myself and surrender. It was hard to turn a whole life of selfishness around, and rebellion did indeed dog my every step. But with the constant support of my sponsor, the Steps, and a God of my understanding, I slowly changed.

These days, when I have a decision to make, I still think about myself, but I also think about how my actions will impact others. I now have the awareness and willingness to consult others and think through the consequences of my actions. I am aware, for the first time, that I have a choice between my old thinking and selfish choices versus the right way to handle things. Today, I think about what the right thing to do is, and with God's help, I do it.

NOVEMBER 11

"Praying is talking to God, and meditation is listening for the answer."

I n Step Eleven, we "Sought through prayer and meditation to improve our conscious contact with God as we understood Him." For a long time, I wondered what the difference between prayer and meditation was, and then I heard this quote. While it immediately made sense, there were important distinctions I soon had to learn.

In the beginning, my prayers were all about what I wanted to see happen for me and other people. I was busy telling God what to do: "Please let me get that job," "Help my friend get better," "Don't let me lose [. . .]." It took me a long time to realize that God's will for my life and others far exceeded my limited vision and best intentions.

After years of developing faith through experience, I finally see the wisdom in the second part of Step Eleven: "praying only for the knowledge of God's will for us and the power to carry that out." That knowledge is the answer I listen for in meditation. My faith today comes from my experience in knowing that God's will for myself or others is always better than what I could think up. Today, I sincerely pray for the knowledge of God's will, and I listen for the best ways to carry that out.

NOVEMBER 12

"A God defined is a God confined."

Long before the program, and even many years into it, I had a need to understand who and what God was. I was sure that if I was "good" and acted the way I thought God wanted me to act, then I would get what I want—and in this way I could exert some control over my life. I didn't know it then, but what I was trying to do was manipulate and impose my will upon God and make it seem like it was His will.

As you can imagine, this never worked out. The harder I tried to control people, places, and things, presuming God's will was in alignment with what I secretly wanted, the more uncontrollable my life became. And the more life didn't turn out my way, the more I began to resent others, myself, and God. It took many years for me to truly surrender my will and my life to God, but once I did, I discovered a faith that went beyond understanding.

Today, I am truly willing to turn my life over to the care of God. My experience confirms that God's will is infinitely better for me and others than I could ever plan, scheme, or make up on my own. By constantly affirming, "Thy will, not mine, be done," I enjoy the freedom that comes from surrendering to the power and love of God. Today, God is no longer confined by my need to define Him, and as a result, I get to be a witness to His unlimited miracles as they unfold around me.

NOVEMBER 13

"The secret to my recovery is no secret."

When I was new to recovery, staying sober—even one day at a time—was occasionally a seemingly impossible task. Old triggers lurked around every corner, and feelings descended on me without warning. While I was in a meeting I was okay, but in between them, while out in the real world, it was touch-and-go. When I saw people celebrate a year of sobriety, I wondered with awe how they were able to hang on that long.

As I got past ninety days and the fog cleared a bit, I began to acknowledge that there were people who had seven, fifteen, even twenty years of sobriety and more! This was unfathomable to me. How could they not drink through all those New Year's Eves, weddings, and tragedies? When I asked my sponsor what their secret was to long-term sobriety, he told me it was simple: "You don't drink or use, one day at a time." I came to find out this was the basis of it, but there was more to the secret. . . .

In over twenty years of recovery now, I've learned that for me to not take a drink, I had to have a spiritual experience. And the way I did that was by working the Twelve Steps of the program with my sponsor. By doing this, I've developed a relationship with a Power greater than myself, and as a result, the man who writes this quote today is a very different man from the one who crawled into the rooms all those years ago. My secret to recovery remains the same: I still go to meetings, I still work the Steps, and I still don't drink, one day at a time.

NOVEMBER 14

"Gratitude is the shortest path
between me and God."

I used to take everything in my life for granted. At the height of my "big-shot-ism," I had a lot of property and a lot of prestige. Rather than appreciating what I had, all I thought about was getting more or better or bigger. What I didn't know was that I also had alcoholism, and the growing hole I felt inside me would never be filled with any of these outside things. When I hit bottom, I was surrounded by a lot on the outside, but I was empty on the inside.

When I started going to meetings, I heard other people talk about the same hole, and I began to hear about a different way to fill it. It started by developing an "attitude of gratitude," and by taking reliance off myself and placing it on a God of my own understanding. They told me I already had everything I needed to be happy, joyous, and free. My job was to become "right-sized" by working the Twelve Steps so that I could appreciate all God had done and was doing for me.

As my humility grew, I found I truly had much to be grateful for. I hadn't died or destroyed my life through my alcoholism, and I was now sober and on a spiritual path. When I looked at the abundance of everything I already had—a loving family, a wonderful new fellowship of friends, my health, and more—I came to appreciate the real richness of my life. As my gratitude continues to deepen, so does my relationship with God. Today, I just think about ten or fifteen things I have that property and prestige can't fill to realize how blessed I am. Today, I know that gratitude is the shortest path between me and God.

NOVEMBER 15

"Learning to live life one day at a time . . ."

My girlfriend went into her office today and found that fourteen people in her department had been laid off that morning. And while home recovering from a gallbladder operation, I found out that I may need three additional surgeries—painful ones at that—for other things. It's easy to get overwhelmed with what's going on in the world and in our lives, and that's when I remember that I can get through anything, as long as I take it one day at a time.

It didn't always used to be like this. Before I had the tools of the program, even the smallest things would overwhelm me. I constantly lived in a state of anxiety, and when something did happen, panic wasn't far behind. I have a mind that is good at painting dark scenarios, and I have lived each imagined scenario to its bitter end. My life was pretty unmanageable.

One of the gifts of recovery has been learning to live in the present. When I can keep my mind in the same place as my feet, then I always find I'm all right. I'm taken care of, I have everything I need, I'm safe, and I can even find things to be grateful for. Once I focus my attention on what is happening now, I can experience the peace and joy in my life that are always present when I can slow down enough to acknowledge them. And it all comes from learning to live one day at a time.

NOVEMBER 16

"God's rejection is God's protection."

Recently I had an opportunity that I was really excited about fall through unexpectedly. At first I was disappointed, then I grew angry, and then I began to examine my part. After determining, with the help of my sponsor, that my side of the street was clean, I began to feel like the universe was against me and that I might never get what I wanted. And that's when I heard this quote.

Today's wisdom immediately reminded me that I had turned my will and my life over to the care of a God of my understanding, and that after I took the appropriate actions, the results were no longer up to me. Despite my expectations, hopes, or desires, I was reminded that turning it over meant accepting God's will for me, even if (and maybe especially if) things didn't turn out the way I thought they should.

This realization soon brought about a new surrender. And for me, after many years in the program, I generally find that what I am surrendering is my limited vision for one that is grander, more fulfilling, and more appropriate for the person God intends for me to become. In hindsight, I find that God always has a better plan for me than any I can think up for myself. And today, rather than being frustrated by God's rejection, I've come to value the protection He offers.

NOVEMBER 17

"Don't forget that the world record is twenty-four hours."

When I was new, I remember watching people take anniversary cakes for five years, seven years, and more, and thinking that they had something I didn't—the ability to stay sober. When I shared about this, I was told that we all have the same amount of time: today. As I kept going to meetings, I started to see people with long-term sobriety go out, and I learned how important it was to value and concentrate only on today.

As I got a few years under my belt and began trying to figure out what to do with my life, I once again grew impatient when I saw that others had accomplished so much and seemed to have many of the things that I also wanted. When I shared this, I was once again reminded that the world record was just twenty-four hours, and that if I set a goal and took the next indicated action, then I could also accomplish anything I set my mind to.

Over the years, I've come to see the immense wisdom and simplicity in today's quote. When tasks or goals seem impossible to accomplish or overcome, I remind myself that while I may not be able to keep it up or do it over a lifetime, I *can* do it just for today. And what I've found is that when I take the right action, one twenty-four-hour day at a time, obstacles are overcome, and dreams do come true.

NOVEMBER 18

"Trying to pray is the same thing as praying."

I didn't pray or meditate much before I got sober. If I did pray, it was either to keep me from getting into trouble or to get me out of the trouble my selfish or self-seeking behavior got me into. As far as meditation went, my mind was way too busy for that. Besides, I had parties to go to. As my life spun out of control, I had very few tools to help me deal with the emptiness and desperation I felt much of the time. Finally, alone and afraid, I reached my final bottom, and that's when I surrendered.

When I began attending meetings, I heard a lot about prayer and meditation. I thought I was doomed because I didn't know how to do either one. My sponsor was very patient with me and asked me if I was at least willing to try. When I told him I didn't know what to pray for, he suggested that in the morning I simply ask God to keep me sober that day, and in the evening to say a prayer of thanks for helping me get through the day without drinking.

Because I didn't have any better ideas around this, I followed his direction. Each morning, uncomfortable as it was, I tried to quiet my mind and I asked God to keep me sober that day. In the evening, I said a prayer of gratitude for another day without a drink. After months of sobriety, I realized that it was working and that my prayers were being answered. What I learned is that trying to pray is the same thing as praying and trying to connect is how we establish the connection to our Higher Power.

NOVEMBER 19

"Would you rather have justice or mercy?"

When I got to the program, I complained to anyone who would listen about how unfair life was. I blamed my parents for screwing up my childhood by moving around the country so much. I blamed the rest of my family for not understanding me and for treating me so callously. I resented not having enough money and having to work for a living. I even justified the illegal career I had and blamed it on my bosses and the industry. Life was not fair, and when I got sober, I wanted justice!

I can still remember being outside the bungalows at a junior college on a Friday night before my regular meeting. I was going on and on about how unfair life was and how everything would be better if there was justice in the world. The guy I was speaking to listened carefully to me, and then said simply that he was grateful there was more mercy and forgiveness in the world than justice. He told me that if justice was the rule, then he might be dead right now instead of at an A.A. meeting.

This stopped me in my tracks. Suddenly I thought about all the illegal things I had gotten away with, and was still getting away with, and I considered how my fate would be very different if I got the justice that was coming to me. After this talk, I paid much more attention to the Steps and began earnestly working my program. As the year progressed and I worked through my Fourth Step and made my Eighth Step list, I felt grateful there was more mercy and forgiveness in the world than there was justice. And that's when I realized that it was up to me to offer forgiveness as well—rather than judgment and justice.

NOVEMBER 20

"Negativity is my disease asking me to come out to play."

I used to have just one voice in my head. Sometimes it was encouraging, even optimistic, but most of the time it was negative and defeatist. It told me things weren't going to get better, so why try? It said things were bad, so why not at least feel better by drinking and using? Toward the end, the positive part of that voice went away, and all I heard was how bad things were and how much worse they were going to get. It's no wonder I hit bottom.

When I entered the program, I heard a lot of talk about the disease. At first, my voice told me that wasn't true, and that instead I was just bad, weak-willed, or a loser. But as I got better, and the positive voice returned, I discovered it was separate from the negative one. I realized there were actually two voices inside my head, and I began to understand the disease of alcoholism.

It's taken a long time to nurture and grow the positive voice of recovery, but now I recognize it as the truth spoken to me by my Higher Power. The negative voice is still there sometimes, and it surprises me when I hear it, but I know it's just my alcoholism. Thankfully, the program has taught me to acknowledge it, thank it for sharing, and then ignore it. Today, I know that negativity is just my disease asking me to come out to play, and I know now how to decline its invitation.

NOVEMBER 21

"There are some days when I say,
'What program? God who?'"

L ast week my business website was hacked, my site was taken down, and my account was suspended. For hours, while I lost revenue and customers, I pleaded, begged, and threatened my hosting company's technical support people. For the most part I was polite and professional, but I was cursing under my breath, anxious, and pissed off. After it was all over, I was a wreck. Later that evening, I wondered why I hadn't brought God into it and why I hadn't worked my program.

What I realized is that fear is still the chief activator of my lingering character defects, and prime among them is fear of losing something I have or of not getting what I demand. As I furiously instant-messaged and emailed their support team, I saw eight years of working on my business go down the drain, felt the pain of starting over, and grew increasingly resentful. Thankfully everything was resolved in a few hours, but for a while I was alone and spiritually vulnerable.

As I reflect on the experience, I'm amazed at how quickly I can abandon my program when I'm in fear. I completely understand when I hear of people who pick up a drink after twenty years and can't explain why. I know that alcoholism is cunning, baffling, and powerful, and I'm constantly reminded that I must remain vigilant. Even after all my time in recovery, there are some days when I say, "What program? God who?"

NOVEMBER 22

❧

"It is always easier to take someone else's inventory."

I was a master at blaming others before I entered the program. Everything that was wrong about my life was somebody's or something else's fault. I didn't succeed at work because the company or the economy was terrible. I didn't have the relationships I wanted because no one understood me. On and on I went, in every situation, detailing the things that were wrong. Rarely did I stop to consider that I was the common denominator in it all.

As I started writing inventories in recovery, and was introduced to the fourth column of the Fourth Step called "my part," I was taken aback. When my sponsor suggested that I begin taking my own inventory and owning up to my part of what was wrong in my life, I was even a little resentful. "But look at what my parents did," I complained. "And at work they still skipped over me for that promotion," I moaned. By carefully focusing on my behaviors in those situations, though, a different pattern emerged.

The freedom the program offers me comes from recognizing, owning, and finally changing the only thing I do have some power over—myself. Once I clearly see where I am at fault—perhaps the company didn't promote me because I had a bad attitude and showed up late most of the time—I can begin to make changes that finally influence my life in a positive way. By being willing to own my side of the street, and by asking God to help me keep it cleaner, I've been able to let go of always judging and blaming others—and that allows me to have a much better life.

NOVEMBER 23

"What Step are you on?"

B efore recovery, I had very few tools to handle the problems, challenges, and situations in my life. And the tools I did have weren't very helpful. My go-to solution was drinking. Whether things were going well (rarely) or poorly (more often the case), I escaped into a bottle of alcohol. It didn't take long for this solution to become part of, and then the main, problem in my life. Out of options, I surrendered and entered the program.

Once in recovery, I was given a whole treasure chest of new solutions. These were spiritually based tools that fit into what my sponsor called my "spiritual tool kit." They included things like working the Twelve Steps, taking commitments, reaching my hand out to others, praying and meditating, and so on. These new tools were incredibly helpful in changing my life for the better, but I soon learned something very important: They only worked when I worked them.

Throughout my recovery, I have found that it is easy to slide back into old behaviors, and that whenever I do, I start to experience my old feelings again. This isn't a good thing. Whenever I find myself on my pity pot, wondering, "Where's mine?" my sponsor brings me back to the solution. He simply asks, "What Step are you on?" When I then ask myself which Step applies to the current situation I'm obsessing over, I see the way out. The tools of a gratitude list, calling another alcoholic, working the Eleventh Step, and so forth never fail to restore me to sanity. Whenever people are struggling in recovery, I know to ask them what Step they are on.

NOVEMBER 24

"God doesn't care what you think about Him,
only that you think about Him."

I've spent a lot of my life struggling with the concept of God. For many years my God was on a throne, judging my thoughts and actions, and I did my best to keep on His good side. When I sinned, I'd try doubly hard to be good again, and all the while I was trying to keep track of my good/bad ledger. *If I die tonight, where will I end up?* I thought regularly before going to sleep. By the time I got sober, I was pretty sure where I was going. . . .

In early recovery, I was terrified of the thought of turning my will and my life over to the care of God as I understood Him. I was sure God didn't care much for me, and I was afraid that if I abandoned myself to Him, then he would exact His just revenge. I secretly resented God, and when I finally admitted this to my sponsor, he gave me the solution.

"Talk to God and tell Him exactly how you feel," he suggested.

"But I'm really angry about a lot of things, and He's not going to like it," I warned him. "Believe me, He's big enough to take whatever you've got," he said. When I finally began an open and honest dialogue with God—telling Him of my anger, resentments, fears, and disappointments in *Him*—that's when my connection with and faith in a Higher Power began. And that's when my real recovery began as well. Today, I've learned that God doesn't care what you think about Him, only that you think about Him.

NOVEMBER 25

❧

"I'm really grateful to be here."

Whenn I finally hit bottom and surrendered, I didn't think my life could get any lower. But then I started attending A.A. meetings. Here was a group of people who had nothing better to do on a Friday or Saturday night than to sit in a room and talk about "the good old days." And they talked about, of all things, God, making amends, and their feelings—lots of feelings! I was pretty sure my life was over for good.

I resisted and rebelled for a long time, but I worked the Steps and kept coming back. I still didn't agree or understand when someone began sharing by identifying as a "grateful alcoholic." *Grateful for what?* I'd think. But subtly and powerfully, I began to change. I became more humble as I recognized my part in things, more grateful when I realized how fortunate I had been, and more hopeful because of the new life I'd been given. Soon, I even looked forward to going to meetings.

Years down the road of recovery, I live from a place of sustained gratitude. My life today is nothing like the hopeless, resentful state it once was. Today, I have a purpose and a new freedom I never had before. I'm immensely comfortable in my own skin—an incredible gift for an alcoholic like me. I'm not only grateful for all I do have in my life, I'm grateful I still have a life—something alcoholism nearly stole from me. Today, I can honestly say, I'm really grateful to be here.

NOVEMBER 26

"Recovery is an education without a graduation."

One of the first things I asked my sponsor was how long I would have to go to meetings. I had been going to meetings every day—ninety in ninety—getting commitments, showing up early to greet, and so on. I was neglecting things at home and was wondering when I might "graduate" to not needing them anymore. He told me that when I got to the point where I enjoyed meetings, that's when I could decide whether to attend them or not.

While that didn't make sense to me—secretly I never thought that I would *enjoy* meetings—I followed direction and kept coming back. As I learned more about the disease of alcoholism, I learned that I could never cure it. What I had was a daily reprieve from the insanity of the first drink, as long as I maintained and fortified my spiritual condition. Each night, I was told, while I slept, alcoholism progressed, getting stronger and stronger. This scared me, so I kept my commitments and meetings.

By following my sponsor's suggestions, I have been able to achieve long-term sobriety and much peace and serenity in my life. When "normal" people ask why I still go to meetings, I explain that it's like someone who was overweight and out of shape. When these people go to the gym, exercise, and eat better, they tend to get fit. In order to stay that way, they need to continue going to the gym and eating well. Same thing for me: If I want to keep my recovery, I need to keep going to meetings and not drink. Today, I enjoy going to meetings because I appreciate what I have.

NOVEMBER 27

"If I'm invested in the outcome,
I've kept God out of it."

The first time I heard this prayer, while working the Eleventh Step, I experienced a great surrender. Although compact and seemingly simple, it is one of the purest ways of working this Step. In the first part, "God, help me to go from where I am," I am strengthening my conscious contact as I partner with my Higher Power and invite Him to guide me on my spiritual journey.

The second part, "to where I need to be," reveals the wisdom of this prayer as it shows that I have truly turned the result of my journey over to God. Like all great spiritual treatments, the power here comes from me getting out of the way, thus removing any limited thinking and self-will. Once my selfish designs have been discarded, I can allow God's limitless power and infinite resources to do for me what I cannot do for myself.

The last part, "for who I am," reinforces the power of my faith. Trusting that God's ultimate knowledge and will for me will be the most fulfilling for me and countless others, I arrive at the surrender of Step Eleven. Through prayer and meditation, I ask Him to reveal my true purpose, and I ask only for the strength to carry that out. By doing so, I am granted a great gift of recovery: peace and purpose.

NOVEMBER 28

"Everything I have is the property of A.A."

When I heard someone share this in a meeting one day, I was struck with an immense feeling of gratitude for all I have been given in recovery. This morning as I write this, I am on a business trip in Atlanta, Georgia, having been flown in by a company to work with their employees. I am highly respected (and paid) today. This is a sharp contrast to the unemployed (and unemployable) thief I was when I crawled into the rooms many years ago. Every area of my life has been transformed as well.

Today, I have meaningful relationships that are healthy and fulfilling. I have a fellowship of people who trudge the road of happy destiny with me—sincere people who would be there for me if I needed them. I am happily married to a wonderful woman who loves and accepts me for who I am. I also have close friends outside of the program who respect and value my opinion, and me, theirs. Compare this to the lone wolf who had been abandoned by most people, including myself.

Recovery has also given me something I didn't even know I wanted or could have: peace and serenity. I feel comfortable in my own skin today, something I never felt before. All this comes from my relationship with a God of my own understanding. Contrast that with the confirmed agnostic and sometimes atheist who came into the rooms all those dark, drunk years ago. I have more, so much more, in my life today, and I owe it all to the program of Alcoholics Anonymous. Everything I have, and that I am, is truly the property of A.A. And for that, my gratitude knows no bounds.

NOVEMBER 29

"God, help me to go from where I am to
where I need to be, for who I am."

I was a big ball of self-will before I entered recovery. In most things, it was my way or the highway. If I couldn't get my way, I'd change jobs or relationships, or I'd move. When I planned something, I'd start with the outcome I wanted, and then invest my time and effort making sure I got it. The trouble was, I often did get what I wanted, but it turned out that it was either never enough or the wrong kind, or ultimately it wasn't what I wanted after all.

When I entered the program, I learned an entirely new way of living. The biggest change was to put my will aside and instead ask what God's will was for me, and then try to follow that. This was as hard as it sounds, because all I knew was dependence on self. But by praying, meditating, and running things by others, I could often distinguish my selfish will versus what God would have me do.

One of the surest ways I have of testing how much I have truly surrendered to God's will today is to ask myself how invested I am in the outcome. If I have planned everything out to the last detail, I can be pretty sure I'm into self-will. But if I instead take the necessary actions, and then suit up and show up to be of service, then I remain open to God's will. And ultimately, if I'm truly willing to be open, I find that what God has in store for me is always better than what I could have wanted for myself.

NOVEMBER 30

*"If you're having trouble making a decision,
maybe you shouldn't."*

When I got sober, I suddenly found that I had a lot more options and choices in my life. Now that I wasn't drinking all the time, I could decide to do many other things: go to meetings or fellowship, fix up the house, visit family and friends again. Soon I decided that I needed to make big changes: move to a new city, change relationships and careers, and more. And that's when my sponsor suggested that I don't make any big changes during the first year of recovery.

While this didn't make any sense to me, he explained that while I may not be the person I was while drinking, I was still not the person I would yet become. What I needed to do was work the Steps, get some clarity, and then begin making changes and decisions slowly and with God's help. He suggested I pray over things first and wait to see what God's will might be for me. This advice has served me well over the years.

These days, I've learned that I no longer have to impulsively act on what I think I want to do. In fact, I've found that if I'm having trouble making a decision, then that means I need to pray over it more until I get a stronger sense of direction. I've also learned to not fear making a mistake, because I know that decisions aren't forever. Today, I struggle less over making decisions and know that I'm not alone. God is my partner in life today, and as long as I am willing to go to Him for advice and follow the direction I receive, things turn out for the best.

DECEMBER 1

❧

"Spirituality is the ability to get
our minds off ourselves."

E arly in recovery, all I thought about was me. *How was I going to
not drink tonight or tomorrow? How was I going to work the
program if I didn't believe in God? Who was going to pay my bills
if I couldn't find work? What if that bump on my neck turned out
to be cancer?* Every morning, I woke up in a cold sweat as all those
thoughts of myself descended upon me. I was so heavy with self-
obsession, it was sometimes hard to get out of bed.

Once I got to a meeting, I felt better. For the hour I spent listening to others, or interacting and helping in some way, I forgot about
myself and felt free. I often went to fellowship where I would listen to
the experience, strength, and hope of other sober people, and I felt a
part of something larger than myself. As I worked through the Steps,
I acquired tools for getting outside myself: things like sponsoring
others, and being of service at meetings or at work or even at social
gatherings. And most of all, I learned to turn to God.

I was taught early on that I could not be in fear and faith at the
same time. Whenever I find I am in fear, it is usually because I am
thinking about myself. The solution is to shift my focus and aware-
ness to God. I begin by repeating all that I know about my Higher
Power: that right now, I am surrounded by the loving presence of
God; that God has infinite resources at His disposal; that God is love.
By thinking about God, I cease thinking about myself, and that's when
I experience the peace and serenity of spirituality.

DECEMBER 2

"I know I have another drunk in me, but I don't know if I have another recovery."

A shiver shot down my spine when I first heard this quote. I know how easy it would be for me to pick up a cold Heineken or glass of Cabernet Sauvignon at a nice restaurant. And my disease even tries to convince me I could handle it now. "It's been years since you've had a drink," it whispers. "You can handle a glass of wine and enjoy it like others do," it says.

As I think that first drink through, I know I might get away with it, but inevitably I would end up drunk. I know myself well enough to know how obsessive I still am—I can prove that with a large bag of M&M's. I know I've easily got another drunk in me, but I can't say the same thing about recovery. That's why this quote resonates so deeply and still gives me the chills.

Getting sober and working the Twelve Steps was a lot of work. Good work, to be sure, but it took countless surrenders, unparalleled willingness, and a humbling of my ego that only the desperation of the drowning can understand. If the embers of alcoholism were lit again, I don't know if I'd ever be able to contain them. That's why I pray to God in the morning to keep me sober another day, and I thank Him at night for doing so. I know how easy it would be to get drunk again, but I don't know if I have the grace and willingness for another recovery.

DECEMBER 3

*"The most spiritual thing you can
do is to help someone."*

One of the most important things I've learned in the program is that whenever two alcoholics get together, God is present. I feel the energy of God flow through me as I talk with, listen to, and help another person. Because I can get wrapped up in myself, it sometimes takes contrary action for me to reach out. But I am always rewarded with a sense of peace and serenity when I connect with and help another.

It wasn't always like this. Selfish and self-centered to the extreme, I crawled into the rooms of recovery emotionally bankrupt and in a state of perdition. I had alienated most of the people in my life and spent much of my time alone with the disease of alcoholism. I dammed God's energy up inside me, twisting it to serve only my interests, and it almost destroyed me. Even today, I have to guard against my tendency to isolate and self-obsess.

A precious gift I've been given in the A.A. program is a spiritual tool that enables me to escape from the pit of self. Working with others is not only part of the solution for their sobriety, but also a crucial part in my own continuing recovery as well. Today, I have discovered the primary purpose of God's love, and so my purpose as well: to be of service to others. Each time I extend myself, we are both rewarded by the presence and love of God. Service is the way out of the prison of self, and it always sets my and the other person's spirits free.

DECEMBER 4

*"Sometimes you don't realize that all you need
is God, until all you have is God."*

Even after years in recovery and with all my sober experience, I'm still amazed by my tendency to put so many things before God. Many times, I'm convinced that if only I were retired or had enough money to travel more, or if my wife would do what I wanted, then my life would finally be better. If only I could get what I wanted, then I would be happy.

My stubborn reliance on this myth can be pretty disappointing. I've been reminded in meetings that anything I place before God will be taken from me. I can show you inventories of the many things I have put before Him, and obsessively chased and then lost, to prove this is true. It's painful when it happens, but the result is that it always leads me back to God.

The greatest gift I have today, and the one constant source of strength and hope in my life, is my relationship with my Higher Power. My Higher Power has the answers and solutions to the problems I face, and He has a deeper love and caring for me than I'll ever comprehend. When I'm connected to God, there are no worries, no wants, and no needs. When things get stripped away, as they will be, and all I'm left with is God, it's then that I remember: All I ever needed *was* God.

DECEMBER 5

*"If I keep doing what I was doing,
I'll keep getting what I was getting."*

I remember when I was new to recovery I was very willing to follow direction. I went to ninety meetings in ninety days, got a home group, got a minimum of four commitments at various meetings, got a sponsor, and began working the Twelve Steps. I did a lot and I got a lot. My life improved, I felt better, and I started to recover. Even the promises began to come true.

Now that I'm deep in recovery, I find that I'm not as active as I used to be. Oh sure, I still go to meetings, and I even have a couple of commitments, but I find I'm not doing all the things I used to do. And I've also found that I'm not getting out of the program what I used to get. When I heard this quote, I immediately made the connection.

When I spoke with my sponsor about this, he reminded me that I didn't need to "go out" to restart my program. There are always newcomers who need sponsors and meetings that need help, and I could always add a meeting or two. The good news is that as soon as I start doing what I did, I start getting what I got. So, if you're not feeling it these days, just think back to what you used to do when you were new and start doing it again.

DECEMBER 6

❦

"If you don't like what you hear at a meeting, then say what you need to hear."

A t a question-and-answer meeting I attend, I often hear people comment that they either don't enjoy meetings or don't think a particular meeting gives them what they need. "It's always the same people saying the same things," they complain. In response, another member shared this quote and suggested they participate and "say what they needed to hear."

In itself this is great advice, but it also addresses a fundamental issue—being of service. So many people (myself included) go to meetings to get something from them and to feel better afterward. And most of the time we do. However, sometimes we may forget that meetings are also a perfect place for us to be of service. Often what we gain from a meeting is in direct proportion to what we contribute to it.

These days, whenever I'm feeling annoyed or disinterested at a meeting, I ask myself what I'm doing to add to it. Am I cleaning up, or reaching out to a newcomer, or contributing something useful? Looking for what I can add works so well that I now do this at work, at home, and even at the market. Service truly is the answer in my life today. The best part is that there is always, everywhere, an opportunity for me to be useful and to contribute.

DECEMBER 7

*"Relapse begins a long time before
you pick up that first drink."*

I am a three-meeting-minimum-a-week kind of guy. Anything less than that and I begin feeling, well, kind of vulnerable. Oh, not that I'm going to pick up a drink, but vulnerable to what my head tells me, and vulnerable to feeling more irritable, restless, and discontented. I'm quicker to judge things, and I begin storing resentments. While I may not be thinking of drinking, I no longer feel threatened by the thought of it.

After a few weeks of that, it begins to get harder to make even two meetings a week. Soon I'm not answering my phone very much, and calling my sponsor doesn't even occur to me. Work pressures mount, and on the way home I'm more frustrated by people not driving right, parking lots that are too full, and a slow Internet speed when I get home. Suddenly the world is out of whack, and the idea of a drink seems not only natural but completely reasonable as well.

I can't tell you the number of times I have heard people who relapse tell a story similar to the one above. It always scares the heck out of me because there have been times when I've begun to go down that same path. Thank God for my commitments, a strong support group, regular meetings I look forward to, and sponsees who continue to call me. These days, I have four meetings a week I go to, whether I need them or not. I want to keep the distance between me and a relapse as wide as possible.

DECEMBER 8

"If you baby them, you bury them."

P eople in recovery are a stubborn lot, used to running their lives on massive amounts of self-will fueled by old ideas. It's hard for us to take direction, and "rebellion dogs our every step." We are constantly looking for a way around things. For instance, I'm reminded of the story of W. C. Fields, who, lying on his deathbed, was asked why he was only now reading the Bible. "I'm looking for the loopholes," was his reply. I can sure relate to that.

The first question my sponsor asked me when we began working together was, "Are you willing to go to any lengths to get sober?" I was able to answer yes because I had reached my bottom, and it was this desperation that gave me the willingness to follow his suggestions and direction. He was firm with me, and I learned about contrary action very quickly. Learning to follow his direction rather than my will saved my life.

I have sponsored a lot of guys over the years, and my experience has taught me that those I have to baby or make "lite" suggestions to are simply not ready to go to any lengths. They are the ones who don't get this, and some have gone out and dug their own graves. Only when you are through looking for the loopholes do you have a chance to recover. And it's my job as a sponsor to make that perfectly clear.

DECEMBER 9

❦

"Quit with the thinking, and start with the doing."

It took me a long time to learn that I can't think myself into feeling better. If I sit at home depressed, waiting until I feel like going to a meeting or calling someone, it means I'm going to be at home depressed a long time. Early on, I learned about contrary action, and when I take it and get out of my head, I always feel better.

My sponsor showed me a chapter in the Big Book called "Into Action," and told me to notice there isn't one called "Into Thinking." He taught me that feelings always follow actions, and every time I take a positive action, I get positive feelings. The opposite is also true. If I stay in my head, I almost always feel bad or grow more depressed.

One of the best actions I've learned to take in the program is to work with or help another. The power of this action is that while helping another, I'm immediately out of thinking about myself and into being of service. And the magic of service is that while I'm helping another, I'm also helping myself. Today, it's much easier for me to get out of thinking and get into doing, and afterward I'm glad I did.

DECEMBER 10

"The key to happiness is usefulness."

This quote really resonated with me the instant I heard it. I immediately thought about how serenely happy I am right after working with a sponsee, or after being helpful in other ways, and how that feeling can last for hours. The secret, of course, is being of service, and the happiness comes from taking the emphasis off myself and focusing instead on being useful to another.

What is amazing about this is not that it works every time (which it does), but that I so often forget and even resist it. Being selfish and self-centered to the core, my default is to be alone and to self-obsess. When I find myself in that state, I'm not useful to myself or anyone else. And I'm certainly not happy.

"People rot out faster than they wear out" is another quote that seems to tie into this quite well. The bottom line for me is that when I'm into action, working with others, or being of service in the program in another way, I'm out of myself and I finally feel fulfilled. My experience continues to teach me it's no coincidence that the key to happiness is usefulness.

DECEMBER 11

"You may be the only Big Book anyone ever reads."

As I was leaving a meeting at a church near my home the other night, I saw one of our members bring his cigarette onto the church parking lot (smoking is not allowed on church property) and then throw it on the ground as he got into his car and drove away. This made me angry as I thought about how this would reflect on the rest of us, and I wondered how he could be so self-centered and insensitive.

About a week later, I found myself at my bank dealing with an online banking error. I was resentful I had to take the time out of my day, indignant they hadn't been able to fix it over the phone, and I was generally a pain in the ass to the guy who was trying to help me. After he resolved the issue and I calmed down, I thought about the kind of example *I* was setting and quickly made amends to him for my behavior.

On the way home, I thought about Step Twelve and the importance of practicing these principles in all our affairs. I realized how easy it is for me to still be self-centered and insensitive, and how the Tenth Step helps me guard against these character defects. I also realized that I have a responsibility to the program because I am an example of us all. Today, I work all the Steps to the best of my ability because I know that I may be the only Big Book anyone ever reads.

DECEMBER 12

❧

"I want my Higher Power to live in my heart full time, but He'll only take a twenty-four-hour lease."

It's amazing how good I feel when I get connected to my Higher Power. I do this by praying and meditating in the mornings, or by speaking with or helping someone in the program. I also get this feeling by attending meetings or going out to fellowship. I love the peace I feel, the sense of belonging I have, and the feelings of being comfortable in my own skin.

It's also amazing how I can wake up the next day and feel so disconnected. There are some mornings when I feel the same old dread and anxiety I lived with while drinking. It's as if I had never heard of the Twelve Steps. I've often asked my sponsor why I can't stay connected, and he tells me it's the same reason I can't stay full after I've eaten a meal. When I ask him to explain, he says:

"Because we are spiritual beings, we all have a hunger to connect with our source. Once connected, we are filled with the peace and serenity that are the nourishment of this union. As we go about our day expending energy—the biggest energy drain caused by thinking and worrying about ourselves—we quickly become depleted and hungry. That's why we need to continually take actions to restore our connection and move God back into our hearts." And once I do that, I am full again.

DECEMBER 13

❦

"Keep doing the things that got it good,
not the things that got good."

I was in a meeting the other day when a guy took a newcomer chip for seven days sober. Before he sat down, he shared that he had twelve years but had gone out. He said it took almost five years to get seven days again, and that during those five years he went through hell. He lost his house again, his family, his career, and almost his life. He said he knew about meetings, about the program, about the disease, but he just couldn't muster the willingness to get sober again.

After the meeting, I asked him what had happened, and he related a familiar story. At twelve years sober, life was great. He owned a big house and had all the toys. He was near the top of his career, and slowly the trappings of success became more important. Suddenly, golfing with his buddies took the place of his Sunday meeting, and after a while he stopped calling his sponsor and reduced his meetings to once or twice a month. Then he stopped going altogether. At a barbeque someone handed him a cold beer, and he was off.

As I left the meeting, I was chilled with fear. My life was going pretty well, too, and there were times when I stayed home to watch football on my massive LCD TV instead of going to *my* Sunday meeting. I couldn't remember the last time I had spoken to my sponsor or if I even had one anymore. And that's when I heard today's quote: "Keep doing the things that got it good, not the things that got good." I vowed right then to reconnect and recommit to my recovery. After all, I remembered that you don't have to go out to start over.

DECEMBER 14

*"It's not about letting God in today,
it's about letting God out."*

For years, I hoarded all the good that was inside me. The capacity I had to be of service, and to truly make a difference in other people's lives, I diverted to serve and advance my own selfish needs and wants. When you needed help, my first thought was, *What's in it for me?* If I couldn't find a compelling answer to that question, I wouldn't bother to extend myself. This attitude left me barren of feeling, alone, and self-destructive.

In early recovery, I was still pretty shut down and unwilling to help or participate. When others offered to help me, I was suspicious of their motives. *What's in it for them?* was my reaction, and I remained distrustful for quite a while. It took contrary action for me to follow my sponsor's direction to be of service and take commitments at meetings. Although I was convinced I would get nothing out of it, over time I found I was wrong.

There is a saying in the rooms that recovery is simply a matter of one alcoholic helping another. The miracle of the program is that this simple act of giving, without the expectation of getting anything back, is how it all works. The innate capacity in us to love, to give, and to be of service reflects the same qualities of the God within us all. The magic and healing of recovery come from letting this energy of God out, rather than damming it in to benefit ourselves. As the poet Robert Browning said, the ultimate goal of us all is to "set the imprisoned splendor free."

DECEMBER 15

"Age will take care of your ego."

When I was young, I was filled with piss and vinegar—and ego. It was all about what I wanted and what I thought I deserved, and I didn't think twice about how I got it. As my drinking got worse, my ego only seemed to grow. Isolated in the prison of self, with only self-seeking and self-centered motives, I finally hit a bottom. In that brief moment of desperation, my ego was temporarily defeated, and I surrendered enough to enter the program.

As I began working the Steps, and as my life got better, my ego rebounded. It was a constant struggle to rein it in. Thankfully, with the help of my sponsor and the support of the fellowship, and by working the Twelve Steps, I was able to humble my ego enough to grow beyond its insatiable demands. I am grateful for how the Steps are structured, especially Steps Ten through Twelve, which allow me to keep my ego in check.

Now that I'm older and in a different stage of my life, the things that were so important to me—money, property, and prestige—are more in the rearview mirror, and I am glad I've grown past them. Today, being comfortable in my own skin and grateful for what I have is much more satisfying than any of the things my ego thought I needed to be happy. I heard someone say that when you get older only two things really matter: having health and time. When I was younger, those two things weren't even on my list. But now, with a little bit of wisdom and a lot of recovery, I see the truth in today's quote: Age does take care of your ego.

DECEMBER 16

"Are you willing to be amazed?"

By the end of my drinking, my life had gotten very small and there wasn't much that excited me anymore. My existence had been reduced to a singular focus—getting loaded. The wonder and possibilities of life, the joy and anticipation of new friends, new opportunities and experiences were crowded out by my overwhelming obsession to drown myself in alcohol. As I slipped deeper into the abyss, I no longer cared if I lived or died. I had reached the end.

Once I surrendered and entered recovery, I discovered that the end actually led to a new beginning: the start of a sober life. As I worked the Twelve Steps, I found that they acted like a ladder that allowed me to climb out of the dark pit of self. With each Step, I built a bridge back to other people, and back to life itself. As I learned to focus on my Higher Power and on being of service to others, the feelings of uselessness and self-pity disappeared and I became reborn.

Recovery has awakened me to a life beyond my imagination. At first, I just hoped to stop drinking, but as I worked the program, I got more than I could ever have asked for. The promises have come true for me and so much more. The wonder and opportunities of life have returned, and I wake up each morning open minded to what God has in store for me. I have discovered and pursued possibilities I never knew existed. I have had wonderful experiences like meeting and marrying my soul mate, and today I have peace and serenity. Now, when I hear a newcomer complain about his life, I listen and then ask, "Are you willing to be amazed?"

DECEMBER 17

"I may not always know what God's will is, but I always know what His will is not."

I n the beginning of my recovery, I had a hard time figuring out what God's will for me might be. It helped when my sponsor explained that turning "my will and my life over" meant turning my thoughts and my actions over to God's care. But listening for and understanding what direction He wanted me to take sometimes left me confused and frustrated.

As I continued to struggle with this, I heard today's quote, and I suddenly had my answer. Now, when I'm considering many courses of action or trying to make a decision, I keep it simple. Instead of wondering which choice would be in alignment with God's will, it's much easier to ask which one is clearly *not* His will. If I'm honest and able to put self-seeking aside, the answer is always clear.

It's like when I pull up to a four-way-stop sign and look around, wondering whose turn is next. While I may not know for sure, it's easy to know when it's *not* my turn. It is the same thing with figuring out God's will today. Any choice that puts my wants and needs first is not God's will. Once I've identified and eliminated those options, it's easy to decide which action or decision to make.

DECEMBER 18

"If you want to keep it, you'll have to give it away."

I used to believe that I needed to accumulate and hoard things if I wanted to have and keep them. I was stingy with my money and never gave to charity, because I thought if I did, I'd have less for me. In my sales job, I stockpiled leads, believing that if I shared them, it would diminish my chances of success. In relationships, I kept my feelings to myself, fearing that if I let someone know how much I cared, that person would use it against me. In general, fear led my life, and in the end I was alone, resentful, and drunk.

In recovery, I heard the darnedest thing: if I wanted to keep my sobriety, I had to spend time working with others, giving away what I had found in the program. I argued against this, especially in the beginning, claiming that I needed the help and support first, and only later would I be able to be of service in that way. My sponsor told me that if I had even a day of sobriety more than a newcomer, then I could share my experience, strength, and hope. And that's when I began giving it away.

Rather than diminish my recovery, I discovered that the more I shared, the more enriched I became. Each time I helped another, I was helped just as much—if not more. I began applying this lesson in other areas of my life, and soon I was recognized at work and even promoted into management. I practiced giving all my love to my partner, and that relationship has turned into an amazing marriage. I also keep giving away what I find in the rooms. As such, my sobriety is solid, my spiritual life keeps expanding, and I am truly happy, joyous, and free.

DECEMBER 19

"Alcoholism . . . cunning, baffling, powerful."

The other night, my wife and I decided to take in some holiday cheer at a very exclusive hotel lounge. Dimly lit, with Christmas piano music drifting in from the bar, it was cozy. After dinner, my wife wanted dessert, and we decided to try something new: smoked maple sabayon. Sounded so innocent, so delicious. It arrived in two bowls, one of which looked like vanilla pudding. I took a tablespoon and dived in. As it hit my palette, my first thought was: alcohol. What happened next is when today's quote took over . . .

Without hesitation, I went for another, bigger scoop. I vaguely remember thinking that it tasted strong, but that it was also the holidays, and only a dessert, and that I should try it again just to be sure. As my spoon was about to plunge into the pudding, my wife said, "There is a lot of alcohol in that." I slowed the descent of my spoon. She continued, "I think I just got a buzz from that first bite." She looked at me and said, "I don't think you should have any more." I put my spoon down, flagged the waiter, and he said, "Oh yes, there is uncooked rum in that."

On the drive home, I tried to explain to my wife that my alcoholism has a mind of its own. Even with twenty-plus years of sobriety, it is cunning, baffling, and powerful. I thought nothing of taking another bite and didn't even consider the consequences. I told her that she saved me from making a serious mistake, and that she needed to continue to be vigilant for me, especially on those rare occasions when I'm not. What I learned is that I can't forget the word that comes before today's quote: "remember."

DECEMBER 20

"How can I help you?"

It used to be all about helping myself. At parties, I helped myself to your alcohol and party favors. At work, I helped myself to your leads and referrals and territory. In relationships, I took as much as I could, and I only thought about giving back if it would help me to get more. As my drinking progressed, I helped myself to larger quantities of alcohol until finally someone suggested I get help in A.A.

When I came into the program, everyone seemed so willing to help me. People gave me their phone numbers, they offered me rides, and they invited me to fellowship. Someone offered to be my sponsor and take me through the Steps. It was great! But I soon learned that if I wanted to get well, I would have to help another. It was suggested that I take commitments, go to ninety meetings in ninety days, and help clean the room. At first, I resisted helping someone else. After all, I was still new and needed help myself. But then I learned the great truth about this program.

As I began talking to newcomers after meetings, listening to them and sharing what little experience I had, I began feeling better. I found that whenever I was having a tough time, the way out was always to help someone else. As I began sponsoring others, I found that I got just as much out of it as they did. In fact, it felt so good to help others that I began looking for ways to help in other areas of my life. These days, whenever I'm feeling anxious about a situation or uncomfortable in general, I simply ask how I can help. When I do, I see the wisdom in the saying "It is always better to give than to receive."

DECEMBER 21

"Today is the tomorrow you worried about yesterday, so live in the now."

When I came into the program, I was so consumed with worry for my future that I couldn't even talk about what I was doing in the present. "But what happens if I lose my house. How about my career? What if I go to jail?" These and other future events were my new obsession once I put the alcohol down. I had completely lost the ability to feel any joy or contentment in my life.

When I tried to tell my concerns to others in the program, they gave me suggestions that seemed ludicrous at the time. "Help stack the chairs after the meeting," they told me. "Collect the coffee cups and go into the kitchen and help the others clean up," they advised. "Aren't you listening?" I wanted to scream at them. "I have some serious issues here!" Instead, I washed cups and helped clean the kitchen after the meetings.

It has taken years to finally learn the lessons they were trying to teach me, but it's clear now. Today, I have everything I need to be happy, joyous, and free. And if I take care of the things in front of me today, then one day at a time my life can and will improve. I now know that today is the tomorrow I worried about yesterday, so now I make the most out of living today. And this way, my life not only takes care of itself, but it improves as well.

DECEMBER 22

*"I don't have to like the situation, but it's
important that I like myself in it."*

When I first got sober, I took a job in Beverly Hills as an investment broker selling municipal bonds. I hated getting up at 4:45 AM to drive to work, hated making cold calls all day, and hated making just enough to get by. What I hated most, though, was myself. Selling bonds wasn't who I was, but it was all I knew to do at the time. And because my identity was tied to what I did, if I hated that, I hated myself. Because of this, I spent many dark days in the abyss of self-pity and self-loathing.

When I look back on it, I'm surprised I didn't just go back out. Thankfully, the bottom I hit was worse than my day job, and so each night I dragged myself to a meeting to try to find a better way. My sponsor listened patiently as I wallowed in my misery and finally said, "Your job isn't about you or who you are. It's simply a vehicle for you to be of service and to help others. And until you see all of life that way, you will never be happy no matter what you are doing."

It took me years of working the Steps and working with others before I saw the wisdom in what he said. Today, I understand the importance of being of service, and I find that I like myself a lot more when I'm trying to give rather than get. Because of this, I'm able to separate myself from what I have and what I'm doing, and in this way, I've learned to live comfortably in my own skin. Today, I may not like all the situations in my life, but I've learned to like myself in them.

DECEMBER 23

❧

"The only thing we can take with us when we leave this world is what we gave away."

For years, I thought the goal in life was to get as much stuff as I could. I spent endless hours shopping for cars, clothes, and tech devices. I loved when UPS came, and for a few hours I almost felt satisfied. I still remember, however, the moment I pressed the buy button on yet another Amazon order and thought about the package arriving and putting the new, unread books on the shelf next to the other new, unread books. In that moment, I hit another bottom.

When I was new, I was told that if I wanted to feel better, then I had to get out of myself by being of service. While I argued that mopping the floor couldn't have anything to do with my recovering or feeling better, I did what I was told. Eventually, I was instructed to sponsor others. While I resented getting up early on Sunday mornings to meet with a newcomer before a meeting, I always felt the deepest satisfaction and feeling of self-worth when I did. Finally, I had found a way to fill the hole inside of me.

What I've learned after many years in recovery is that it's not about me. It's not about how much I earn or how much I can get. Instead, it's only about how much I can give away. The truth in my life today is that I'm happiest when I'm being of service. I'm in fear less when I'm thinking of others, and ultimately, I know that the only thing that really matters now is how much I can pack into the stream of life. I finally understand the last line of St. Francis' prayer: "It is by dying (of self) that one awakens to eternal life."

DECEMBER 24

"I've been here a few twenty-four hours."

When I was struggling to get 120 days sober, I watched a guy take an anniversary cake for seven years. I honestly thought there was no way he had stayed sober for all seven years straight—that was obviously impossible. Perhaps he had a margarita in Mexico a few times, or on New Year's Eve he celebrated with a glass of champagne. As he blew out his candles and walked back to his seat, I wondered what the secret was.

While discussing this with my sponsor, he told me that the secret was that we took our sobriety one twenty-four-hour period at a time. There were many days when I really wanted to drink, and I remember his answer was always the same. He would ask me, "Can you just not drink today?" "Yes," I'd say. "But I'm drinking tomorrow." He'd reply, "Fine. I'll buy you that drink tomorrow, but just don't drink today." The next day I'd be in a different place, and because I didn't drink I'd be one more day sober.

Fast-forward over twenty years, and I'm still sober. I didn't drink while out of the country, and I've spent many New Year's Eves without champagne. In fact, when I turned twenty years sober, my friend even called me an old-timer. Imagine that: me an old-timer! People newer than me ask how I've been able to stay sober so long, and I tell them the secret—just don't drink today. I tell them I know it works, because I've been here a few twenty-four hours.

DECEMBER 25

*"We are always just an arm's length
away from active alcoholism."*

Over the holidays, I came uncomfortably close to accidental slips. First there was that rum dessert. Then there were those liquor-filled chocolates we got for Christmas. And when I heard today's quote, it scared me and snapped me back to reality. What I remembered is that some people slip by mistake and then indulge in the belief that they can probably control and enjoy their drinking again. After all, they think it's been years since they had a drink, and surely it won't have the same effect.

It is truly terrifying to realize that I am indeed just an arm's length away from disaster. Alcohol is all around me. And after long-term sobriety, it's easy to let my guard down. But when I think it through, what I know for sure is that if I pick up, it won't be long before I'm in a state of pitiful and incomprehensible demoralization. No one glass of wine for me. I would be all in, and I shiver as I remember what *that* was like.

Thank God I still work my program. I know that I am not cured; rather, I only have a daily reprieve based on my spiritual condition. And this requires maintenance to keep up, as well as constant vigilance. Alcoholism remains cunning, baffling, and powerful. I must continue to do the things that gave me the gift of sobriety: work the Steps, pray to my Higher Power, be of service, and go to meetings. When I do, I have access to the strength I need to resist temptation. And if I don't, then active alcoholism is just an arm's length away.

DECEMBER 26

*"It is a pity we can't forget our troubles the
same way we forget our blessings."*

I used to wake up reviewing all the bad things in my life. I often had a deep hangover—the kind where your head hurts when you move it just an inch. I'd wonder how I was going to work that day, and if the boss would make good on his threat to fire me if I called in late again. Next, I'd review my dwindling bank balance and worry about my bills. By the time I reached for coffee, I was pretty much defeated.

In early recovery, I still woke up and reviewed all the bad things in my life. I had lost that job, and I was living on borrowed money. I was now sentenced to A.A. meetings and forced to work the Steps. I was pretty sure my life was over. My sponsor wasn't having any of my pity party. He suggested I write a gratitude list which started with things like (1) I was alive and not in jail, (2) I was sober today, (3) I actually owned a home I could borrow on, and so on. Turns out, I *did* have a lot to be grateful for.

These days, the pity pot doesn't get used as much, but I can still get into fear and worry. When I do, I review all the things sobriety and my Higher Power have blessed me with: my life, long-term sobriety, spiritual tools that allow me to live comfortably—even serenely—in my own skin. And I have a lot of "outside" stuff as well. Today, I try to forget the temporary troubles that come and go, and instead stay focused on the blessings that are always with me. When I do, I live a very happy and contented life.

DECEMBER 27

"I can't do God's will my way."

I remember driving home drunk after parties, window open, one eye closed so the lane would stop moving. I'd pray to God to get me home safe, promising I would behave the next time. The next morning when I came to, I'd have some juice and coffee, my head would clear, and I would think that next time I would control my drinking better, and that I didn't need God's help after all. And then I'd be driving home from a party again. . . .

When I worked the Steps in the program, there was a lot of talk about God's will, and turning my will and life over, and praying for the knowledge and power to carry that out. It was confusing for me because I was still trying to use His will to secretly fuel and further my own. For many years my ego was still in charge, and I was able to deceive myself into thinking that if I wanted it, then it must be God's will as well. I wasted a lot of years trying to do God's will my way.

My experience has been that once I am truly ready to seek a "Higher" way—usually through a surrender because my will has failed to get me what I want—that is when the miracle happens and my life changes. It happened when I finally let go of my old ideas around drinking, it happened when I finally surrendered my ideas about a relationship, and it happened in many other areas of my life as well. The truth is that God's will is always better for me, and once I stop trying to twist His will to fit my own, my life and those of everyone around me improve.

DECEMBER 28

"Be kind, be loving, be quiet."

I used to have a lot to say. At parties or gatherings, I had to make sure everyone was listening to the stories or jokes or opinions I had because, don't you know, I knew everything. And after a few drinks, I became the obnoxious attention-seeker whom people avoided. I was so self-absorbed that I didn't even notice I was not getting invited to things, and by the end of my drinking, I didn't care anymore.

In early sobriety, I couldn't wait to give my opinions. When I was called on to share, I'm sure many people rolled their eyes as I told them why alcoholism wasn't really a disease, and why I was there to just dry out and learn how to drink normally again. "Keep coming back," was a phrase I heard often. Finally, my sponsor suggested I listen more and share my thoughts with him one on one after meetings. After many inventories, much Step work, and a lot of time, I understood the wisdom of this advice.

I'm a completely changed man today. I am sincerely interested in other people's journey and experiences, and today I look to be of service whenever I can. I understand the value of kindness, and I look for opportunities to practice love and tolerance. I also appreciate the gift of remaining quiet and letting others express themselves. I love to listen to their stories and learn from their unique points of view. Today, I'd rather listen than share, and as such, both I and others enjoy our interactions more.

DECEMBER 29

*"I can't turn back the clock, but
I can wind it up again."*

One of the fears I had when I got sober was that I had ruined vast parts of my life, and that the damage I had done was permanent. I spent many nights wishing I could go back in time and make different, better decisions. As I went over and over these things, I was overcome with shame, remorse, and resentment. At times, I felt like my life was over and that things would not turn out okay for me.

In working the Steps, I began to come to terms with the things I did, and I discovered the causes and conditions for why I did them. As I took the focus off others, and even off the past, I concentrated on making things right in the present. I built a relationship with my Higher Power, I cleaned house and made amends, and soon I found that I had built an archway through which I could once again connect with other people.

The gift of the program for me came when I realized that I was given a second chance at a new life. I felt the joy they talk about in the program when I found that while I couldn't change the past, I could create a new future. One day at a time, I took the right actions, and each time I did, my life changed. I became a new man, and soon I found I was living in the sunlight of the Spirit. Each day, the clock of my life winds up again, and today I have the freedom to make my life the way I truly want it to be.

DECEMBER 30

*"Serenity is paying attention to
what I'm doing right now."*

I have a mind that races ahead of where I am, plans outcomes, anticipates obstacles, and prepares for the worst. It's a busy mind. If it's not in the future, then it's reviewing the past, coming up with wouldas, shouldas, and couldas. Drinking offered a respite from this obsessiveness, and for a few hours I was mostly concerned with what was happening in the present. But then my bottom forced me to get sober, and even in the program I found I still had a restless mind.

My endless thoughts wouldn't let me alone during early sobriety. I woke up in fear, worried most of the day, and at night I'd lie awake imagining dark futures fueled by what ifs. Thank God for my sponsor and the fellowship. They had many suggestions, like when they told me to keep the Big Book at my bedside because reading a few pages would definitely put me to sleep. It worked! They also taught me about being of service, prayer, and building my spiritual tool kit. That all worked—when I worked it.

Many years have passed, and while I'm recovered from the obsession to drink, my mind still likes to get into the future and look for danger. This is the path to insanity for me. Thankfully, I'm much better at reining it back in and focusing it on what I'm doing, what I have, and how fortunate I am right now. I have more than I need to be happy, joyous, and free. And most of all, I have a God of my own understanding, and I have serenity in the here and now. How's that for the future I used to worry about?

DECEMBER 31

*"God handed me the menu. He didn't tell me
to choose the moldy sandwich."*

This quote seemed appropriate for the New Year because it reminds me that in recovery, with a relationship with my Higher Power, I have a world of opportunities open to me. In meetings every week, I hear others share about going back to school, changing careers, or starting a family—all miracles of recovery and all part of the new life available to us through the program.

This quote also reminds me that while there are many new and wonderful opportunities available, it is still up to me to choose the right path. Do I choose to work my program today? Do I choose to turn my will and my life over to God, and pray for knowledge of and power to do His will today? Or do I stay isolated, not go to meetings, drink too much coffee, and spend my time regretting the past or fearing the future? What do I do with the menu God gives me today?

As I look toward the New Year ahead, I have an overwhelming feeling of possibility and hope as I acknowledge with gratitude the new menu of life I've been given in recovery. I make resolutions to make better choices, and I ask God to guide me and to release me from the character defects that lead me to reach for the wrong kind of sandwich. Today, I will use my power of choice to make this year the best one yet.